Reading Henry James

ALSO BY GEORGE MONTEIRO

Robert Frost's Poetry of Rural Life (McFarland, 2015)

*Elizabeth Bishop in Brazil and After:
A Poetic Career Transformed* (McFarland, 2012)

Reading Henry James
A Critical Perspective on Selected Works

GEORGE MONTEIRO

McFarland & Company, Inc., Publishers
Jefferson, North Carolina

ISBN (print) 978-1-4766-6585-6
ISBN (ebook) 978-1-4766-2550-8

LIBRARY OF CONGRESS CATALOGUING-IN-PUBLICATION DATA

BRITISH LIBRARY CATALOGUING DATA ARE AVAILABLE

© 2016 George Monteiro. All rights reserved

No part of this book may be reproduced or transmitted in any form or by any means, electronic or mechanical, including photocopying or recording, or by any information storage and retrieval system, without permission in writing from the publisher.

On the cover: Henry James, ca. 1910 (Library of Congress); *background* open book © 2016 itchySan/iStock

Printed in the United States of America

*McFarland & Company, Inc., Publishers
Box 611, Jefferson, North Carolina 28640
www.mcfarlandpub.com*

Table of Contents

Preface   1

1. The Manuscript   5
2. The Californian   13
3. Madame Merle   21
4. Fathers and Sons   29
5. Lessons of Browning   33
6. The Destructive Self   41
7. Portraits of Friends   53
8. Artifice in "The Real Thing"   69
9. "The Pupil" Rejected   72
10. New Christians and "The Liar"   79
11. The Poynton Marbles   93
12. The Caretaker   95
13. Figure in the Carpet   98
14. Identity Theft   105
15. Great White Hunter   108
16. The Example of Late James   120
17. Quest for Truth   130
18. The Spirited Daisy   134
19. The Wings of Doves   136
20. Innocence or Experience   140

21. Fathers and Daughters 146
22. The Double Bind 150

Chapter Notes 155
Bibliography 167
Index 173

Preface

Over time Henry James's work has been put to many uses. He has been championed as the historian of fine consciences and attacked as the spokesman for social privilege. His Americanness has been questioned by nativists and defended by Brahmins. Even ardent supporters have been amused by the wit of those who first divided his career into three royal parts: James I, James II, and James the Old Pretender. But numerous others have had difficulty with his style, even that of the lucidly complex *Portrait of a Lady*. "It's not that he bites off more than he can chew, but that he chews more than he bites off," as a Cambridge contemporary complained. Although he was acknowledged in his final decades as a master by followers such as Ford Madox Ford and Percy Lubbock, James had long since seen his always selective and narrow readership dwindle away.

At the time of his death he received handsome tributes that were informed critical assays of his work and importance from the likes of T. S. Eliot and Ezra Pound. In January 1918 *The Egoist* devoted its four pages to pieces on James by Eliot, Pound, Enrique Gomez, and Arthur Waley. Seven months later, in August, *The Little Review* published eleven pieces in a total of sixty-four pages, including work by Ethel Coburn Mayne, A. R. Orage, John Rodker, and Theodora Bosanquet (James's amanuensis and typist), as well as, again, T. S. Eliot and Ezra Pound. Both numbers can of course be considered memorials to James, who died on the 28th of February 1916. But these intelligent tributes were not enough in themselves to sustain interest in his work during the 1920s, a decade which saw in its early years the publication of Van Wyck Brooks's *The Pilgrimage of Henry James*, an attack on the expatriate writer for his un–Americanism conceived as a counter-example to Brooks's *The Ordeal of Mark Twain*. Periodic attempts to resuscitate James's reputation enjoyed little or no success.

In 1934 *Hound and Horn*, the precocious Lincoln Kirstein's journal, bucking the rising tide of proscriptive and prescriptive social-economic concerns among intellectuals and writers of all stripe, devoted its spring issue to James. "In expressing its admiration for Henry James," writes its editor, "*The Hound & Horn* does itself and its contributors great honor, for there is no American artist who can serve as such an admirable point of departure for an inquest into the present condition of our literature. An attempt has been made to illuminate the several facets of his genius as they have attracted individual writers who have felt the pressure of his influence. As a whole, this tribute comes from a younger generation who, as yet have not expressed their gratitude to the great novelist." The list of contributors, reading like a who's who of modern letters, included Marianne Moore, Edmund Wilson, Francis Fergusson, Stephen Spender, Newton Arvin, and R. P. Blackmur. Unfortunately, not much was accomplished by Kirstein's noble gesture beyond encouraging the faithful to continue to keep the flame.

In 1943, the centenary year of James's birth, F. W. Dupee published *The Question of Henry James*. This thoughtful collection of essays, if not the sole source for the reassessment and celebration of James that has continued to this day, undoubtedly had a good deal to do with the James revival. In the same year appeared the special James number of the *Kenyon Review*, edited by Robert Penn Warren and presenting nine essays. Two of them were the work of holdovers from the *Hound and Horn* issue of 1934, Francis Fergusson and R. P. Blackmur. The newcomers included Katherine Anne Porter, Jacques Barzun, John L. Sweeney, F. O. Matthiessen, Austin Warren, David Daiches, and Eliseo Vivas.

Since 1943 James's stock among readers and scholars has grown exponentially. The scholarship on James is enormous. There have been several special issues of academic journals devoted to his work, including *Modern Fiction Studies* and *Modern Language Studies*. He is the subject of one of the most impressive multi-volume biographies of the twentieth century. There is an active, lively Henry James Society. The University of Nebraska Press has agreed to publish a complete edition of James's letters, a project that is expected to run to twenty-five volumes or more to be edited and published over fifteen to twenty years. He has survived the various critical fashions and sometimes heavy cultural pressures. *The Turn of the Screw*, *The Ambassadors* and *What Maisie Knew* (to name only three titles) continue to be read and taught in college classes. A good deal of his work has been adapted for the theatre, movies, and television—some titles more than once. Off the top of my head, I can recall several treatments of *The Turn of the Screw* available and at least two *Portraits of a Lady*, along with a *Bostonians*, a *Daisy Miller*, one *Europeans*, and even an "Altar of the Dead." *The Heiress*, a 1945 play based on *Washington Square*, was turned into what has become a celebrated motion picture and has itself been revived on Broadway in the mid–1990s. It has become a commonplace to say that James, who failed miserably with his own plays, wrote fiction that lends itself beautifully to dramatic adaptations in virtually any medium. But there is still much to do in this area. No one, to my knowledge, has yet filmed *Guy Domville*. Even the Master was known to nod on occasion.

This selection of writings on the subject of Henry James, some published for the first time, several revised for inclusion in this book, reflects the belief that literary scholarship matters. It sets a record straight, permits access to documents, offers a interpretive slant. Moreover, apart from the "news" that an individual piece of scholarship brings at the time of its publication, it also becomes part and parcel of the historical record of response to Henry James's life and work.

Acknowledgments are due to the editors who have consented to my use in *Reading Henry James* of material, much of it now revised, that first appeared in the journals *American Literary Realism*, *Massachusetts Review*, *Modern Language Studies*, *Nineteenth-Century Literature*, *Texas Studies in Literature and Language*, *Wallace Stevens Journal*, and *Western Humanities Review*. Henry James's letters are quoted by permission of Bay James and Harvard University.

1

The Manuscript

Several years ago the *Hartford Courant* published a piece titled "A Busy Day at the Archives." It turned out to be not one of those mildly interesting pieces that editors squirrel away toward some anticipated future use as newspaper filler, but a chapter in *The Resurrection of Caleb Quine*, a novel appearing serially in the *Courant*. Chapter twenty-one opens:

> At the archives of the Guine-Hatcher Memorial, the librarians confiscated all pens and replaced them with pencils so that people couldn't absent-mindedly doodle a big indelible psychedelic orchid on a thank-you note from Henry James.
> The archives were brightly lighted and pleasant, and if one got lucky, one might get one of the six tiny roomettes where one could close the door and be spared some of the maddening peculiarities of the more antique antiquarians.

The writer then dutifully turns to some of these antiquarians: "These included 82-year-old amateur historian Newell Griswold who had been humming something—guesses among the librarians ranged from Beethoven sonatas to 'I've Got a Gal in Kalamazoo'—in low rusty tones every day at a paper-cluttered table for 26 years. Not to mention Tuffett Skethering, who was somehow able to combine the handling of complex genealogical materials with knitting and who, when she felt she had hit upon some especially nifty family connection, would produce a klaxonian whoop of excitement."

It was, he notes, "a busy day in the archives": "There was usual ruckus of scholars and high-culture groupies troweling and trolling for nuggets about Iphigenia's friendship with Degas or the luxuriant weekends with William Dean Howells and Archibald MacLeish and Aeneas Cathcart or Geoffrey Hatcher's explorations of Venezuela and Australia, etc."[1]

Scholars of my generation—certainly those in the Humanities—we have all been there. The scholar is under scrutiny. After all, scholars have been known to steal documents, mark them up, spindle, fold, and mutilate surreptitiously. But I wish to address the matter of some of the other uses of custodial vigilance. And here we get to something that has changed greatly since my salad days. It has been some time since I have myself run into the type of the big-time owner of an author's manuscripts and his or her powerful ally, an institutional guardian of those manuscripts.

Well do I remember the first days I worked at Harvard University, in the (at first) imposing and intimidating reading room at the Houghton Library. (Later, because of special circumstances that made my work useful to the library, I was permitted to work daily in the lower depths of the Houghton, but that is a story for another day.) But my experience begins earlier. It was the language requirement for the PhD in English at Brown University that started me on my long Jamesian journey toward this book. Attempting to learn German in a summer course taught at the University of Rhode Island, I met a fellow student of German, who, as things would have it, surfaced a couple of years later as a "Special Collections" librarian at Brown working on, among many other things, I suspect, a recent gift to the library of papers belonging to John Hay, Lincoln's secretary and Theodore Roosevelt's Secretary of State. Remembering me from classes at U.R.I. where she learned German and I barely learned to count to ten in German (don't try me) she invited me to come in some day and read recently acquired Henry Adams letters to John Hay. Thus the first bite of the apple.

While a student at Columbia University I had marveled at the information that Daniel G. Hoffman had been brought in to write a dissertation on recently acquired Stephen Crane materials, but it had never occurred to me that an ordinary mortal might be given access to such treasures. Hence my pleasure at having someone on the inside extend such an invitation. I had no ulterior motives in going to read those letters beyond the never really extinguished thrill of looking, for the first time, into a folder of genuine letters. Had I stopped after reading and listing Adams's letters, most of which, as I discovered, had already achieved print in book form, I dare say that I wouldn't be raking over some old memories. But, as luck would have it, Henry James was another of Hay's friends, and the Hay papers included a batch of James letters. So I went on to read those.

Unlike Adams's letters to Hay, however, James's letters I soon discovered were unpublished or even unknown to James scholars. As an exercise and a challenge, I set about the task—I was avoiding several responsibilities, including trying to learn German—of transcribing these letters, dating them, and annotating them. At first I saw my work as a disinterested exercise that was interesting and somehow useful to my development as a teacher (although I didn't know how, exactly). I cannot remember if I already had dreams of publication—it would have been a heady matter, in any case—on that cloudy, rainy day in November when the Special Collections librarian walked a stranger over to the table where I was working on the James letters. He was short, dapper, sported a small mustache, and was about fifty. He was Leon Edel, that last of "the big-time owners," as *Time* magazine would later call him. I had never seen him before, but I knew his name, having heard the distinguished Jamesian F. W. Dupee, a couple of years earlier at Columbia University, refer to him, on the basis of the first volume of what would turn into a five-volume work, as the definitive biographer of Henry James. To me, that afternoon, Professor Edel was courteous, seemingly affable, pleasantly inquisitorial. He asked me what I had found in the James correspondence and I, happy to show off a bit, told him all I knew. He thanked me and offered me a bit of advice to the effect that if I intended to "do something" with the letters that I should follow good, ethical procedure in such matters by writing to James's descendant and executor, William James, the son of the psychologist-philosopher and the nephew of the novelist. To make it easier for me he gave me William James's Cambridge address. Whereupon he moved to another table, and I left so that he could look at the James correspondence at his ease. Possessing now the approbation of Professor Edel himself, as I thought, not to mention his unasked-for help, I continued my work on the James letters. I now had to run down the John Hay part of the correspondence.

And that took me to old Route 1, the Boston Post Road, and the Houghton. John Hay's letters to Henry James, the few that survived James's 1907 bonfire at Lamb House to which he consigned all the letters he had accumulated over the decades, were part of the James Collection. I do not remember what they asked me at the reception desk but because I was already a "publishing" scholar—a couple of term papers on William Faulkner turned articles in professional journals—I passed muster and was allowed to see the Hay letters. So far so good. Then I asked to see the letters of Constance Fenimore Woolson, the American writer of stories and novels who was sometimes James's companion in Europe. I not known such letters existed but when 1 found them listed in the directory to the James Family papers I thought how serendipitous, for there was at Brown University a James letter to Hay devoted entirely to the strange circumstances of Miss Woolson's death and its immediate consequences. Perhaps there would be something in these Woolson letters at Harvard that I might use in my introduction to the James-Hay correspondence.

No sooner had I got the letters when swooping down on me was the supervisor of the reading room. She asked me, breathlessly, why had I asked to see those particular letters, what did I intend to do with my "knowledge" of them, that I must not take notes, and that—here was my first encounter with a privileged scholar's archival gatekeeper—these letters (and much else among the James family papers) were reserved for the exclusive use of Professor Edel. It was a scene that, mutatis mutandis, would be replicated elsewhere, notably at the Alderman Library, University of Virginia, where the Xerox copies of James letters to Sir John Clark that were shown to me in the morning were, after lunch, rather shamelessly recovered from me because the assistant—or assistant-assistant librarian who had not only allowed me to see the letters but had copied three or four of them for me had not known that the expired date shown on the folder along with the indication that the letters were reserved for Professor Edel's use had been extended.

My telling of this James saga could go on at great length, for incidents relative to it appear and reappear over several decades, but suffice it say at this moment that when, following Edel's advice, I did write to William James for permission to publish Henry James's letters, James's executor informed me that he had long ago deferred to Edel in such matters and suggested that I might write to him. You have already anticipated my story, I suspect. The good professor's answer to my request, a request couched in deferential terms reminding him of his words to me that cloudy and rainy November afternoon in the John Hay Library, was that I was not, absolutely not, to try to publish James's letters to Hay. After all, were he to accede to such requests, he informed me, his own work on James would be anticipated "monthly," in bits and pieces, and he could not allow that to happen.

No scholar, of course, is ever totally innocent in matters of this nature, for he does pry into the lives of his subject and all those within his subject's ken. The question of his own privacy when he is under scrutiny in the reading room (even when he has the approbation of the keepers he remains under their eyes; they do know what he is doing, in what directions his scholarship will take) pales, of course, before the personal and familial privacy that is the right of all those whose papers end up in some archive. But whose duty is it to protect such rights? It has been a good move on the part of institutions to get totally out of the consenting and permitting business.

But good taste and decency are alien to legislation and even privacy remains a vexed matter. After all, the biographer and the scholar who will edit and publish journals or correspondence is very much in the business of violating privacy, even though he works out of the highest motivations, in taking what was originally private communication and turning it public. Even the unwitting, budding scholar—as I was for a few moments when I first read the Adams letters to John Hay—soon enough becomes professionalized as his mind turns to thoughts of publication.

Consider Henry James's melodramatic portrait of the "publishing scholar" the editor in *The Aspern Papers*. The now aged lover of the Byronic poet Jeffrey Aspern is close to dying, and the editor, who in disguise has taken rooms in her Venetian palazzo to get access to the so-called Aspern papers (which he thinks exist, though he is never certain) finds himself for the first time in the old dying woman's sitting-room. He is alone, full of curiosity and cupidity, and speaks his own narrative:

> I stopped in front of the secretary, gaping at it vainly and no doubt grotesquely; for what had it to say to me after all? In the first place it was locked, and in the second it almost surely contained nothing in which I was interested. Ten to one the papers had been destroyed, and even if they hadn't the keen old woman wouldn't have put them in such a place as that after removing them from the green trunk—wouldn't have transferred them, with the idea of their safety on her brain, from the better hiding-place to the worse. The secretary was more conspicuous, more exposed in a room in which she could no longer mount guard. It opened with a key, but there was a small brass handle, like a button, as well: I saw this as I played my lamp over it. I did something more, for the climax of my crisis; I caught a glimpse of the possibility that Miss Tina [Juliana Bordereau's niece] wished me really to understand. If she didn't so wish me, if she wished me to keep away, why hadn't she locked the door of communication between the sitting-room and the sala? That would have been a definite sign that I was to leave them alone. If I didn't leave them alone she meant me to come for a purpose—a purpose now represented by the super-subtle inference that to oblige me she had unlocked the secretary. She hadn't left the key, but the lid would probably move if I touched the button. This possibility pressed me hard and I bent very close to judge. I didn't propose to do anything, not even—not in the least—to let down the lid; I only wanted to test my theory, to see if the cover *would* move. I touched the button with my hand—a mere touch would tell me and as I did so—it is embarrassing for me to relate it—I looked over my shoulder. It was a chance, an instinct, for I had really heard nothing. I almost let my luminary drop and certainly I stepped back, straightening myself up at what I saw. Juliana stood there in her night-dress, by the doorway of her room, watching me; her hands were raised, she had lifted the everlasting curtain that covered half her face, and for the first, the last, the only time I beheld her extraordinary eyes. They glared at me; they were like the sudden drench, for a caught burglar, of a flood of gaslight; they made me horribly ashamed. I never shall forget her strange little bent white tottering figure, with its lifted head, her attitude, her expression; neither shall I forget the tone in which as I turned, looking at her, she hissed out passionately, furiously:
>
> "Ah you publishing scoundrel!"[2]

James, of course, is not the only one to see the scholar as a "publishing scoundrel." Scholars with self-knowledge as well as librarians know who and what they are. The same Houghton Library gatekeeper who zealously guarded the James manuscripts for Professor Edel rather vainly expressed the wish, on another occasion, that scholars would leave "poor Emily" alone when visiting scholars wished to see a Dickinson manuscript or two, since, as she said, Theodora Ward, in her work helping to edit and date the letters and in her own book on Dickinson and the Wards, had done once and for all what could or should be done with the Dickinson family materials. Henry Adams, himself an indefatigable devourer of all sorts of institutional archives, destroyed materials he thought too private to save for the uncontrolled perusal of others. "During summers from 1887 to 1889 he [Adams] was writing and proofreading his History of the United States in the Stone Library at Quincy, Massachusetts," writes Lyman Butterfield, the editor of the Adams papers, "because his widowed and ailing mother had to be cared for.... Surrounded by the vast assemblage of his forebears' diaries, Henry reread and committed to flames his own, kept since college days, leaving, so far as 1 know, only the single gathering of sheets that recorded his systematic destruction."[3] In his decision, Adams was not only anticipating his friend James's bonfire at Lamb House, but following Nathaniel Hawthorne, whose so-called American notebooks include the following entry: "I burned great heaps of old letters and other papers, a little while ago, preparatory to going to England. Among them were hundreds of Sophia's maiden letters—the world has no more such; and now they are all ashes. What a trustful guardian of secret matters fire is! What should we do without Fire and Death?"[4] Sad to say—to the scholar or archivist, of course—no phoenix has ever risen from such ashes. Fortunately, when writers have not taken it upon themselves to destroy their manuscripts—not of their books, of course, for these have either a great value already or may acquire great value in the future—their heirs have seldom in modern times, it seems, resorted to destruction. Sealing up papers until some future date seems to have worked in the past. Yet one recalls that Samuel Clemens's daughter set aside her father's restrictions and published his materials several hundred years before the date he had set, and Mary Hemingway, as his executor, permitted the publication of a hefty selection of her famous husband's letters even though he himself had forbidden such a publication, But there seem to be no standards, rules or firm guidelines in such cases; hence we had Bernard Malamud's daughter wringing her hands in the most public way as she agonized over what to do with her father's papers, and we had the not-yet-posthumous J. D. Salinger successfully blocking even the paraphrase of letters preserved in several different library collections. Of course, when a writer's papers are too "valuable" to burn—that is, the dollar value placed on them is great enough—what is the "family" to do? When literary talent has translated itself to the next generation, a writer's children—Susan and Benjamin Cheever—may themselves turn into "publishing scoundrels," publishing their father's letters and diaries themselves after "outing" him posthumously on the basis of those very documents. Or a daughter, taking her cue from the one of the least possibly private poets—Anne Sexton—releases to the biographer the tapes of her poet-mother's privileged sessions with her psychiatrist. Scandalous as the biographer's publisher thought the matter was, only the psychiatrists, it turned out, were bothered by this egregious act of accessibility extended to the biographer. Many literary scholars, I suspect, merely saw this act as opening another door to scholarship, providing, perhaps, another source of archival material that might be exploited in other cases. In the case of Sylvia Plath questions of accessibility to materials amid the *parti pris* nature of executive and familial "authorization" has spawned a new and different genre: the biography meditation or the biographer's *mea culpa apologia* in which the ostensible subject of the biography has become the necessary but not sufficient occasion for a biography.

Fortunately, however, we drones of literary study, who despite our essentially low-keyed efforts do sometimes produce studies and biographies that are brilliant, insightful, informative, even pleasant to read. Historical study and literary biography have survived the sometimes frontal, sometimes seemingly incidental attacks of the most brutish of contemporary literary theories. New generations of scholars continue to experience that inimitable thrill when those first folders containing manuscript materials are turned over to us, who feel that rush when the hitherto unknown Browning poem directed to his son at college is found (even if it be doggerel) or the menu for the private dinner at the *Lion d'Or* in Paris, signed by John Hay, Clarence King, Ferdinand Rothschild, and Henry James—a document that clears up a puzzling reference in a James letter—pops up, out of the blue.

In James's tale it turns out that Jeffrey Aspern's surviving lover has a portrait of the poet that she wishes to turn over for cash. She sets a high price on it because she thinks there will be some "amateur" who will want it enough to pay her price. Her use of the word "amateur," which in her mind does not seem to make it the opposite of "professional," seems wonderfully appropriate. I should like to present it as indicative of my view of the literary scholar on his best behavior.

The heroine of Margaret Drabble's novel, *The Realms of Gold*, is an anthropologist who boasts without bluster. Frances Wingate discovers Tizouk, "the city of her imagination": "All alone she had worked it out, putting bits together from here and there—the tablets at Carthage, the strangely Meroitic lion in Kano, the curiously Nok-like face on the table in Kush. A phrase or two from Athenaeus, who said that the Cartaginians had crossed the Sahara eating barley." Bit by bit she fleshed out vision: "A sentence from Herodotus, a remark by Heinrich Barth, a visit with the children to the Ethnological Museum, a conversation about *négritude* with Joe Ayida, a vague memory of a heap of ruins, glimpsed like so many heaps from a passing Land-Rover, in mountainous country near the Chad-Libyan border, going north. And then, one night, sitting at Rome airport waiting for a delayed flight home ... sitting there, gazing at the relief of the mountains, suddenly she knew exactly where to look." It was all right there, within her grasp, so to speak: "She knew with such conviction that it was like a revelation—the evidence was all there, it was simply that she alone had produced the correct interpretation of it, and being correct, of course it had fitted. It was as simple as that.... She had known that the city was there, she had gone out to dig for it, and she had found it."[5]

The dreams of the most responsible scholars resemble the fictional Frances Wingate's, and they are no less immodest. They do not go snooping for evidence of scandal or some bit of forbidden knowledge, but they do not suppress such information if it is appropriate to their projects. A fact is a fact. They dream to find in the documents the one genuine order that is in them, the overall sequence and form that result from the radiating out of facts from any document taken as center. This hope (or illusion) is in some way related to the scholar's weakness for letters. It is always his hope that a correspondence will tell its own story, form its own pattern, with its own sense of beginnings, middles, closings.

In the poem "Connoisseur of Chaos" Wallace Stevens writes: "A great disorder is an order." Maybe for a poet. But the scholar will not settle for that. Nor is the scholar's order quite the order that William Carlos Williams finds when making a house call, but it is not entirely different either. Williams is there to deliver a baby. The house is, by any standard, a mess: "I have seldom seen such disorder and brokenness—such a mass of unrelated parts of things lying about. That's it! I concluded to myself. An unrecognizable order! Actually—the new. And so good-natured and calm. So definitely the thing! And so compact. Excellent. And with such patina of use. Everything definitely 'painty.' Even the table, that way, pushed off from the center of the room."[6]

Exactly, though things do not always work out, of course. But when I visit Henry James's papers at Harvard or Roy Campbell's at Texas or Fernando Pessoa's in Lisbon, I am always ready—poised, alert, hopeful—to discover the genuine ore, to expose the true order in what, to some others, might look like mere dross. It is a search that will in all probability not turn up the lost city of Troy, an unknown Beowulf manuscript or an anthropologist's "city of the imagination," but it has the potential to bring into being a new thing—"so definitely the thing"—emerging (with selection and some arrangement, of course) from those inviolable and unburned survivors we know and value as manuscripts and documents.

2

The Californian

In the fall of 1875 Henry James arrived in Paris, with, as he later recalled, "plans of indefinite residence."[1] Commissioned by the *New York Tribune* to do a weekly letter, he was able to get down immediately to quick-paying work. Working at his fiction, for him still a comparatively speculative form of writing for pay, would follow soon. In fact, within the month, the determined expatriate was hard at work on *The American*.

James's intentions in this novel, his third in five years, were, from the beginning, clearly patriotic. He hoped to present his readers with a creditable portrait of a genuine American type. A decade earlier he had written, expansively, to his friend Thomas Sergeant Perry that as a critic—he was not then thinking of himself as a novelist—he must "let all the breezes of the west blow through me at their will."

> We are Americans born—*il faut en prendre son parti*. I look upon it as a great blessing; and I think that to be an American is an excellent preparation for culture. We have exquisite qualities as a race, and it seems to me that we are ahead of the European races in the fact that more than either of them we can deal freely with forms of civilization not our own, can pick and choose and assimilate and in short (aesthetically etc.) claim our property wherever we find it. To have no national stamp has hitherto been a defect and a drawback.... We must of course have something of our own—something distinctive and homogeneous—and I take it that we shall find it in our moral consciousness, our unprecedented spiritual lightness and vigour.[2]

Surprisingly, when he sat down to work out the details for his fictional American, he chose to make him a millionaire—a millionaire from California who was at once vulnerable to the scorn and ridicule of the European and worth defense at home as a type of a uniquely American "new" man. Using the more specific term "Californian" to stand for "western" and all that the word then implied—including the "horribly Western," as one of his expatriated Americans puts it—James's task was to give shape and color to "an intensely Western story" of the self-made American man as a sub-type of the millionaire.[3] He was among the first novelists, if not the first, to undertake that task in a major work. After all, if "Americans in Europe are outsiders," wrote James shortly after the publication of his novel about a commercially successful man, it is "for excellent reasons." "We are the only great people of the civilized world that is a pure democracy, and we are the only great people that is exclusively commercial."[4] In Paris, in 1876, he discovered, he recalled later, that he would never be anything but "an eternal outsider."[5]

One James critic has observed, I think shrewdly, that *The American*—intended to justify "American ways against a European caricature of them"—was "essentially a reply to a satire that had been completely missed in America."[6] That "missed" satire, in its French version at least, emerges in several places in James's novel, often, dramatically, in statements addressed to the Western hero Christopher Newman. It is announced by Mrs. Tristram, Newman's fellow-American: "You are the great Western barbarian stepping forth in his innocence and might, gazing a while at this poor effete Old World, and then swooping down on it." It comes through, genially, in the voice of Valentin Bellegarde, the younger brother of Claire de Cintré, the widow Newman proposes to marry. Valentin reports to Newman what his sister-in-law has said about him: "Madame de Bellegarde said that if she had not been told who you were, she would have taken you for a duke—an American duke, the Duke of California ... you couldn't help it if you were not a duke. There were none in your country; but if there had been, it was certain that, smart and active as you are, you would have got the pick of the titles."[7] Less genial, perhaps, are the remarks of a duchess—"with her little circle of beholders" she reminds Newman of "the Fat Lady at a fair"—who, not entirely tongue-in-cheek, pretends to see Newman as a larger-than-life American:

> Oh, you have your *légende*. We have heard that you have had a career the most checkered, the most bizarre. What is that about your having founded a city some ten years ago in the great West, a city which contains to-day half a million of inhabitants? Isn't it half a million, messieurs? You are exclusive proprietor of this flourishing settlement, and are consequently fabulously rich, and you would be richer still if you didn't grant lands and houses free of rent to all new-comers who will pledge themselves never to smoke cigars. At this game, in three years, we are told, you are going to be made president of America.[8]

Newman himself helps the satire along. To Mrs. Tristram he announces: "I want the biggest kind of entertainment a man can get. People, places, art, nature, everything! I want to see the tallest mountains, and the bluest lakes, and the finest pictures, and the handsomest churches, and the most celebrated men, and the most beautiful women."[9] It is not surprising that the *Athenaeum*, getting it wrong though within the logic of the case, identified the title of James's book as *The American Abroad*.[10]

In each of these instances James plays with the European's distorted notions of the character and putative exploits of the typical American millionaire who has made his fortune in some banal or ridiculous way—"it is very disagreeable to know how Americans have made their money," says Mrs. Tristram. Interestingly, the satire emerges at the expense, simultaneously, of both the American Newman, who in his mid-thirties is traveling well outside his natural Western milieu, and his French hosts, who are complacently secure in theirs. Acknowledging that in many ways Newman's experience reflects James's own "Parisian life of action" in 1875–1876, James's biographer cautions that the Californian possesses "a strong and vulgar streak of materialistic self-satisfaction" which the author, otherwise his defender, "had understood from the first and to which many American readers preferred to close their eyes."[11]

In 1907, in James's preface for Scribner's New York Edition volume of *The American*, the novelist recalls the moment his subject first occurred to him. He gives no evidence that he was of two minds about his typical American millionaire and highly dubious about the manners and morals of the French nobility he introduces into his fable:

> It had come to me, this happy, halting view of an interesting case, abruptly enough, some years before: I recall sharply the felicity of the first glimpse, though I forget the accident of thought that produced it. I recall that I was seated in an American "horse-car" when I found myself, of a sudden, considering with enthusiasm, as the theme of a "story," the situation, in another country and an aristocratic society, of some robust but insidiously beguiled and betrayed, some cruelly wronged, compatriot,… I was charmed with my idea, which would take, however, much working out; and precisely because it had so much to give, I think, must I have dropped it for the time into the deep well of unconscious cerebration.[12]

And there it persisted, to do its work, James tells us, until 1875–1876, the year he lived in Paris. It was at that time that he conceived of his hero, Christopher Newman, his millionaire businessman from California:

> It was all charmingly simple, this conception, and the current must have gushed, full and dear, to my imagination, from the moment Christopher Newman rose before me, one perfect day of the divine Paris spring, in the great gilded Salon Carré of the Louvre. Under this strong contagion of the place he would, by the happiest of hazards, meet his old comrade, now initiated and domiciled; after which the rest would go of itself. If he was to be wronged he would be wronged with just that conspicuity, with his felicity at just that pitch and with the highest aggravation of the general effect of misery mocked at. Great and gilded the whole trap set, in fine, for his wary freshness and into which it would blunder upon its fate. I have, I confess no memory of a disturbing doubt; once the man himself was imaged to me (and that germination is a process almost always untraceable) he must have walked into the situation as by taking a pass-key from his pocket.[13]

While James names no sources for *The American*, literary or otherwise, I would suggest that he found the germ for his novel in the work of Gustave Flaubert. James, who, shortly after his arrival in Paris, was introduced by the Russian novelist Turgenev to Flaubert's famous Sunday afternoons, provided an introduction for an English-language translation of *Madame Bovary* in 1902. Calling Flaubert "the novelist's novelist," James wrote that "he was formed intellectually of two quite distinct compartments, a sense of the real and a sense of the romantic," with *Madame Bovary* and *L'Éducation sentimentale: Histoire d'un Jeune Homme* on the side of the former and *Salammbô* and *La Tentation de Saint-Antoine* on the latter.[14] Of *Madame Bovary* and its heroine, James had a good deal to say over the years, including this comment in his 1907 Preface to *The American* in the New York Edition: "It would be impossible to have more romantic temper than Flaubert's Madame Bovary, and yet nothing less resembles a romance than the record of her adventures."[15]

It is no surprise that James considered *Madame Bovary* to be Flaubert's greatest success, though the French critics themselves chastised him for praising the novel. In *The Nation*, for instance, one such reviewer, unnamed but self-identified as French, wrote disapprovingly: "Mr. James has done an unmerited honor, I believe, to our modern French literature in praising, as he has done, the author of *Madame Bovary*. Madame Bovary has been but a shooting star. If M. Flaubert's novel goes down to posterity it will be because it will be illustrated, as it well deserves to be, with indecent engravings. It will be admired as we admire some poems of Dorat. I have never been able to admire this realistic history of the Fall transported to a vulgar Norman town."[16]

But it was not Flaubert's *Madame Bovary* but his *L'Éducation Sentimentale* (1869), described by James as "that indefinable last word of cold and joyless execution," that started him out on *The American*.[17] That he considered *L'Education sentimentale* to be one of the French master's failures, however, would be puzzling, if James did not explain the matter himself. "How much more interesting a man may be by his failures than by his successes," James writes, continuing:

> The successes somehow disconnect and dismiss him; the failures keep him in relation. Thus it is that, as the work of a "grand écrivain," *L'Éducation*, large, laboured, immensely "written," with beautiful passages and a general emptiness, with a kind of leak in its melancholy, moreover, by which its moral dignity escapes—thus it is that Flaubert's ill-starred novel of manners is a curiosity for a literary museum. Thus it is also that it suggests a hundred reflections, and suggests perhaps most of them directly to the intending labourer in the same field. If, in short, as I have said, Flaubert be the novelists' novelist, this performance does more than any other towards making him so.[18]

Chronicling the modest career and gradual diminishing of Frédéric Moreau's chances as he fumbles about in Paris and elsewhere, always more or less in search of his illusive fortune, Flaubert's consummately ironic novel provided James—as one of those "hundred reflections"—with the idea to write a novel about a wealthy American widower in Europe, in search of cultural experience and, as one might now put it, a trophy wife. With money accumulated in California, James's hero is on extended holiday from his more natural habitat, the world of business.

2. The Californian

A brief digression, before we turn to the particulars of James's specific indebtedness to Flaubert's *L'Éducation sentimentale*. James's 1885 novel *The Princess Casamassima*, it has been shown, owes its overall structure as well as the character of its hero, Hyacinth Robinson, to mainly French novels detailing the type of story centered on the "Young Man from the Provinces." "*The Princess Casamassima* belongs to a great line of novels which runs through the nineteenth century as, one might say, the very backbone of its fiction," writes Lionel Trilling. "These novels, which are defined as a group by the character and circumstance of their heroes, include Stendhal's *The Red and the Black*, Balzac's *Père Goriot* and *Lost Illusions*, Dickens's *Great Expectations*, Flaubert's *Sentimental Education*." The "Young Man from the Provinces" has the following key features: "He need not come from the provinces in literal fact, his social class may constitute his province. But a provincial birth and rearing suggest the simplicity and the high hopes he begins with."[19] If this paradigm fits Hyacinth Robinson, it is also true that it suits the "American," Christopher Newman, as well, with the crucial exception that Newman has become rich. Socially and culturally provincial he remains, but he is as one of the nouveau rich, as rich as he can possibly be, preferring copies of the Old Masters—even mediocre or bad ones—to the originals, paintings he peers at in the museums.

The single most fruitful hint for James's Californian occurs in *L'Éducation sentimentale*. It must have struck James as no more than "the merest grain, the speck of truth," but to him that would be enough.[20] Flaubert's hero, Frédéric Moreau, visits an art gallery and "factory" for the manufacture of great art. While there he witnesses a scene in which the proprietor, one Jacques Arnoux, berates one of his workmen for having botched the "authenticating" signatures he has added to paintings purporting to be the work of the old masters. They can no longer be sold in Paris or, presumably, any other European market: "Arnoux ... was telling off a seedy-looking old man wearing blue spectacles. 'Well, what a bright boy you are, old Isaac! That makes three works completely discredited and on the scrap heap! Everyone's laughing at me! What am I going to do with them now people know all about them, I ask you! I'll have to ship them over to California! To hell with it! No, I won't listen to you!' This character's specialty was providing such pictures with old masters' signatures. Arnoux was refusing to pay him and sent him packing with a flea in his ear."[21]

From this scene one can infer something of the views of the French toward the American nouveau riche in the years following the California Gold Rush. Simply put, the fake paintings bearing botched signatures can still be disposed of in the United States, specifically in California. Given the Californian's reputed lack of knowledge and taste in the matter of European art, ignorant and stupid millionaires in the American West comprise the final lucrative market for such otherwise worthless forgeries. In addition, there was always the Californian's natural vulnerability to exploitation as he yearned for the trappings of high culture and the things of genuine gentility. "San Francisco's gilded age witnessed an almost frenzied enthusiasm for the drama, opera, and music," noted one historian. "Wealth meant a new stake in gentility. It is reported that the first miner to strike gold at Gregory's Gulch in Colorado, in 1859, flung down his pick with the exclamation, 'Thank God! Now my wife can be a lady—and our children can have an education!'"[22] James's fictional Christopher Newman, a member of the next Western generation, sets his sights higher. His accumulated wealth enables him to desert his business (temporarily) for Europe, "to rest awhile, to forget the confounded thing, to look about me, to see the world, to have a good time, to improve my mind, and, if the fancy takes me, to marry a wife."[23]

Anticipating the nativist leanings and patriotic example of Van Wyck Brooks in *The Pilgrimage of Henry James* (1925), speaking, as well, for others, many readers faulted James for his ignorance about his own country, of any place west of the Hudson River, with the possible exception of the provincial upstate cities of Schenectady, Utica, or Albany. *The American* provided the usual case in point, offering what was considered to be rich and unmistakable evidence that James did not know his own country. James had been unable to fill in the details, in any creditable way, so ran the argument, of what his hero had done in California to earn his fortune. This view was a continuation of a long-standing argument that had begun with the first reviewers, who questioned James's right to set up his version of a Western millionaire as the American. *The Galaxy*, a New York journal to which James contributed frequently at the outset of his literary career (and in which he had originally hoped to serialize *The American*), found James's novel deficient in several ways, including its title and "the inferences which it measurably warrants abroad":

> Mr. Christopher Newman is certainly a fair representative of a certain sort, and a very respectable sort, of American; but he is not such a man that Mr. James, himself an American living in Europe, is warranted in setting him up before the world as "The American." Men like Newman are already too commonly regarded as the best product, if not the only product, of two hundred and fifty years of American life, and a hundred of republican institutions. But let us argue a little ad hominem, and ask Mr. James if Christopher Newman fairly represents the larger number of his associates when he is at home. We fancy not. Why then put him forth thus set up on the pedestal of the definite article? If Mr. James had chosen to write his novel with Newman for hero, and to call it by his name, or Mme. De Cintré's, or any other, and to let Newman go as a representative of a certain kind of American who gets rich in California, very well; but to have an American hold this man up to the world as the American is not highly satisfactory."[24]

The *New York Times* (May 21, 1877) refined on the charge. Newman's "conduct is not that of so unsophisticated a man," it noted as the serialization in the *Atlantic Monthly* came to a close, "we learn that he impresses others with his barbarism, but he does not act or talk like a barbarian. The sensations, likes, and dislikes which Mr. James attributed to him are those that he, Mr. James, might have, but not a Californian handler of stocks, who has to learn French at the age of 36."[25]

The fictional Christopher Newman did have his defenders, however, then and later. That one of them was William Dean Howells, who as editor of the *Atlantic Monthly* decided in favor of serializing *The American*, is hardly surprising. When John Hay asked Howells, rhetorically, "Is not the American astonishing, even to us who always believed in him," Howells countered with the observation that "the fact that Harry James could write likingly of such a fellow-creature as Newman is the most hopeful thing in his literary history, since Gabrielle de Bergerac"—a story James published in the *Atlantic Monthly* in 1869.[26] Five years later, Howells recalled that while, admittedly, Newman "is not the 'cultivated American' who redeems us from time to time in the eyes of Europe," he is "unquestionably more national"; "an adequate and satisfying representative of Americanism, with his generous matrimonial ambition, his vast good-nature, and his thorough good sense and right feeling. We must be very hard to please if we are not pleased with him."[27]

Praise from Howells, John Hay, and others notwithstanding, James could never set aside the instances of adverse contemporary criticism aimed at his perceived presentation of Christopher Newman as the American. That criticism was not far from his consciousness, when a dozen years later, at the behest of the theatrical producer and actor Edward Compton, he agreed to turn his novel into a play. On May 12, 1889, he set down his thoughts for such a play, which he intended to rename:

> His proposal is that I shall make a play of *The American*, and there is no doubt a play in it. I must extract the simplest, strongest, baldest, most rudimentary, at once most humorous and most touching one, in a form whose main souci shall be pure situation and pure point combined with pure brevity. Oh, how it must not be too good and how very bad it must be! À moi, Scribe; à moi, Sardou, à moi, Dennery!—Reduced to its simplest expression, and that reduction must be my play. *The American* is the history of a plain man who is at the same time a fine fellow, who becomes engaged to the daughter of a patrician house, being accepted by her people on acct. of his wealth, and is then thrown over (by them) for a better match; after which he turns upon them to recover his betrothed (they have bullied her out of it), through the possession of a family secret which is disgraceful to them, dangerous to them, and which he holds over them as an instrument of compulsion and vengeance. They are frightened—they feel the screw: they dread exposure; but in the novel the daughter is already lost to the hero—she is swept away by the tragedy, takes refuge in a convent, breaks off her other threatened match, renounces the world, disappears. The hero, injured, outraged, resentful, feels the strong temptation to punish the Bellegardes, and for a day almost yields to it. Then he does the characteristically magnanimous thing—the characteristically good-natured thing—throws away his opportunity—lets them "off"—lets them go. In the play he must do this—but get his wife.[28]

When James got down to the actual reworking of *The American* into a play, he at first abandoned the title. As revealed in his journal on February 6, 1890, he was calling his play *The Californian*, influenced, perhaps, by the critical reviews of his novel.[29] Later, of course, probably because he realized that the novel's title would bring more immediate public recognition to the play, he changed its title back to *The American*. But he continued to emphasize Christopher Newman's Western characteristics as a "candid Californian," as Valentin Bellegarde whimsically addresses him, to the expense of his more sensitive characteristics so evident in the novel.[30] Newman's frontier roughness is further played up, if only jokingly, when Valentin accuses him: "I daresay you've got a bowie-knife somewhere"—to which Newman answers, jokingly, "Yes, somewhere in a cupboard, in California."[31]

In 1877, in an unsigned editorial note, *The Nation* had complimented James for taking the "self-made American" type seriously.

> The self-made American, who has suddenly grown rich by "operations" of one kind or another, and has taken himself and his wealth to Europe, is a familiar enough character in literature, but usually the character has been made a comic one, and we have been called upon to laugh at the ridiculous figure cut by our compatriot in the gilded saloons of the effete but critical Europeans, or at his shocking display of ignorance and barbarism as he wanders through "specimen ruins" and "specimen galleries." Mr. James, however, has placed before himself a very different task. He has undertaken to make use of this same type as a serious character in a love story. Newman, as we understand him, is a man who by means of a God-given talent for making money has, while still a young man, accumulated a great fortune we confess to a sneaking curiosity as to which side of the market he operated upon, and while being in externals an entirely untrained and unsophisticated person, is possessed of that tact and adaptability to circumstances and refinement of mind which have always been set down as distinguishingly American traits by such unbiased observers as the English.[32]

Much of this favorable characterization was steadily compromised in the play as James rewrote it to suit Compton and his sense of what would please audiences, including a new fourth act with a conventional happy ending. Tellingly, he called his attempts at adapting his novel for the theatre "histrionics."[33] What he ended up with, precisely, was a crudely conceived "American," one closely approximating the caricature of the Californian—consonant with Arnoux's remark in *L'Éducation sentimentale*—that James was trying to repudiate in the first place when he conceived the character of Newman as he walked about the Louvre. But when James permitted Compton to coach theatre audiences by dressing Newman rather outlandishly in "a Noah-ark coat of yellowish brown, with blue facings and mother of pearl buttons almost as large as cheese plates," his Californian—very like one of Mark Twain's innocents abroad—became, it has been observed, very "nearly a caricature of the American tourist, complete with tag line—'That's just what I want to see.'"[34] Hoping he had managed to supply a piece that would appeal to "this Philistine provincial public"[35]—his not entirely joking assessment of his audience—he had succeeded only in turning a fine novel into a rather commonplace melodrama.

3

Madame Merle

In a discussion of the pleasure human beings take in resemblances, Wallace Stevens chooses for his exemplary text the familiar lines from Ecclesiastes: "'the silver cord be loosed, or the golden bowl be broken, or the pitcher be broken at the fountain, or the wheel broken at the cistern—.'" The effect of these images or symbols can be explained, according to Stevens: "When we read Ecclesiastes the effect of the symbols is pleasurable because as symbols they are resemblances and as resemblances they are pleasurable and they are pleasurable because it is a principle of our nature that they should be, the principle being not something derived from Narcissism since Narcissism itself is merely an evidence of the operation of the principle that we expect to find pleasure in resemblances."[1]

Of course, human beings "find pleasure in resemblances"—the reader takes pleasure in noting that not merely Stevens, but Henry James before him, the novelist whose work most resembles Stevens's poetry, has recourse to the symbols of this passage in Ecclesiastes, particularly the break in the barely discernible crack in the golden bowl that is given to Maggie, the only daughter of the American businessman-millionaire, Adam Verver, in *The Golden Bowl*. But what Stevens does not address in his meditative essay is the notion that distinctions also bring pleasure to those who see them. If we are weighing the relations between Stevens and James, we would do well to keep in mind that the resemblances depend on the distinctions and, surely, vice-versa.

In order to clarify one of those distinctions, let me begin by going off on something of a tangent. When Stevens and Robert Frost had their famous exchange, there was something behind it more than merely the subject matter of their poetry. If Frost "wrote on subjects," as Stevens charged, Stevens wrote "bric-à-brac," fired back Frost. In this exchange, John Ciardi saw the central difference in the two poets. "Some poets, Frost notable among them," wrote Ciardi in 1954, "write poems which have their references, at least in large part, in a recognizable external world; to the extent that we knew beforehand something at least about what they are describing, our understanding of the poems is made easier. Stevens, on the other hand, insists on the poem as its own imagination and subject; a thing made of itself in the saying; a self-entering, self-generating, self-sealing organism, a thing of its own nature."[2] Of course, it was not just "subjects" that interested Frost, but "persons" as well, both of which—subjects and persons—Stevens brushed aside as unsuitable or irrelevant to the kind of poetry he was bent on writing. It goes without saying, moreover, that those persons who interested Frost were ordinary folk, more often than not, of the rural or farming species. When a young novelist, looking for a patron, informed Stevens of his intent to support himself by farming, Stevens warned him (without offering to become his patron): "there doesn't seem to be much chance for you as a writer if you are going to engage in farm work."[3]

If Henry James was no farmer, he was not a businessman either. What for the moment both Stevens and Frost ignored—Stevens astonishingly so—was the supreme role of the imagination in creating art out of persons and bric-à-brac, just as James might have failed to appreciate the poetry of business—something he tried to make up for, clumsily, in "The Jolly Corner," and more sympathetically, if belatedly, in the late fragment of a novel, *The Ivory Tower*. Stevens, on the other hand, if he took satisfaction in business as legitimately a place for the active imagination (even as farming was to others), he chose not to tackle the matter in his poetry.

Judging from the evidence so far available as to Stevens's reading of James, it can be safely noted that he did not read widely in James, which should come as no great surprise, but that the little he did read he seems not to have read with much appreciation or profundity. For example, on a dreary winter day in 1909, while still living and working in New York City, he wrote to Elsie Moll, the woman who would become his wife:

> Our first day of snow, although, in fact, it has been thawing since morning; and most of the day it has been dropping rain. I left the office at five and went to several book-stores for something to read. The shops were just closing and the crowd, the lights, the cars, the machines and horses in the street, together with the mist and the casual rain, made a flawless city night.—I imagined (if I might, Bo) that I was going home to you. No such luck. But I picked up a novel and have finished cutting the pages and expect to dip into it to-night. Last night I read Coleridge until midnight, after writing a little to you.—It is heavy work, reading things like that, that have so little in them, that one feels to be contemporary, living. My novel is Henry James' "Washington Square." I think I'll send it to you if it is good. It was written almost thirty years ago, when Henry James was still H. J. Jr. and had tales to tell.[4]

Before going on to see what Stevens thought about the novel after he read it, it is useful to note that Stevens was well aware of James's literary reputation at the time, to wit, that the author of *The Wings of the Dove* and *The Ambassadors* no longer had the capacity or will to "tell" interesting stories, particularly, one surmises, tales involving persons. But Stevens implies more. The Anglo-American writer was not quite "Henry James" when he published his modest New York City novel in 1880; he was merely "H. J. Jr.," not dropping the "Jr." until after the death in 1882 of the family patriarch, the maverick philosopher-theologian, roughly coincident with the publication of *The Portrait of a Lady*. Stevens read *Washington Square* immediately, and three days after acquiring the book he was ready to report to Elsie that James's modest novel had not impressed him much. "The 'Washington Square' was not specially good," he wrote.

> [It is] altogether an exhibition of merely conflicting characters. It is such an old story that the neighborhood was once suburban but that with the growth of the City has come to be very much "down-town"—the very last place, in fact, in which people live, all below it being exclusively business, except for the tenement intermissions.—Yet it was balm to me to read and to read quickly. I have such difficulty with Maeterlinck. He distracts by his rhetoric. Indeed, philosophy, which ought to be pure intellect, has seldom *if ever*, been so among moderns. We color our language, and Truth being white, becomes blotched in transmission.—I think I'll fall back on Thackeray.[5]

It would be easy but misleading to look too deeply into Stevens's remarks. But there is something valuable here on the surface. Despite his having a few days earlier remarked on James as a teller of tales, Stevens says nothing about the tale (read plot) or about the characters in this trenchant novel. Rather he speaks about the story as one of demographic and sociological transition, neglecting to acknowledge that the story of Dr. Sloper, his daughter Catherine, and Morris Townsend, her fortune-hunting would-be lover, is the moral one of the consequences of emotional violence among the principals in a possible marriage. Such matters never being Stevens's strong suit, at least not in his poetry, it is not surprising that he moves on quickly to a comment on Maeterlinck's rhetoric and generalizations about philosophy, intellect, language, and truth—matters with which he would always be more comfortable than with persons, his reference to Thackeray notwithstanding. It should be noted, however, that the elliptical nature of Stevens's remarks on *Washington Square* may also reveal that he was avoiding something even more personal: Stevens's father (like Dr. Sloper) disapproved of his choice of Elsie as a marriage partner. They fought about it in late 1908 and never spoke again. The plot of James's novel would hardly be comfortable reading for Stevens and Elsie in 1909.[6]

In 1945, decades after setting down his reactions to James's *Washington Square*, Stevens found in F. O. Matthiessen's *Henry James: The Major Phase* (1944) the following sentence from James's notebooks: "'To live in the world of creation—to get into it and stay in it—to frequent it and haunt it—to think intensely and fruitfully—to woo combinations and inspirations into being by a depth and continuity of attention and meditation—this is the only thing.'"[7] An ethic of aesthetics for the creator, this refinement of the legacy of Walter

Pater, spoke eloquently to Stevens the poet. In fact, it can be seen to be directly related to what was his great and virtually exclusionary subject at the last: what he called, somewhat triumphantly in the poem "On Modern Poetry" with conclusive contentment, "The poem of the mind in the act of finding / What will suffice." The notion, it should be noted, does not oblige the poet to focus on the minds of individualized characters—there is in Stevens no Duke of Ferrara, say, or no J. Alfred Prufrock or Isabel Archer—but solely on his own. It was, of course, his own mind at work that caught Stevens's creative attention. When James turned his attention to his own creative mind, he wrote his remarkable set of prefaces to the volumes of the so-called New York Edition in the first decade of the twentieth century.

Long before that prolonged inquiry into mind and memory that are his New York Edition prefaces, James had written narratives centering on characters searching for facts and truth. A case in point is Isabel Archer's night of questioning, remembering, and discovering (chapter 42). "For a long time, far into the night and still further, she sat in the still drawing-room, given up to her meditation," but when she arose, she had discovered what she considered to be the true relationship of her husband, Gilbert Osmond, to Madame Merle, and in the course of that discovery the useful truth about herself. Writing in the preface about his conception of *The Portrait of a Lady*, James recalled:

> "Place the centre of the subject in the young woman's own consciousness," I said to myself, "and you get as interesting and as beautiful a difficulty as you could wish. Stick to that—for the centre; put the heaviest weight into that scale, which will be so largely the scale of her relation to herself. Make her only interested enough, at the same time, in the things that are not herself, and this relation needn't fear to be too limited. Place meanwhile in the other scale the lighter weight (which is usually the one that tips the balance of interest): press least hard, in short, on the consciousness of your heroine's satellites, especially the male; make it an interest contributive only to the greater one.... To depend upon her and her little concerns wholly to see you through will necessitate, remember, your really 'doing' her."[8]

The reminder to himself to really "do" Isabel, to dramatize her inward life—remembering always that her relationship to her "satellites" must not be pressed lightly—was all well and good, but the proof was still in the pudding, and it all needed doing. James explains how the "doing" might be brought off. But James is already in complete possession of his story, a story that will center on a personage who is not yet in complete possession of an understanding of her situation. That she will arrive at the knowledge necessary to such an understanding is the point of the vigil scene James has conceived for her. For James, making his subject the central consciousness of his narrative clarified his theme and provided him with a structure. In the mind of the novelist-critic who wrote the prefaces for the collective edition of his works in the first decade of the twentieth century, his achievement in *The Portrait of a Lady* was not unrelated to what he was able to do in later works such as *The Sacred Fount* and, preeminently, *The Ambassadors*.

> I might show what an "exciting" inward life may do for the person leading it even while it remains perfectly normal. And I cannot think of a more consistent application of that ideal unless it be in the long statement, just beyond the middle of the book, of my young woman's extraordinary meditative vigil on the occasion that was to become for her such a landmark.... She sits up, by her dying fire, far into the night, under the spell of recognitions on which she finds the last sharpness suddenly wait. It is a representation simply of her motionlessly seeing, and an attempt withal to make the mere still lucidity of her act as "interesting" as the surprise of a caravan or the identification of a pirate. It represents, for that matter, one of the identifications dear to the novelist, and even indispensable to him; but it all goes on without her being approached by another person and without her leaving her chair.[9]

Now to turn to Isabel's dark pseudo-benefactor, Madame Merle. There is more than one way to look at Madam Merle, as Isabel, sitting alone before the fire during that long night into morning, discovers. But the truth for Isabel, it turns out, must be but one truth, not multiple truths to be weighed in the balance. She says in all but words, "Here is what the woman did, what she said, what she implied, what it is legitimate to infer, and I must get it down to the one truth. Ah, Osmond's manner when she entered the room, that time, and from that observation I uncover the nature of their intimacy. It's easy now, no shadows or chimeras, philosophical conundrums, the parsing of images, the poison of notions, thoughts that lead nowhere—only the truth." Here is the fruit of the act of the mind in finding what will suffice. One of the brilliant things about James's chapter on Isabel's solitary thinking at this point is that the reader already knows pretty much what there is to know about the nature of Madame Merle's involvement with Osmond, knowledge gained from chapter 22, in which the meeting of the two—Merle and Osmond—where they discuss Pansy's future, takes place before Osmond and Isabel meet for the first time, and thus the reader is able to appreciate just how, at a later date, Isabel comes to the same conclusion. Now the question becomes: what is Isabel going to do, since knowing something that Osmond and Merle do not know that she knows, though advantageous, brings its own responsibilities. Thought brings on passion, new thoughts, new passions—and a new plot.

Embracing the romantic truth that what is imagined is the closest one can come to what Emerson called the "not me," Stevens was content (in his native and chronic discontent) to exploit the ingenuity of his imagination to offer the ingenious variety of his blackbirds. But James, witting or unwitting follower of his brother William's useful precept that what obtains is not truth per se but the consequences of believing that something is true, espouses an idea that does not even come into play for the poet in "Thirteen Ways of Looking at a Blackbird." With Stevens the game of imagining is usually the sum and whole of everything. Madame Merle is Isabel Archer's "blackbird," but Isabel cannot afford to see her thirteen different ways. She comes to the one—fictionally accurate—way of viewing her, for the shape and quality of her life from that moment on depends on her discovery of the truth.

T. S. Eliot said famously that James had a mind so fine that no idea could violate it. It was not that James's mind was not receptive to ideas, far from it, but that it was proofed against violation. Something similar could have been said about Stevens, who embraced ideas—the idea of a supreme fiction, for instance, or the integrity of the imagination in confronting whatever reality there is—but who did so, unlike James, to the exclusion of much else, including something of human sympathy. With this sort of thinking in the background, let me now take the risk of turning briefly to a consideration of Gilbert Osmond—the aesthete Madame Merle has chosen to be Isabel's soul-mate. He, too, was intended to be, in James's thinking for his novel, merely a satellite, viewed once in a while as it circles the cynosure who is Isabel. But when James's older brother objected to his depiction of Osmond even as the novel was being serialized, James defended his work. Asking her to thank William for "his remarks on my novel—especially on the character of the depraved Osmond," he wrote to Alice, William's wife: "I am afraid it won't be in my power, however, to change him much at this late day. As however he was more intended than Wm appears to have perceived, to be disagreeable & disappointing, it may be that the later numbers of the story have already justified my first portrait of him. I think on the whole he will be pronounced good—i.e. horrid."[10] As James makes abundantly clear, Isabel's husband—collector, watercolorist and connoisseur—lacks the ability to feel the deeper human sympathies.

The modern reader is tempted to see in Osmond a prefiguring of the type of modernist poet engaged in near-exclusive activity that is not unlike that of James's fictional character—absorbed in coloring-in a small painting or intently tracing the outline and modulations of an ancient coin, well away from human contact—reading, composing poems, meditating on art. The biographical Stevens was no Gilbert Osmond, of course; but he did share with James's fictional aesthete the propensity to shrink into the solitude of the self. That in Stevens's case this was not just a late-in-life affectation is suggested in Alfred Kreymborg's account in 1925 of his first encounter with Stevens:

> Of the poems he [Kreymborg] had read in *Rogue*, the thing he liked best was a bit of vers libre called Tea, by Wallace Stevens:
>
> "When the elephant's ear in the park Shrivelled in frost, And the leaves on the paths Ran like rats ..."
>
> Colyumists [sic] had riddled it so often alongside things of his own that he felt a fellowship with the author and on the way to the Nortons hoped most of all to meet him. He visualized a slender, ethereal being, shy and sensitive. The man he was introduced to

was shy and sensitive, but so broad-shouldered and burly that Krimmie [as the diminutive Kreymborg, employing the third person, called himself in this autobiography] was overawed. He tried to refer to "Tea," but the tall man waved a deprecating hand and muttered something sounding like "Jesus." Norton drew Krimmie aside and explained: "Cornering Wallace about his own work isn't done." He thanked his host and vowed never to address the giant about his own work again, nor about anything else for that matter.[11]

To complement this partial view of Stevens, I would adduce another anecdote, one told by Samuel French Morse, one of Stevens's early would-be biographers, in a talk at Brown University in the early 1960s. When Stevens learned that Morse had recently come to Hartford to teach at Trinity College and had not yet been to visit him, he wrote him a chiding postcard. "In Hartford, and you haven't come to see me?" quoted Morse. "That's like visiting India and not going to see the Taj Mahal."[12] The self-directed humor here (the Taj Mahal is, after all, a mausoleum) gives way to one's sense of the poet's view of himself as an imposing and immovable presence.

In contrast with James's interest in the affective reasoning of his women characters—a panoply ranging from Christina Light to Kate Croy—is Stevens's rather consistent lack of interest in the women who surface in some of his best-known poems. It is not that he did not write poems about women, as James wrote novels about them, for that was Stevens's prerogative, but when he put them in his poems they always were in service of the poem's narrator—Stevens himself. Each of Stevens's women is at best a *ficelle*, as James called those ancillary characters who are not "of the true agent" of his purposive narrative.[13] Showing no concern for the woman's mind or affections, Stevens lectures (no, hectors) the titular figure of "A High-Toned Old Christian Woman": "Poetry is the supreme fiction, madame, / Take the moral law and make a nave of it / And from that nave build haunted heaven."[14] The biblical Susanna is projected entirely as a sensual woman, a feast for the male voyeur's eyes and lustful longing in "Peter Quince at the Clavier." In "The Idea of Order at Key West," the "she" is useful to the speaker of the poem as the "maker of the song she sang" and "the single artificer of the world / in which she sang"[15]—but, humanly, she is nothing more to him than a stimulus to his thinking. In the satirical "The Emperor of Ice-Cream," "she" is a lifeless body whose "horny feet protrude" from under the sheet that "cover[s] her face."[16]

Only in "Sunday Morning," which in a far-fetched way recalls Isabel's solitary vigil in *The Portrait of a Lady*, does Stevens offer us what must pass for a woman's thoughts. But she, unlike James's heroine, who thinks—dreams, though what she dreams in these "complacencies of the peignoir" are the dark thoughts of myth and religion.[17] One senses that in substance they serve less to give the woman a character or evidence a mind thinking than to address indirectly matters Stevens prefers not to address directly in his unmediated voice. Stevens never came closer than he did in "Sunday Morning" to replicating Isabel's solitary vigil unless it was, one is tempted to say maliciously, in the single, unadorned, unexplored image of "a woman writing a note and tearing it up" ("An Ordinary Evening in New Haven").[18] For the abstractions in Stevens's poetry, not to mention his affective deficiencies, were alien to James's fiction, so different were the two writers in temperament: Stevens aloof, cold and solitary; James warm, social, and focused on other human beings.

But let us end on a note of consanguinity by quoting Stevens in a moment in which he found himself in total agreement with James: "We do not have to be told of the significance of art. 'It is art,' said Henry James, 'which makes life, makes interest, makes importance ... and I know of no substitute whatever for the force and beauty of its process.' The world about us would be desolate except for the world within us."[19] On this—the sufficiency of art—the poet and the novelist were in absolute agreement.

4

Fathers and Sons

In the last years of the nineteenth century Henry James, even before he began to live outside of London, first as a renter of Lamb House and then as its owner, assumed the role of host rather than guest for visits and weekends. Although only when he moved to Rye did he, for the first time in his life, have the room at his disposal to accommodate family, friends or visitors, he was nevertheless an accommodating host at 34 DeVere Gardens in London. Among his many visitors were his brother William and his sister-in-law Alice, his old friend of pre–Civil War days, the jurist Oliver Wendell Holmes, William and Alice's children, his namesake Henry, the younger William, and Alice. He also received Adelbert "Del" Hay, the oldest child of John and Clara Stone Hay. Indeed, his friends' children were by the late 1890s undertaking their own tours of Europe, making their own, more or less, protracted visits in London and Paris and Rome, even as the Jameses, the Adamses, the Hays, and the Howellses had done so in their time. Del Hay, just out of college, made his obligatory visit to the now avuncular novelist ensconced at Rye, a comfortable distance from daily hurly-burly of London life. One of the things that James could do for parents of sons such as Del Hay was to reassure them of their progeny's social graces and evident high abilities for the affairs of an honorable and useful life. He could also assure worried parents that their children, wandering or rushing through Europe, were still safe from the unwanted lures and attractions of London and Parisian life. So he wrote reassuring letters to his friends whose sons had come to pay their respects, thereby serving a most useful function.

To many parents Paris was not the City of Light but the place of temptation. John Hay had written about the moral and psychological demise of a young American boy who becomes infatuated with the Parisian demi-monde, with drink and the can-can. "Kane and Abel," dating from the late 1860s, grew out of its author's stint as secretary of legation in Paris, shortly after his years in the White House as a secretary to President Lincoln. The melodramatic story reveals the tragic fate of Kane, who despite his brother Abel's best efforts to save him, succumbs to temptations, enticements, and the vices of Paris.[1]

William Dean Howells, who had spent the Civil War years as American consul in Venice and who, over the next thirty years, visited Europe several times, published in the mid–1880s, *Indian Summer*, a genial novel about the romantic charms and attractions to an American, just barely over forty years of age, of both Italy and a young American girl.

Indeed, Colville's situation (his age, his present still unmarried state) does not reflect or foreshadow that of Howells or James or, for that matter, that of any of their friends, but does anticipate that of Lambert Strether of *The Ambassadors*. This fact is no cause for wonderment, of course, for it is James himself who established a connection between his 1904 novel and his friend William Dean Howells. In his 1907 preface to *The Ambassadors*, written when the novel was reissued as part of the New York Edition, James reveals that the donée for the great novel of his so-called "major phase" was a remark by Howells, made at one of James Whistler's free-wheeling artists' parties in Paris in the early 1890s and reported to James at second hand. James quotes Howells's *cri de coeur*, as reported to him by Jonathan Sturges, his advice to Sturges (disabled through polio) that one must live all that one can. That it is imperative not to wait for life, but to live it as fully and as continuously as one can. Howells's remarks, perhaps the most widely celebrated words in all of Henry James, are, as they appear in *The Ambassadors*, "Live. Live all you can. It is a mistake not to"—are spoken by Lambert Strether to John Little Bilham in Gloriani's (read Whistler's) Parisian garden. They are words that James first heard from the lips from his friend Jonathan Sturgis, and which, as set down in his notebooks in 1895, became the germ for his 1903 novel. Here is the notebook entry:

> I was struck last evening with something that Jonathan Sturges, who was staying here for 10 days, mentioned to me: it was only 10 words, but it seemed, as usual, to catch a glimpse of a sujet de nouvelle in it. We were talking of W. D. H. and of having seen him during a short and interrupted stay H. had made 18 months ago in Paris—called away—back to America, when he had just come—at the end of 10 days by the news of the death—or illness—of his father. he had scarcely been in Paris, ever, in former days, and he had come there to see his domiciled and initiated son, who was at the Beaux Arts. Virtually in the evening, as it were, of life, it was all new to him; all, all, all. Sturgis said he seemed sad—rather brooding; and I asked him what gave him [Sturgis] that impression. Oh—somewhere—I forget, when I was with him—he laid his hand on my shoulder and said à propos of some remark of mine: "Oh, you are young, you are young—be glad of it, be glad of it and live. Live all you can: it's a mistake not to. It doesn't so much matter what you do—but live. This place makes it all com over me. I see it now. I haven't done so—and now I'm too old. It's too late. It has gone past me—I've lost it. You have time. You are young. Live!"[2]

James, it is apparent, mulled over this anecdote for years. Right off, it seems, James detected in it Howells's lingering concern over his son John's prolonged stay in Paris—"domiciled and initiated," as James embellished suggestively in setting down Sturges's anecdote.[3] It is of more than passing interest, I think, that the recipient of Strether's Howellsian advice is also named John. But it should be noted that his name doubles down as "Bil." Thus, to put a fine point on it, we have in "John Little Bil[ham]" a not so oblique link to James's real-life source: "John, Little William (Dean) Howells." Of course, at his age—his mid-fifties—Howells bursts out with advice that one might have expected to have been offered by a father to his son. But since he could not get himself to offer that advice directly to his son, in my view, he offered it to an intermediary, knowing, of course, that it would undoubtedly at some point become known to John. He could count on that. But that he chose Jonathan Sturges as the vehicle for that brave advice is intriguing. For Sturges, a graduate of Princeton University and a writer and translator, "had been badly crippled in childhood by poliomyelitis; from the waist up he was a good-looking, broad-shouldered young man, with fine distinctive features," writes James's biographer, but "he liked best to go riding in Hyde Park in an open hansom to conceal his infirmities."[4] It seems to have been rather cruel of Howells to have offered this advice with Sturges uppermost in mind. James himself was wont, as he did in a letter to Edmund Gosse in 1890 to refer to Sturges as "Little Brother Jonathan."[5] It is, of course, another oblique clue into just how James's writer's creative logic brought to book Howells's germinating words.

Interestingly, in recording this Howells anecdote in his notebook, James thought of it, not something that might lead to some piece of writing of large compass such as what *The Ambassadors* would become, but "of something, of a tiny kind, springing out of it, something that would take its place in the little group I should like to do of Les Vieux—The Old. (What should I call it in English—Old Fellows? No, that's trivial and common.)"[6] Nowhere else does James return to this idea of a "little group" of Les Vieux. Finally nothing big came of this idea. But one thinks now of who might have been included in that group. Henry Adams comes to mind, as do John Hay and William Dean Howells, along with Oliver Wendell Holmes (his model for Waymarsh in *The Ambassadors*), and James's brother William. By 1895 they were in their mid- to-late fifties. As Howells had lamented in 1886, when he thought of his next birthday (his fiftieth), "I have heard people say that they are not conscious of growing older; but I am. I'm perfectly aware of the shrinking bounds. I don't plan so largely as I used, and without having lost hope I don't have so much use for it as once. I feel my half century fully. Lord, how it's slipped away!"[7]

Howells's being in Paris in 1895 had had a serious purpose of its own. He was looking in on his son, John Mead Howells, "the domiciled and initiated" young man (as James characterized him). In short, the visit had been undertaken by a concerned parent. Paris, of course, was Paris. And Howells had come alone, and he intended to stay around. As James recalled in his preface in 1907, "There was the dreadful little old tradition, one of the platitudes of the human comedy, that People's moral scheme does break down in Paris; that nothing is more frequently observed; that hundreds of thousands of more or less hypocritical or more or less cynical persons annually visit the place for the sake of the probable catastrophe, and that I came late in the day to work myself up about it. There was in fine the trivial association, one of the vulgarest in the world; but which gave me pause no longer, I think, simply because its vulgarity is so advertised."[8]

That "vulgarity" was also a viable worry for William Dean Howells. On his return to America in 1894 he confessed to young John, who was still in Paris: "Perhaps it was as well I was called home. The poison of Europe was getting into my soul. You must look out for that. They live much more fully than we do. Life here is still for the future—it is a land of Emersons—and I like a little present moment in. When I think of Whistler's garden!" But he quickly turns to a momentary stay of enticement. "but Saratoga amuses somewhat. Here is an image of leisure, if not leisure. I think it would interest you. There are no such intensely American types anywhere, not even in Paris: thin young fellows, sharp, aquiline, definite, pointed for business, not two ideas in their skulls, but mostly good and kind. I suppose something will come of it all."[9] Think Chad Newsome, Parisian poison, and his return to Woollett to run the family business, whatever business that was.

One last (curious) note. While it is widely accepted that James's Louis Lambert Strether owes his given and middle names to "Louis Lambert," a character in a Balzac novel, another possibility is that his name derives from "Louis Lambert," the pseudonym used by the Irish-born Patrick Sarsfield Gilmore, who wrote the song "When Johnny Comes Marching Home" in 1863.[10] How fitting this song for Howells when his John came home to America after having been "domiciled and initiated" in Paris or, for that matter, of Mrs. Newsome when one ponders her anxious wait for her son Chad to return to "the philosophy of Woollett" after his generous portion of Parisian life.[11]

5

Lessons of Browning

Ernest Dowson once observed that Robert Browning's poetry was essentially Jamesian. "As for Browning!" he wrote to Arthur Moore in 1890, "if our Henry, if Turguenef, if Bourget had written their masterpieces in verse they would have been like that. The subtility, the tact of omission, the Morbidezza! 'My Last Duchess,' par exemple, is pure Henry James. I must have read it a dozen times before to-day: but I have only just appreciated the full subtility of it. It is wonderful."[1]

Robert Browning's books had a prominent and permanent place on the James family book-table. There, on display, they would come to stand for many things to the novelist in the family.[2] Over the years Henry James would read everything Browning published, from *Sordello* to *The Ring and the Book*, with *Men and Women* the text he most treasured. It became a standard for measuring excellence in others as well as in himself, a consummate performance that constantly challenged his own narrative and dramatic efforts, and a storehouse rich in what we would now call Jamesian devices, themes, and situations. To James, Browning would always be, simply, "the author of *Men and Women*."[3]

"*Men and Women* (1855) left an early and lasting mark on James's fiction, including "A Light Woman," a poem has been neglected by even Browning's most enthusiastic readers." William C. DeVane, for example, found that "the chief point of interest" in this fifty-six-line poem is "the idea which concludes it,"

> And, Robert Browning, you writer of plays,
> Here's a subject made to your hand![4]

Henry James, on the other hand, found it fare rich enough to levy upon twice over a period of twenty years: initially, for the story "A Light Man" (1869), and then for a second story, "The Lesson of the Master" (1888).[5]

"A Light Woman" exemplifies Browning's uncanny skill at condensing into ordered poems, usually monologues, what in the hands of others (including James) would be the materials sufficient for a novella. Since it ranks among the least familiar of Browning's early poems, it will be useful to recall the poem:

> So far as our story approaches the end,
>   Which do you pity the most of us three?—
> My friend, or the mistress of my friend
>   With her wanton eyes, or me?
> My friend was already too good to lose,
>   And seemed in the way of improvement yet,
> When she crossed his path with her hunting-noose
>   And over him drew her net.
> When I saw him tangled in her toils,
>   A shame, said I, if she adds just him
> To her nine-and-ninety other spoils
>   The hundredth for a whim!
> And before my friend be wholly hers,
>   How easy to prove to him, I said,
> An eagle's the game her pride prefers,
>   Though she snaps at a wren instead!
> So, I gave her eyes my own eyes to take,
>   My hand sought hers as in earnest need,
> And round she turned for my noble sake,
>   And gave me herself indeed.
> The eagle am I, with my fame in the world,
>   The wren is he, with his maiden face.
> —You look away and your lip is curled?
>   Patience, a moment's space!
> For see, my friend goes shaking and white;
>   He eyes me as the basilisk;
> I have turned, it appears, his day to night,
>   Eclipsing his sun's disk.
> And I did it, he thinks, as a very thief:
>   "Though I love her—that, he comprehends—
> One should master one's passions, (love, in chief)
>   And be loyal to one's friends!"
> And she,—she lies in my hand as tame
>   As a pear late basking over a wall;
> Just a touch to try and off it came;
>   'Tis mine,—can I let it fall?
> With no mind to eat it, that's the worst!
>   Were it thrown in the road, would the case assist?
> 'Twas quenching a dozen blue-flies' thirst
>   When I gave its stalk a twist.
> And I,—what I seem to my friend, you see:
>   What I soon shall seem to his love, you guess:
> What I seem to myself, do you ask of me?
>   No hero, I confess.
> 'Tis an awkward thing to play with souls,
>   And matter enough to save one's own:
> Yet think of my friend, and the burning coals
>   He played with for bits of stone!
> One likes to show the truth for the truth;
>   That the woman was light is very true:

> But suppose she says,—Never mind that youth!
> What wrong have I done to you?
> Well; anyhow, here the story stays,
> So far at least as I understand;
> And, Robert Browning, you writer of plays,
> Here's a subject made to your hand![6]

If Browning the dramatist, addressed by Browning the poet, did not take up the hint, Henry James did, though not as a play. From this poem he derived a title and culled an epigraph (the eleventh stanza), and he reworked its basic situation into a story that he would always number among his own favorites.

"A Light Man" can be readily summarized. Maximus Austin, a thirty-two-year-old adventurer, has just returned from Europe. A letter from Theodore Lisle, a close friend, serves to attract him to the estate of a seventy-two-year-old millionaire Frederick Sloane, who is close to death. Almost at once Austin begins to vie with his friend for the approval and affection of the older man, as well as his money. Sloane soon favors the new man. The situation, at least before James revised the story for republication, fifteen years later, suggests the latent homosexuality of its principals. Played out in rooms that abound with the conventional signs of effeminacy, as the narrator is quick to point out, this drama revolves around "a gossip flanked by a coxcomb and an egoist."[7] The tale reaches its climax when Austin, having been requested by the dying old man to fetch his will, finds his rival perusing it. They note that the will is made out in Lisle's favor. When Austin tells Lisle that Sloane has asked him to destroy it, but that he has refused, Lisle's anger turns to remorse and he destroys it. In the meantime Sloane has gone to his reward. Because the will has been destroyed, however, he dies intestate, and his fortune falls to a "discarded half-niece." The narrator indicates that he will now await the arrival of the new heiress.

As in Browning's poem, James's story centers on three individuals, two of whom compete for the favor of the third. In "A Light Woman" two men (one considerably younger than the other) compete for a young woman, while in "A Light Man" two young men compete for an old man. In Browning the young friend stands to get the woman's affection until the older friend makes his move and then the woman drops the younger man for the older man. In James the friend stands to get the old man's affection (and money) until the narrator makes his move and then the old man drops the friend for the narrator. If there is less ambivalence about the motivations of James's characters than there is about Browning's, there is nevertheless the same claim in James's story on the part of the narrator that he behaves unselfishly in preventing his friend, a "belle âme" and a "man of taste," from sacrificing himself to circumstance that there is in Browning's poem. Were the light woman to add his friend "to her nine-and-ninety other spoils, / The hundredth for a whim!" it would be a "shame," decides

Browning's narrator. James's narrator tells us that the light man had "for the past ten years an unbroken series of favorites, *protégés*, and heirs presumptive," but that each, in turn, having "by some fatally false movement ... unjointed his nose," had been dropped at the old man's whim. "The woman was light," Browning's narrator tells us, while James's narrator tells us that although the old man "fancie[d] himself one of the weightiest of men," he was "essentially one of the lightest." Indeed, so closely does James follow Browning that he even adopts and elaborates upon one of the poem's key images. Browning's narrator laments: "my friend goes shaking and white;/ He eyes me as the basilisk:/ I have turned, it appears, his day to night, / Eclipsing his sun's disk." James's narrator asks himself: "Can it be that Mr. Sloane really wishes to drop him? He understands favor and friendship only as a selfish rapture—a reaction, an infatuation, an act of aggressive, exclusive patronage. It's not a bestowal with him, but a transfer, and half his pleasure in causing *his sun to shine is that*—being woefully near its setting—it will produce *a number of delectable shadows. He wants to cast my shadow*, I suppose, on Theodore; fortunately I'm not altogether an opaque body" (emphasis added).

There is nothing in Browning's poem "A Light Woman" to suggest that the older man (the "eagle") and the younger man (the "wren") are writers, nor does James in "A Light Man" insist that his principals are writers. But the years after 1869 wore on and James gradually began to "recast" Browning's poem exactly along those lines, populating his second "version" of "A Light Woman" with two novelists. James himself had been unable to square the Robert Browning he had admired through his poetry with the posturing poet he met frequently at dinner parties. Although others lionized Browning, James was not impressed. He had read the poetry with approval as it emerged from the presses and then had listened to the poet read that same poetry as if he "hated" the words and would like "to bite them to pieces." "Robert B. I am sorry to say does not make on me a purely agreeable impression," he complained. "Strange to say, his talk doesn't strike me as very good. It is altogether gossip and personality and is not very beautifully worded." Sad to say, Browning was "a great chatterer but no Sordello at all." And worse, when this chatterer was not chattering, he was quite amply "dozing." Evidently, he would suggest, not entirely in amusement, that there must be "two Brownings—an esoteric and an exoteric. The former never peeps out in society, and the latter has not a ray of suggestion of *Men and Women*."[8]

The notion that there were "two Brownings"—two separate, discrete, complementing beings—would incubate a while longer, flowering ultimately into the fantastic tale, "The Private Life" (1892). Prior to that fanciful takeoff, however, James came to the more realistic conclusion that Browning as artist and

Browning as social lion were simply irreconcilable. That notion set him on the road to an entirely different tale. A notebook entry early in 1888 records one of the germs for "The Lesson of the Master":

> Another [idea] came to me last night as I was talking with Theodore Child about the effect of marriage on the artist, the man of letters, etc. He mentioned the cases he had seen in Paris in which this effect had been fatal to the quality of the work, etc.—through overproduction, need to meet expenses, make a figure, etc. And I mentioned certain cases here. Child spoke of Daudet—his 30 Ans de Paris, as an example in point. "He would never have written that if he hadn't married." So it occurred to me that a very interesting situation would be that of an elder artist or writer, who has been ruined (in his own sight) by his marriage and its forcing him to produce promiscuously and cheaply—his position in regard to a younger *confrère* whom he sees on the brink of the same disaster and whom he endeavours to save, to rescue, by some act of bold interference—breaking off the marriage, annihilating the wife, making trouble between the parties.[9]

James would trace "The Lesson of the Master" to this conversation, but his conversation with Child was only part of the story. For the blueprint of the achieved tale—an older man's attempt to "save" a younger friend from a potentially harmful marriage—had already served Browning in "A Light Woman."

Narrated in the third person, "The Lesson of the Master" nevertheless has as its center of consciousness, except for the final sentences when the "author" takes over, a younger writer. Its basic story can be quickly retold. At an English country house on a pleasant Sunday in June, Paul Overt, a young writer, meets Henry St. George (the "Master"), St. George's wife, one General Fancourt, and the latter's marriageable daughter Marian. After supper St. George ruefully advises Overt that for the sake of his artistic promise he must never marry. Wife and children, he insists, will only cripple the artist within him. (One thinks here of Browning's way of seeing the failed painter's marriage in "Andrea del Sarto.") Back in London, Overt sees Marian again, promptly discovering that he loves her. When he then visits St. George at home, however, the "Master" once again advises him—even more adamantly this time—to court only the muse. St. George has made his point, and the young writer goes off dutifully alone to the Continent. Working deliberately and conscientiously, he manages to finish a new book. Toward the end of his longish stay a letter from Marian informs him that St George's wife has suddenly died. On his return to London, he is stunned to learn further that Marian herself is about to marry the "Master." Overt and St. George meet, and the young writer charges the older writer with having duped him into renouncing Marian. But St. George insists that his original advice was offered honestly and remains sound: he will never again have the opportunity to write well, but Paul, because he has not married, will achieve greatness.

James's tale follows Browning's poem to a T. The eagle, fearing that the wren's integrity will be compromised and that he will betray his talent, has indeed removed temptation from the path of his flight by marrying the young woman himself. Only the "Master" ("the illustrious *confrère*," his votary calls him) knows that he has not lived up to his fine talent and that, moreover, he never will. At fault in his apostasy, as St. George sees it, is his wife. "I never made him do anything in my life but once," she insists, "when I made him burn up a bad book." And what was that book? "It was," St. George admits to Overt, "about myself," adding: "Oh, but you should write it—you should do me. There's a subject, my boy: no end of stuff in it!"[10]

The difficulty, St. George insists, is that he has sold out. "I've married for money," he confesses; "I refer to the mercenary muse whom I led to the altar of literature. Don't do that, my boy," he cautions, "she'll lead you a life!" For the "mercenary muse" calls for endless obedience. St. George's wife, who cares nothing for perfection, plays the demanding Lucrezia to his compliant Andrea del Sarto, her great stroke having been to invent the "Master's" study. When the disciple visits the "Master," he finds him at work:

> St. George was in his shirt-sleeves in the middle of a large, high room—a room without windows, but with a wide skylight at the top, like a place of exhibition. It was furnished as a library, and the serried bookshelves rose to the ceiling, a surface of incomparable tone, produced by dimly-gilt "backs," which was interrupted here and there by the suspension of old prints and drawings. At the end furthest from the door of admission was a tall desk, of great extent, at which the person using it could only write standing, like a clerk in a counting-house; and stretching from the door to this structure was a large plain band of crimson cloth, as straight as a garden-path and almost as long, where, in his mind's eye, Paul Overt immediately saw his host pace to and fro during his hours of composition.... "Ah, we're practical—we're practical!" St. George said, as he saw his visitor looking the place over. "Isn't it a good big cage, to go round and round? My wife invented it and she locks me up here every morning."
> "You don't miss a window—a place to look out?"
> "I did at first, awfully; but her calculation was just. It saves time, it has saved me many months in these ten years. Here I stand, under the eye of day—in London of course, very often, it's rather a bleared old eye—walled in to my trade. I can't get away, and the room is a fine lesson in concentration. I've learned the lesson, I think; look at that big bundle of proof and admit that I have." He pointed to a fat roll of papers, on one of the tables, which had not been undone.

St. George advocates the early recognition of the masters that he has served and their immediate rejection. "I've touched a thousand things," he cries, "but which one of them have I turned into gold?"

> [For] the artist has to do only with that—he knows nothing of any baser metal. I've led the life of the world, with my wife and my progeny; the clumsy, expensive, materialised, brutalised, philistine, snobbish life of London. We've got everything handsome, even a carriage—we are prosperous, hospitable, eminent people. But, my dear fellow, don't try to stultify yourself and pretend you don't know what we haven't got. It's bigger than all the rest. Between artists—come! You know as well as you sit there that you would put a pistol-ball into your brain if you had written my books!

Shortly thereafter, convinced of the wisdom of St. George's words, Paul Overt goes off to Europe to work at his trade, but to learn, subsequently, the price he will have paid for having been "dosed with the doctrine of renunciation."

Whether or not Marian Fancourt was worthy of the young writer's love is never established. If St. George finds her worth marrying, Overt can no longer be certain that he knows her worth. Suspicion lingers. Browning's Duke had observed of his "Last Duchess," "She had / A heart ... too soon made glad, / Too easily impressed; she liked whate'er / She looked on, and her looks went everywhere ... / all and each / Would draw from her alike the approving speech. / Or blush, at least."[11] Paul Overt now notes of Marian Fancourt that "it cost her nothing to speak to one in that tone; it was her old bounteous, demonstrative way, with a certain added amplitude that time had brought; and if it began to operate on the spot, at such a juncture in her history, perhaps in the other days too it had meant just as little or as much—a sort of mechanical charity, with the difference now that she was satisfied, ready to give but asking nothing."

In a roundabout way, one suspects, James had Browning in mind even when he chose his "Master's" surname: St. George. James's notebooks testify to his writer's interest in names. He searched the pages of the London *Times* for names to give his fictional characters, and he frequently compiled long lists of such names. He chose names on several principles: for sound, oddity, thematic resonance, and mythic links. It is entirely in character, then, that James decided to name the "Master" of his story "Henry" (after himself, though he was not yet in 1888 an acknowledged "Master") and "St. George" (an allusion to Robert Browning and the role Browning himself had "adopted"). The story of Browning's dashing "rescue" of Elizabeth Barrett from her father's home was, of course, the great real-life Victorian love story.

That Browning saw himself as a Perseus—St. George defying dragons to rescue princesses, even before he himself had performed the heroics of rescuing his beloved Elizabeth—has been well established. It is also well-known that judging from the many allusions to the various forms of the legend in his later work, including both *The Inn Album* and *The Ring and the Book*, the ancient legend of England's patron saint continued to cast a persistent spell over Browning.[12]

As the name is used in "The Lesson of the Master," "St. George" is both appropriate and ironic, depending, of course, upon whose point of view is honored. In marrying the young Marian Fancourt, the "Master" saves not a maiden but a young man, and he saves him, he insists, for the sake of his future masterpieces. From the point of view of the young writer who is "saved," however, the possibility nags that it is the dragon itself in the person of St. George who has married the princess and that he, her would-be rescuer, has been shut out: "the door quite slammed in his face."

"The Lesson of the Master" was not to be James's last word on the Browning puzzle. One question nagged him. Just how did Browning's genius survive his "worldliness"? In his story of 1892, "The Private Life," James indulged in the fantasy that his poet-hero was, like Browning, literally two persons. He was both the "Private Poet" and the "Poet of Society," who were, in him, dissociated "as they can rarely elsewhere have been."[13] From his own vantage as the "Master," however, James would see Browning differently. Contrasting another artist's failure with Browning's success, James saw the key to the difference in Browning's exemplary devotion to his art. "The writer's 'relation to his subject'" was for Browning "constitutionally stout and single," he wrote in 1903; for Browning was "neither divided nor dispersed."[14] Yet the striking thing was that Browning had maintained that singular devotion to his art without ever renouncing the things of this world. Indeed, although James did not so put it, he was struck by the irony that Browning had had his art for its own sake, without foregoing his marriage, his child, his public acclaim, and his social triumphs. The "illustrious novelist" holding forth in "The Lesson of the Master" had simply been wrong. Henry St. George's conviction that perfection in art could be attained only by the talented artist who would renounce wife, family, society, and fortune just did not apply to Robert Browning. If Henry St. George saw himself as "walled in to [his] trade," even when working below his potential and against his talent, Browning had miraculously solved the riddle of slipping back and forth between private and social worlds without compromising his integrity. As James described the feat, "the wall that built out the idyll ... contained an invisible door through which, working the lock at will, he [Browning] could swiftly pass and of which he kept the golden key—carrying the same about with him even in the pocket of his dinner-waistcoat."[15] It is small wonder that at the very end of "The Lesson of the Master" we find St. George's young protégé haunted both by the Master's advice and the irrevocable nature of his own Jamesian decision to ransom so very much for the chance to fulfill his talent and to perfect his art.

6

The Destructive Self

In the face of James's own formidable performance in his preface to *The Altar of the Dead* volume of James's New York Edition, it may seem gratuitous to attempt a further definition of the moral and psychological makeup of John Marcher. Although his commentary is unsurpassed at the level of apprehending the isolated, individual personality, James fails to perceive that his creation of Marcher embodies an implicit criticism of a literary type then extant, but about to become even more widely characteristic and symptomatic of the early decades of the twentieth century. Certainly, to dismiss Marcher, the hero of "a great negative adventure," as just another of his "poor sensitive gentlemen," as James does, a little disingenuously,[1] is to ignore the larger cultural and historical references of his achievement. One of the purposes of this chapter is to account for James's central position in the delineation of this type by identifying his work in this vein with a notable literary tradition.

One of the principal means of organization in "The Beast in the Jungle" occurs through a succession of images, metaphors, and references to sight and perception. In this instance it may well be the author's most revealing method of exploring his theme. Our experience of the story is very much shaped by these references to seeing—looking into eyes, facing, confronting, looking "things in the face"—with the result that, for much of the time, we perceive, for all their statements to the contrary, that there is only blind empathy between those individuals who will not see. Yet, although we are told that no one has seen into Marcher's eyes—not even May Bartram—for a very long time, it is a fact that the closeness of their relationship has occurred at the moment she manifests an ability to look at everything through his eyes only, to see the world consistently from his point of view. Henceforth her own perceptions may be dominated by his jaundiced views. To the crowds of life, which to him are stupid, dumb, unseeing, Marcher leads one kind of life; to May he offers a life which she can share with him, unequally, as another pair of eyes focused upon the same void. In *Walden* Thoreau has asked, "Could a greater miracle take place than for us to look through each other's eyes for an instant?"² Thoreau was speaking, of course, of the literal impossibility. James, on the other hand, in grasping at the imaginative possibilities, would see that the miracle could be approximated at crucial moments by personal, sensitive dedication. It is in this fashion that May Bartram does perform the miracle of seeing through Marcher's eyes, a feat that enables her to understand all. And it is from such miracles that Marcher's narrowing and reductive ideal conception of his personality disqualifies him.

Marcher ultimately realizes that he has seen his life only from the outside. This is the reason, simply, for his inability to see the long, continuous visitation of the beast. Even Marcher's few realizations of external change in himself come from his awareness that the appearance of May Bartram, his reflector and spurned guide, has changed perceptibly. His awareness, toward the end, that she is dying is the first definite proof (which she does her utmost to dispel in their "short interviews") that he has been indeed "sold." Later, considerably after her death, he tries to see himself in the middle-aged mourner who appears beside him at the cemetery, and he recognizes the ravages of pain and sorrow caused by the stark betrayal of passion by death that he has not come to possess. In an instant his sight of the mourner, who is no more than a *ficelle*, turns into the culmination of his attempts to recapture—in the famous Jamesian phrase— the "lost stuff of consciousness," which he had "hunted up and down very much as if he were knocking at doors and enquiring of police."³

This flash of understanding, after so many years, allows Marcher to experience what is now merely the memory of the beast. And the way in which such an experience finally takes place sustains James's central image: Marcher is able to get out of himself long enough to look clearly into the eyes of another being. He sees there something, for once, which goes beyond his own familiar reflection. All his life he has beheld his potential experience, not objectively, but as an object. His wait for the beast was matched by his careful guidance of the externals of his own life. Furtively dedicated to the internal life, he is fixed, paradoxically, in the more appropriate, but less congenial, role of keeper to formal appearance. In this, of course, he succeeds admirably. The precise relationship of the elements of distorted perception and superficial formality is made clear in a single passage:

> He knew how he felt, but, besides knowing that, she knew how he looked as well; he knew each of the things of importance he was insidiously kept from doing, but she could add up the amount they made, understand how much, with a lighter weight on his spirit, he might have done, and thereby established how, clever as he was, he fell short. Above all she was in the secret of the difference between the forms he went through— those of his little office under Government, those of caring for his modest patrimony, for

his library, for his garden in the country, for the people in London whose invitations he accepted and repaid—and the detachment that reigned beneath them and that made of all behaviour, all that could in the least be called behaviour, a long act of dissimulation. What it had come to was that he wore a mask painted with the social simper, out of the eyeholes of which there looked eyes of an expression not in the least matching the other features. This stupid world, even after years, had never more than half-discovered. It was only May Bartram who had, and she achieved, by an art indescribable, the feat of at once—or perhaps it was only alternately—meeting the eyes from in front and mingling her own vision, as from over his shoulder, with their peep through the apertures."

Marcher's enormous concern that society's role in his life remain neutral compels him to maintain a mask of social unimportance, of seeming commonness and mediocrity. Of vital importance, besides, is his desperate and selfish hope that his own bit of society never suspects the potentiality of uniqueness which his life calls for. Even with May, his only close friend, the social role must be maintained as a convenience and perhaps as a necessity; their relationship must appear to be no more than the normal socially accepted one of gentleman friend and genteel lady. This, of course, she can give him immediately, and when later in their life together she tells him that she will continue to give him, in this way, protection from society, he can only thank her obsequiously for what he takes to be her disinterested generosity. But awareness of the cuts inflicted by this social role (a role which is all too effective in hiding their tragic empathy and her acceptance of his death-in-life grip over her) begins when at the hour of her death he realizes shockingly that he is of less official importance at her funeral than distant relatives who had meant nothing at all to her. The price of effective social protection has been final exclusion.

Seen abstractly, the thematic emphasis upon the role of each man in shaping his own experience has a limited, but precise relevance to the tradition outlined some years ago in Philip Rahv's highly influential account of "The Cult of Experience in American Writing."[4] Acknowledging specifically James's great teaching that experience constitutes "the rights of the private man, the rights of personality," Rahv points out that the high point of this central doctrine occurs in *The Ambassadors* in Lambert Strether's epochal advice to Little Bilham to live. Strether's own achievement is offered as the finest illustration of acute moral and personal awareness as valid experience. He begins to live finally at the age of fifty-five only because he has become, through his Parisian education, wondrously aware of moral and ethical nuances and reverberations. Yet "The Beast in the Jungle," written immediately after the completion of *The Ambassadors*, stands as a trenchant qualification of Strether's urgent message. Usually accepted as a good in itself, awareness is destructive when the idea of it, becoming essential, is emphasized to excess. For most of his adult life Marcher is unconsciously guilty of such excesses. To say that the idea of experience has become for him a personal cult is to understate the matter badly. The rights of personality have been so selfishly developed and slavishly sheltered that finally even he cannot face up to what he has done to his life. Even his desperate, but hollow hope that his suffering "would only be decently proportionate to the posture he had kept, all his life, in the threatened presence of [the beast]" is eventually followed by the debilitating realization "that all the while he had waited the wait was itself his portion." The momentary disclosure to Marcher of his "arid end," springing at him not out of the jungle he has watched but from a cultivated "garden of death," is James's corrective to the excesses inherent in Strether's shrill admonition to live for conscious impressions.

Remarkable creation that he is, John Marcher, as a type, has direct antecedents in American fiction in the work of Hawthorne. Several years ago, it was suggested that "The Beast in the Jungle" had its source in a passage from Hawthorne's *Blithedale Romance*.[5] In his critical study of Hawthorne, James quotes: "Hollingsworth scarcely said a word, unless when repeatedly and pertinaciously addressed. Then, indeed, he would glare upon us from the thick shrubbery of his meditations, like a tiger out of a jungle, make the briefest reply possible, and betake himself back into the solitude of his heart and mind."[6] On the basis of James's use of this excerpt, Lucke concludes:

> Thus it becomes clear that one passage by Hawthorne together with its omitted sentence, quoted by Henry James in 1880, was responsible for James's story "The Beast in the Jungle," some two decades later. The passage is responsible, it may be, not only for the title of the story, for the underlying symbolic idea of the springing tiger, for the character of the hero as the egotist deranged by prolonged concentration on his own ideas, but for the philosophy pervading all of James's later work—experience, living, is all that matters, a theme developed in detail in *The Ambassadors*.[7]

Although I see no reason to deny that James probably got his central image from Hawthorne, the full claim as it stands is extravagant and misleading. The most telling qualification results from our recognition of what James made of this source. Judging from his own achievement, I suspect that he would have seen that Hawthorne's image was somewhat out of proportion for Hollingsworth in that it was too much of a psychological image for his relative insensitivity. In this connection it is useful to recall James's regret: "It is a pity, perhaps, to have represented him [Hollingsworth] as having begun life as a blacksmith, for one grudges him the advantage of so logical a reason for his roughness and hardness."[8] It is notable, further, that in Hawthorne this imagery is given as the narrator's, Coverdale's, whereas in James's story Marcher himself conceives his fate in terms of the stalking-beast image. And yet to the characterization of even John Marcher this image seems to be grossly out of proportion the first few times it appears. Of course it is a tribute to James that the culmination of the story completely justifies the use of this image in the terms of Marcher's own life, not merely as ironic disproportion, but in that what does happen to him ultimately is indeed wildly terrifying.

In regard to the question of James's use of this source then, what is significant is not that Marcher's existence is controlled by one idea, but rather that his *idée fixe* differs from Hollingsworth's in quality. Hollingsworth is a vehement social reformer who fails either to analyze or to question the patently superficial social vision that warps his life. Marcher's overwhelming idea is quite something else. He doesn't want to do anything—"to achieve in the world, to be distinguished or admired for," as he puts it; on the contrary, he desires and expects something to be done to him which will be exclusive and personal. This event must come about because, for some inexplicable reason, he is fated to suffer the anguish, pain, and violence necessary to requite his life of ascetic preparation. To May Bartram's question as to whether "it's to be something you're merely to suffer?" he answers in passionately disproportionate terms, "Well, say to wait for—to have to meet, to face, to see suddenly break out in my life; possibly destroying all further consciousness, possibly annihilating me; possibly, on the other hand, only altering everything, striking at the root of all my world and leaving me to the consequences, however they shape themselves."

To Marcher the beast is no more than an approximate and shadowy symbol for the potentially shattering nature of the great adventure. He is directed not by an intellectual idea but by a sensibility overworked into a false prescience of what is beyond the merely imminent. It is misleading, then, to say that his actions are expressive of his will in conjunction with his persistent idea in the way that we can say that Hollingsworth's decisions are made to accord with his controlling social principles, for the very possibility of Marcher's making any meaningful decision is precluded by his immobilizing sense of personal fate. Since his choice of the beast image characterizes his ego above all, we can see that his sensitivity, pitched to decadence, enables him to expect something of great magnitude out of his life; yet, somewhat paradoxically, he is certain that it is to be of a completely personal nature. The substance of Marcher's life, purely of his own making, remains synthetic and spurious.

Through this analysis it becomes clear that actually it is Miles Coverdale, the narrator of *The Blithedale Romance*, who is directly and meaningfully related to Marcher. F. O. Matthiessen has acknowledged the large general effect which the characterization of Coverdale, as the perceiving influence and as narrator through whose consciousness a story is told, had upon James's work. Matthiessen, viewing the primary influence as one of technique, evaluates Coverdale's characterization:

> A long distance separates Miles Coverdale, who seemed unwittingly to contribute something of his own self-conscious coolness to the story he was reporting, and Lambert

Strether, whose rich sense of all that was unfolding enabled James so to center the composition of *The Ambassadors* that he could consider it his best achievement. But the stages of development between these two are precisely those of James' experiments, for which a natural starting point was provided by Coverdale's own recognition of his role.[9]

Yet, strangely enough, he adds that Coverdale is aware of the causes for his failure to contribute to the action of his own narrative: "But what Coverdale has dreaded acutely, that he was becoming inhuman through his analytical detachment, became the increasingly inescapable situation for James's supersubtle observers."[10] The implications of this connection require investigation.

What, precisely, motivates Coverdale's analytical detachment from the life around him? Except for the few oblique hints that Coverdale's function as a poet necessarily causes him to dissect the emotions and behavior of other human beings in the service of his art, and the implied belief that such close analysis can be done well only if he remains dispassionate and apart, we have perhaps no way of answering the question of motivation through explicit statement from the text, for we are contained by the limitations of Hawthorne's rigorously sustained point of view. But once we accept conscious detachment as the register of Coverdale's character, we can make some useful progress toward a satisfactory answer. Sensitive, somewhat intellectual, and excruciatingly self-conscious at all times, Coverdale is refined beyond the point of acting effectually in any emotional capacity. His melodramatic last-sentence confession that he too has loved Priscilla, many years after the failure of the social experiment and certainly long after the death of any hope he may have had for the consummation of this love, remains astonishing; but it is wholly in character. We may, if we so wish, see this profession of love as merely the public revelation of another of the matters that Miles has kept hidden and disguised in various ways. But such an explanation is insufficient; he can never convince us that it is love he has kept secret. Far more likely his confession of love is in reality no more than a half-realized rationalization based upon the assumption (to adapt a cliché) that it is more desirable to appear to have loved secretly and unsuccessfully than never to have loved. At least his feeling that he should have been in love with her—or, for that matter, with anyone at all—is genuine; in any case, he can now claim his love with impunity—and even believe in it—because neither Priscilla nor anyone else is around to question his word. From another aspect, it is possible also that this avowal is another of his deliberate ironies—designed often to counterbalance his sometimes painful social lapses and, at times, to mitigate his extreme candor—in that Coverdale knows a great deal about the quality of his own life; but this knowledge has not freed him from his fear of life. And since his inability to engage himself emotionally commits him to the passive agony of watching others live, it becomes the quality and the necessity of his life that he insulate himself against great passions and great adventures. In the most directly revealing passage in the novel, Coverdale, now middle-aged, assesses himself wearily:

> How strange! He [Hollingsworth] was ruined, morally, by an overplus of the same ingredient that want of which, I occasionally suspect, has rendered my own life all an emptiness. I by no means wish to die. Yet were there any cause in this whole chaos of human struggle, worth a sane man's dying for, and which my death would benefit, then—provided, however, the effort did not involve an unreasonable amount of trouble—methinks I might be bold to offer up my life. If Kossuth, for example, would pitch the battlefield of Hungarian rights within an easy ride of my abode, and choose a mild sunny morning, after breakfast, for the conflict, Miles Coverdale would gladly be his man, for one brave rush upon the levelled bayonets. Further than that I should be loath to pledge myself.[11]

And in spite of his carefully phrased promise to participate under ideal conditions, we are not at all certain that Miles would arrive at his convenient battlefield in time to serve. Sixty years later, in a similar song of love and agony, J. Alfred Prufrock would emphasize wearily that he was no Prince Hamlet. There is not much distance between Coverdale and Prufrock, and John Marcher is a watcher along the way.

Yet Hawthorne's most brilliant evocation of what we have come to recognize, in a form of useful shorthand, as the Prufrockian temper—indeed, in a larger context, the modern temper as delineated most explicitly by Joseph Wood Krutch—occurs in a tale that made its quiet appearance in the pages of *New England Magazine* in 1835. "Wakefield," more so than any other piece by Hawthorne, focuses upon the unlived life.

Hawthorne's claim that he got the idea for this story in an account, "told as truth," from an old magazine or newspaper has been amply documented.[12] Yet in acknowledging that this instance of "marital delinquency [is] ... as remarkable a freak as may be found in the whole list of human oddities," he appeals nevertheless, to our sense of the deeper reality of the situation. On the surface, his *donée* promises to be worthy of no more than melodramatic treatment, but Hawthorne's resilient view of reality is always based upon a profounder psychology of personality involving the irrevocable working of a stern morality. His admission that the item had originally been of topical interest only is made in the face of his necessity to justify artistically his belief that to the incident itself adheres a great moral reality. It is clear that for Hawthorne, as Renato Poggioli has written of Dostoevsky, "an object [did] not cease being symbolic merely because it was found by the poet ready-made, rather than invented anew."[13] Hawthorne himself wrote, in another connection, "I can never separate the idea from the symbol in which it manifests itself."[14] Hawthorne's insistence upon the necessity to move continuously from the realistic to the symbolic existed side by side with his permanent concern with the historical and the topical. For he could just as well have added to "Wakefield" Dostoevsky's own footnote to *Notes from the Underground*—published in the year of Hawthorne's death, 1864—that it was his "intention to bring before our reading public, more conspicuously than is usually done, one of the characters of our recent past. He is one of the representatives of a generation that is still with us."[15]

Yet "Wakefield" has never been accorded the attention that it merits and requires, both as a document and as the organic, closely structured piece of fiction that it is. The crux has been clearly a matter of its form. From a limited aspect, "Wakefield" seems to be little more than a not unsuccessful mixture of essay and fiction. If we examine it closely, however, we shall see that the essay portions are really part of the fictional process in that the story is a palpable demonstration of investigation by an artist into the materials suitable for literature. In a sense, Hawthorne's story is a tour de force in which the materials seem to be incompletely exploited, but are actually quintessentially rendered in just a few pointed scenes—scenes of crisis. In effect and by design, the story is a justification of the kind of knowledge which the art of fiction can give us. Our failure to emphasize this has resulted, clearly enough, from our reluctance to admit that there is, intentionally, a difference between the author's voice, which draws the clear-cut moral and is official in tone, and the meanings achieved through the rendering of scene and action. The official voice in this case, however, differs from that of an omniscient or intruding author, for what seem to be intrusions are actually attempts to understand the materials as they are turned into the incidents of fiction. In part, "Wakefield" is a parable of literary art in its concern with the process of discovering the realities of personality and the social meanings inherent in an old news account of a strange defection. The limited action that Hawthorne chooses to render may then mean, at least partially, what he says it means, but then again it may not. In any case, the author's observations, external to the fictionalized portions, do not exhaust meaning. Consequently, in this respect, we can see that Hawthorne's emphasis upon the idea, for example, that "it is perilous to make a chasm in human affections" is inadequate as a statement of meaning, for the achieved character of Wakefield shows us precisely that in no meaningful sense was he ever a party to genuine human affections. To forget that Hawthorne's opening promise—for the reader "there will be a pervading spirit and a moral, even should we fail to find them, done up neatly, and condensed into the final sentence"—is stated somewhat facetiously limits meaning in just the way that Hawthorne knew it could not be limited. Successful rendering of materials is in itself the act of investigation, but total meaning finally evades abstracted statement. The fragmentary surface quality of this story is functional in that the intentional gaps in the narrative suffice to suggest the emptiness of Wakefield's life during his twenty-year hiatus. To have filled it in with more details and scenes might have given his narrative the semblance of more life than Wakefield could have felt.

What, then, can be said of the portion of life that is his? Because he is disappointed, or at least uninterested, in the course of his present life, it occurs to Wakefield to do something adventurous, something eccentric. His extended plans to remove himself from his normal surroundings to a room in a nearby street for a short, but undetermined period are made in the attempt to measure the effect which his controlled experiment will have upon his wife—what, precisely, will be her reaction to the inordinate continuation of his unexplained and seemingly unmotivated absence? At one moment Hawthorne says that Wakefield acts "with a cold but not depraved or wandering heart." This is tentative and eventually misleading. Of course, in Hawthorne's terms, Wakefield is a man of reason as opposed to heart, but his experiment is particularly cruel in that it deals with the deepest emotions of another person. Implicit in this exercise of authority is his assurance that he possesses great power over the terms of his wife's existence. Characteristically, he overestimates both the effect of her grief and the duration of her sense of loss. Hawthorne is aware that Wakefield does not know, as James was later to observe about one of his own heroes, "it is so rarely, alas, into our power that anyone gets"[16]; but we know that the desire for such power is the sure sign of a heart depraved and without reason. Notably, both Hawthorne and James relate this lust for power over others to impotence. Yet May's ultimate awareness of just what her friend's experience has been frees her from his power, and Mrs. Wakefield unwittingly sheds all traces of domination and all effects of her husband's sadism when she survives the crisis of her illness at the outset of his absence to resign herself to a long period of comfortable and secure mourning.

Wakefield's departure from home is the beginning of his adventure, the beginning, in effect of his portion of life. His attempt to define his relationship to his usual world by absenting himself from it is not explained by his selfishness and vanity alone. Wakefield is enamored with the idea of doing the eccentric, the unmotivated, the unexplainable. Although he wants the dramatic thing to happen because of him, he acts negatively, by not doing. He wants to know "how the little sphere of creatures and circumstances, in which he was a central object will be affected by his removal"; but he can be best defined by his omissions. His personal disaster occurs, however, when, inevitably losing his tenuous control over his will to return, the objective experimenter is drawn into the vortex of his experiment. His life has lost, in the course of his attempt to watch it at its center, whatever significance it had possessed. In the beginning, because he is a creature of habits, habit alone nearly takes him home; but "the scraping of his foot upon the step" shocks him into the realization that his return at that very moment will destroy the effect of his experiment. Having effected a "wonderful escape" on this occasion, he does not get that close for another twenty years. Yet Wakefield, during all that time, remains "faithful to his wife, with all the affection of which his heart is capable, while he is slowly fading out of hers." The justified irony is that her life continues to develop, to adapt to the course of normal change, while his is cut off at the moment he realizes that it is no longer within his power to choose his moment of return. He is farthest from his own life when, in a flash of absurd fear, he accidentally encounters her in the street, for without recognition on her part "the throng eddies away, and carries them asunder." Hawthorne observes sadly that it is part of Wakefield's "unprecedented fate to retain his original share of human sympathies, and to be still involved in human interests, while he has lost his reciprocal influence on them." But Wakefield is never entirely aware that this fate has been triggered by his translation of his implicit conception of self into action.

Finally, after twenty years, his timidity in the face of a chance shower combines with an accident of location to send him back up the steps to his home in a moment of unmeditated decision. Outside, "quite penetrated with its [the shower's] autumnal chill," he has watched the mocking and, to him, "grotesque shadow of good Mrs. Wakefield," visible before the fire, as it "form[s] an admirable caricature, which dances, moreover, with the upflickering and down-shaking blaze, almost too merrily for the shade of an elderly widow." Even "the placid mien of settled widowhood" has been permanently transcended. Feeding upon the comfortable memory of loss in the course of the years, she has become a "portly female"; while he, in turn, existing in the midst of continuing loss, has grown "meagre." No longer does his foot scrape on the step to warn him from his salvation; now "he ascends the steps—heavily." As he returns to pick up whatever life is left to him, he is unaware that the "sole home" left him—the only end for his twenty-year wake—is the "grave," an anticipation of May Bartram's tomb in "The Beast in the Jungle." Wanting to watch his own life for a few days at the most, he has been trapped into observing nothing less than its death.

In summary, it may be of some use to begin by making a final attempt to define even more closely the crucial judgment and evaluation which Hawthorne and James contribute to this tradition. Wakefield's and John Marcher's necessary divorcement from the center of their lives through their secret conceptions of self occurs, in a sense, because, no less than Lambert Strether and Miles Coverdale, they want genuine experience. Consequently, each attempts at the outset of his adventure to apprehend and then to shape the meaning of his life through an act of will. Yet even though it is the lived life above all that he seeks, each is unaware that the kind of experience he eventually calls forth results necessarily from his having made a cult of personality. In Marcher's case, because his compulsive receptivity to the quality of experience he desires—and to that quality only—precludes the possibility of his being quick to any other kind of experience, his ideal conception of self is, in its consequences, as morally destructive as Wakefield's attempt to measure and evaluate his social and personal self through calculated experiment.

The extent of Hawthorne's contribution has already been suggested, but we would do well to establish even more precisely its relationship to James's work. Of pertinence here is the observation made by Matthiessen and Kenneth B. Murdock in their edition of James's private journals to the effect that "James' absorption, to the end of his career, with giving embodiment [especially in "The Beast in the Jungle"] to such a formalized spiritual and psychological pattern is again a token of his enduring kinship with Hawthorne. But," they continue, "James had progressed beyond Hawthorne's method of presenting, as in Ethan Brand, an allegory of the Unpardonable Sin."[17] Considering the current taste for realistic rather than allegorical symbolism, there is no doubt that *qua* method James had gone beyond "Ethan Brand" (so had Hawthorne, for that matter). But in conception and achievement James was never able to equal Hawthorne's Wakefield, whose physical withdrawal was, in effect, the final decadent flowering of the kind of life that had always been his, whose "eyes, small and lustreless, sometimes wander[ed] apprehensively about him, but oftener seem[ed] to look inward," whose absurd absence should have revealed to him the emptiness and meaninglessness of his life, but whose confusion at the last far surpassed his understanding. Certainly, in prefiguring one of the major aspects of the modern image of man, as he appears in the work of such representative twentieth-century writers as Kafka, Camus, Gide, Hesse, Faulkner, and—in a special way—Conrad, Wakefield is unmatched in the literature of nineteenth-century America.

Of their treatment of this type, it does not seem unfair to say that Hawthorne and James have based their work upon a consideration of the idea that a secret conception of self, by its very nature, tends to destroy the possibilities for genuine moral experience. John Marcher's complaint, "It wouldn't have been failure to be bankrupt, dishonoured, pilloried, hanged; it was failure not to be anything," suggests strongly that the valid test of any conception of self may require action, perhaps great actions. But it was Hawthorne's discovery that such conceptions could, and in some cases would necessarily, destroy the possibilities that the individual might have for meaningful actions of any efficacy. Allen Tate has ventured that "it is a fact of curious and perhaps of important historical interest that Hawthorne was the first American writer (he may have anticipated anybody in Europe) who was conscious of the failure of modern man to realize his full capacity for moral growth."[18] To this it may be added that it was also Hawthorne who first perceived the necessity for modern man to recognize that total blame for this failure lay in the destructive egocentricity of his personality. The account of Wakefield's experiment marks the beginning in America of the enduring literary concern with the nexus of the critical failure of personality and the destruction of the individual capacity for moral growth. Hawthorne's achievement in this story is neither accidental nor eccentric; it stands as the astonishingly complete detection of one of the prevailing modes of modern man.

7

Portraits of Friends

It is hardly surprising that Henry and Marian Hooper "Clover" Adams would make several appearances in Henry James's fiction, either as lightly disguised characters or through quotations of their words and sentiments. The preeminent stories in this regard—"The Point of View," "Pandora" and "The Modern Warning"—date from the 1880s.

It is well over a century since Henry James's epistolary story, "The Point of View," first achieved print in the pages of the December 1882 *Century Magazine*. It was reprinted, in book form, along with the title story and "The Pension Beaurepas," in *The Siege of London*, which was published three months later, in February 1883. It was, from the beginning, a controversial story. Indeed, when it was published in the *Century*, observed the *Boston Evening Transcript*, it rivaled *Daisy Miller* in the comment it elicited.[1]

It is not difficult to see why "The Point of View" should have created a stir. The causes are clear enough, but the response now seems excessive. In the background was the accruing general bad feeling over James's portrayal of the American Girl abroad (the A. G.) in *Daisy Miller*. In 1879 the magazines and newspapers had not been immediately excited over what would become James's best known story; they were more interested, actually, in praising his New England novel, *The Europeans*. But with the reading public it was another matter. In the *Atlantic Monthly* alone, for example, there were several anonymous readers' notes, pro and con, printed in the "Contributors' Club" between January and June 1879. And then with the appearance of James's treatment of Hawthorne in the English Men of Letters series, it became clear that future attacks upon James were to be oriented around the question of his patriotism or, to be more exact, his lack of it.

Certainly in an era of much economic, political and geographical development, satire, and honest criticism confused with satire, may not have been the most genial mode a young writer could have chosen. But even in this period of national hyper-self-consciousness, a Mark Twain could bring off satire. One difference between Mark Twain and Henry James was, of course, that the former, a "Westerner," directed much of his satire at Europe, and when not at Europe, at the eastern United States. At least so it seemed then. John Hay, a friend to both of them, was right when he said about James that "if he lived in Chicago he could write what he likes. But because he finds London more agreeable he is the prey of all the patriotisms."[2] What the strident nationalists of every stripe could not accept was the combination of James's expatriation and his talent for acute satire.

"The Point of View" is composed of a series of eight letters. The correspondents are the Americans Aurora Church and her mother, Miss Sturdy, Marcellus Cockerel and Louis Leverett, along with the Honorable Edward Antrobus (an English M.P.) and M. Gustave Lejaune, who is French. Of course these letters reflect in some detail the many new impressions of America that James had gathered in 1881–1882 during his first visit home in six years. James had stayed a while in Washington, a frequent visitor at the home of his friends, the Adamses. It seemed to whet his appetite for piercing social observation and for the mordant *bon mot*. It appeared to him, at the time, that Henry and Marian "Clover" Adams were always the center of a distinguished circle. It is no wonder, then, that a good deal of the material in James's story came from the Adamses and those attracted to their company. "Clover" Adams personally admitted some involvement, albeit unwittingly. "By the way, the only letter in Harry James's 'Point of View' in the last *Century* that can hit me is that of Hon. Marcellus Cockrell," she acknowledged. "Some of the remarks—as that about 'Hares and Rabbits Bill and Deceased wife's Sister'—I plead guilty to, but that it should be spotted as 'one of mine' I can't imagine."[3] She was of course right. Rather than crediting her (or anyone else) with the opinions and attitudes expressed throughout "The Point of View," contemporary reviewers, whether favorably disposed toward James's story or manifestly in opposition to it, were pretty much unanimous in crediting James himself with all the opinions expressed. *The Literary World*, for instance, insisted that the "letters are all strangely alike, so to speak, in their handwriting," the problem being, thought the reviewer, that "Mr. James did not sufficiently disguise his penmanship in composing this correspondence."[4] Even Horace E. Scudder, always good for a bit of generous praise for James's work ("Mr. James's subtlety never appeared to better advantage than in this clever bundle of letters"), admitted in the *Atlantic Monthly*: "One generally feels that, however elaborately the various characters are dressed, the voice is always the voice of Mr. James, and that the blessing intended for the character falls upon the head of the spirited wit who has planned the disguise."[5]

Some of James's more perceptive readers were not so sure about this, however; and their task for a long time, seemed to be that of identifying and isolating James's genuine voice, as well as distinguishing among those voices that were not his. John Hay thought that "the Howling Patriot['s]" mistaken view was that "'Miss Sturdy is James himself.'"[6] Miss Sturdy, the brusque and brash precursor of Dr. Prance of *The Bostonians*, seems hardly the persona through whom James would reveal his own actual views. Sympathetic James might have been to some of the hard-nosed views expressed by Miss Sturdy, but there are too many of his own sentiments scattered among his other speakers for any reader to see her as James's alter ego in this story. But neither, for that matter, is Hay's own guess as to who might be James's spokesman any more acceptable. His conclusion that "the author gives his sympathy only to the Roaring American" reveals more about Hay, one suspects, than it does about James. Certainly James's young American's occupations and jobs suggest a slight kinship with the so-called "ring-tailed roarer" of the American frontier, but it is no more than a suggestion. Yet even James's deliberate use of a characternym—he is called Marcellus Cockerel—indicates that we are to see him as the lusty, spirited product of the American West with his cockalorum Americanism reaffirmed by his "exhaustive" (and exhausting) three-year tour of Asia and Europe. Countering, seemingly, James's own complaints that America lacked traditions and institutions (evident in his *Hawthorne*), Marcellus as chauvinist writes to Mrs. Cooler ("*née* Cockerel"): "The vastness and freshness of this American world, the great scale and great pace of our development, the good sense and good nature of the people, console me for there being no cathedrals and no Titians."[7] Although he admits to "an immense deal of plainness" in America (515), he nevertheless boasts: "you'll call me a bird o' freedom, a braggart, a waver of the stars and stripes; but I'm in the delightful position of not minding in the least what any one calls me" (512).

In Marcellus Cockerel—the two names in themselves form a curious combination until one spells his surname Coquerel—is embodied the residue of the frontier tradition. By 1880 the frontier hero, it seems, has acquired a national self-consciousness. No longer is the battle perceived as one between ill-accommodated man and a real and demonic nature, but rather it is the bravado battle, fought through the media of the day, between the denizens of the new and of the old world. Cockerel is what is left of Natty Bumppo in a post–Jacksonian nation in which the frontier's natural setting has been translated into social and cultural terms in an international arena. Cockerel's scarcely hidden suspicion of such internationalism stands behind his overstatement of the virtues of the United States. Even the American newspaper, one of the durable banes of James's existence, comes in for its encomium: "Delightful country, where one sees everything in the papers—the big, familiar, vulgar, good-natured, delightful papers, none of which has any reputation to keep up for anything but getting the news!... Here the newspapers are like the railroad trains; which carry everything that comes to the station, and have only the religion of punctuality" (509).

The moral of this, of course, is clear enough. No one totally speaks for James; it is precisely his point of view that is missing. Louis Leverett is the deracinated American who has espoused most of the pseudo-aestheticism of Europe, and the young girl, Aurora Church, is intentionally presented as being less sensitive than even Daisy Miller, whom she resembles. Her European veneer spoils her for the likes of Marcellus Cockerel but it would appear that it will not stand in the way for very long—not even in the Oshkosh she offers as the very heart of the American provinces. In fact, the one who in some way comes closest to speaking for James (and about James) is M. Gustave Lejaune, the least American member of the group, who writes:

> They have a novelist with pretensions to literature, who writes about the chase for the husband and the adventures of the rich Americans in our corrupt old Europe, where their primeval candor puts the Europeans to shame. *C'est proprement écrit:* but it's terribly pale. What isn't pale is the newspapers—enormous, like everything else (fifty columns of advertisements), and full of the *commérages* of a continent. And such a tone, *grand Dieu!* The amenities, the personalities, the recriminations, are like so many *coups de revolver.* Headings six inches tall; correspondences from places one never heard of; telegrams from Europe about Sarah Bernhardt; little paragraphs about nothing at all; the *menu* of the neighbor's dinner; articles on the European situation *à pouffer de rire:* all the *tripotage* of local politics. The *reportage* is incredible; I'm chased up and down by the interviewers. The matrimonial infelicities of M. and Madame X. (they give the name) *tout au long,* with every detail—not in six lines, discreetly veiled, with an art of insinuation, as with us; but with all the facts (or the fictions), the letters, the dates, the places, the hours. I open a paper at hazard, and find *au beau milieu à propos* of nothing, the announcement— "Miss Susan Green has the longest nose in Western New York." Miss Susan Green (*je me reseigne*) is a celebrated authoress: and the Americans have the reputation of spoiling their women. They spoil them *à coups de poing* [506–07].

Only a year earlier, among the many newspaper paragraphs about himself preceding his two visits to America in the early 1880s, James could have read the following tidbit in the "Personal" column of the *New York Tribune,* a newspaper read faithfully by the Jameses:

> Mr. Henry James, Sr., metaphysician and philosopher, is described as a man bright-looking in spite of his many years, short in stature, erect in form, with keen gray eyes, and modest yet distinguished bearing. His father, an Irishman by birth, a Presbyterian and a merchant at Albany, was successful in business and left a great deal of money to his son, who was graduated at Union College in 1831. Mr. James, during one of his visits to England, wrote some remarkable letters to The Tribune. Of Mr. James's four sons, the eldest, Dr. William James is professor of philosophy at Harvard. Of the two younger sons one is an artist and the other a business man.[8]

Clearly a typical, if moderate, example of what James, in 1883, would call "the invasive impudence of the papers here."[9]

But we must notice that there are indications of M. Lejaune's bias, not the least of which is his name, suggesting, as it does, "jaundice." If so, then we must see that his attacks upon the newspapers—and also upon the novelist who resembles James himself as some of his readers saw him—are not to be taken entirely at face value. It is the one-sidedness of his view of America that reveals his limitation, just as it is the "roaring Yankee['s]" (516) blindness to the limitations of the results of the American democratic experiment that removes him from James's camp.

Satire is not always handled as cleverly as this. Something of James appears in every letter, but no letter is exclusively or even principally James's. Expressed sentiments, especially when taken out of context, can be traced to James, but in "The Point of View," *pace* Scudder, James manages to tie each opinion to its proponent. Behind the shield of these strictly defined points of view James has preserved these umbilical cords. Many of the readers of the day, however, failed to see how skillfully James had skirted the problems of chauvinism and strident Americanism as well as those of Europe's own provincialism. In translating his impressions and experiences, James remained faithful to his original impulse: "Description of a situation, or incident, in an alternation of letters, written from an aristocratic, and a democratic, point of view;—both enlightened and sincere."[10] This notation was made before James's visit to the United States in 1881–1882, but he was able to fulfill his original intention to offer both aristocratic and democratic points of view, enlightened and sincere. It would be some time before James would be able to convince his own reading public that in his own mind he himself had, by 1882, paraphrasing Taine's remark about Turgenev, "so perfectly cut the umbilical cord that bound the story to himself."[11]

In effect, most of the readers of the day penalized James for having an acute ear. The warning, clear enough in the story's title, that all opinion and commentary depended upon the vantage from which anything was viewed, was, of course, bypassed. What was clear to the average reader of the day was that James's letter-writers, in the main, deprecated American morals and manners. Obviously they must also have been unhappy at what they considered Marcellus Cockerel's inadequate defense of his country. Their failure was that they did not see the author's double-edged rendering of character, that every opinion expressed called forth or countered its counterpointing opposite in another speaker. The aesthetic reality for the writer lay not in the sentiments expressed by his characters, but in the appropriateness of each sentiment, given the particular character. Consequently, it is clear that while many of James's own observations and complaints are given in the letters, James is always cautiously aware of the shortcomings displayed by each of his seven correspondents. If M. Lejaune says much of what James himself felt about American newspapers, for example, it is also evident the M. Lejaune, unlike Tocqueville (to whom he is compared in the story), has no affection for America, even less, seemingly, than did Mrs. Trollope. His attack is largely one-sided, just as is Cockerel's, on the opposite side. What "The Point of View" does, then, is to render as subject, almost programmatically, what was already one of James's main technical interests: the dramatizing of a multiple reality dependent upon a variety of points of view. By design, James's own point of view defies location. If the reader wants that, he would do better to look for it in James's letters, journals and travel literature. If he looks there he will see, of course, that James's views about America were never unmixed—which, to adapt the notion to this story, is to say that there is some kernel of truth in what every letter-writer has observed. His readers accepted satire, but seldom, naturally, at their own expense. National feeling in particular, because of its precariousness and tentative validity, could not afford laughter, especially not when it was provoked by an expatriate.

When James was visiting in Washington in January 1882, "Clover" Adams sized him up in rather supercilious terms: "Thursday, Henry James put in an appearance; that young emigrant has much to learn here. He is surprised to find that he can go to the Capitol and listen to debates without taking a license, as in London. He may in time get into the 'swim' here, but I doubt it. I think the real, live, vulgar, quick-paced world in America will fret him and that he prefers a quiet corner with a pen where he can create men and women who say neat things and have refined tastes and are not nasal or eccentric."[12]

James remembered his visit to the Capitol and when it came time to write M. Lejaune's letter, he incorporated it in this way: "You go into the Capitol as you would into a railway station; you walk about as you would in the Palais Royal. No functionaries, no door-keepers, no officers, no uniforms, no badges, no restrictions, no authority—nothing but a crowd of shabby people circulating in a labyrinth of spittoons. We are too much governed perhaps in France; but at least we have a certain incarnation of the national conscience, of the national dignity. The dignity is absent here, and I am told that the conscience is an abyss. 'L'etat c'est moi' even—I like that better than the spittoons" (508).

There is no evidence that Mrs. Adams was amused, though she did acknowledge the cleverness of a thing or two from the Cockerel letter—"the suggestion that 'an aristocracy is bad manners organised' is very good," she admitted.[13] Still, overall, it can be said that her response to James's Americanism was more or less typical. And when she and her husband surfaced, a year later, as the Alfred Bonnycastles of James's Washington tale, "Pandora," she ignored the genial satire at her expense, as well as the irony of the story's first appearing in the *New York Sun*, an American newspaper. It is not without import, by the way, that despite James's strong feelings about the papers, he was willing in this instance to accept, according to Charles A. Dana, the *Sun's* editor, the then very generous payment for "Pandora" of between eleven and twelve hundred dollars.[14]

In "The Point of View" James made his best effort to show how much he had got into the "swim" of things. But it was a no-win situation, one that would scarcely change in his lifetime, for not even his friends would entirely come round to his point of view. Listen, for example, to S. Weir Mitchell, writing as late as 1905, on the occasion of James's late visit to America: "I was very glad to hear news of Henry James and when he comes to write what my son John calls his 'depressions of America,' I shall be interested to see what he will say about his historic visits with you and me."[15]

Reacting patriotically to the unexpectedly mixed English reviews of Henry James's novel *The Portrait of a Lady*, George Washburn Smalley arrived at a debatable conclusion "Nobody would say that Mr. James would be consciously unfair; even to his own countrymen," wrote the *New York Tribune*'s London correspondent. "It is more just to suppose that his long residence abroad has deprived him of those opportunities for close observation and accurate study of the good American which he would have enjoyed at home." Then he appended a fond wish: "Now that he [James] has returned to his native land, one may fairly hope to find true American patriots in his next book—less flattering to the Briton and more just to the American."[16]

By late 1881 British readers, having welcomed *Daisy Miller* (but not, notably, the story's "English" equivalent, *An International Episode*), had themselves become noticeably discomfited by what they took to be James's rather crude designs on English society. Concomitantly, resentment in America at what was viewed as James's Anglophilia ran exceedingly high. An anecdote making the rounds of newspapers shortly after James's first visit to Washington, D.C., early in 1882 is instructive and typical. "Henry James, while in Washington lately, is wickedly said by *The Boston Gazette* to have asked a clever young lady if there was not a river near the city called the Potomac. 'Oh, yes,' said she, 'and I should think you would know all about it, because there is a place on it called Mount Vernon, where a man named Washington lived. You are sure to have heard of him, you know, because his father was an Englishman.'"[17]

James's visit to the United States in 1881–1882 followed a stay of six years abroad, the last five in London. He saw his return as a time for updating his impressions of his native land with ample opportunity for re-encountering the "good American" (as Smalley had advised) in his many habitats. Eager for new experience, James put aside his usual inhibitions. Visiting with the Adamses he surprised and shocked them by defying their rather narrow social conventions. He accepted invitations, averred Mrs. Adams, that he should not for a moment have otherwise considered. Unfamiliar with the ways of his own nation's capital and its vast gathering of public officials, James had no qualms about visiting James G. Blaine or George Maxwell Robeson—abominations both to the Adamses. "Henry James passed Sunday evening at Robeson's," wrote Marian "Clover" Adams, "and dines tomorrow with Blaine. 'And a certain man came down to / from Jerusalem and fell among thieves ... and they sprang up and choked him.'"[18] In short, although James was himself no great social success—the triumphs that season were all Oscar Wilde's—he was more attentive than entertaining, industriously cultivating attitudes, and storing up materials.[19]

The time was also right for personal stock-taking. James was particularly struck with the news that his *Daisy Miller: A Study* (1878) had emerged as something more than a seasonal sensation. Hitting a public nerve, the tale had evoked both an immediate and, as it turned out, a lasting response in its American readers. Even when the initial furor over James's *"succès de haine"* had abated and most of the women James had "waked up" had calmed down, the *New York Tribune* was calling loudly for more fiction like *Daisy Miller*—"more work in the same style."[20] Privately, however, "Clover" Adams reported that she found it necessary to continue defending the poor author of *Daisy Miller* from the charges of irate New Yorkers and Chicagoans who continued to excoriate the expatriate for his rendering of the American Girl.[21] Another young lady, still fuming over the real and imagined slights of James's *Hawthorne* (1879), particularly his strictures on Concord, announced that she would "die happy" only if she could see James "desperately in love and married to a perfect Daisy Miller."[22] Daisy Miller, as a type, would not go away. Five years after the book's publication James was greeted at the Saturday Morning Club, in Boston, with "a bouquet ingeniously illustrating the name of his little heroine." The modest bouquet was "formed of white daisies and surrounded by leaves of the grayish plant known as 'dusty miller.'" 'I see I have hundreds of Daisy Millers here,' said the author."[23] If James's pleasure on the occasion was somewhat restrained, he seems to have kept his public equanimity.

Given the success of *Daisy Miller*, then, it is not surprising that among James's first thoughts about future fictions was that Daisy Miller could serve as a model in a story about Washington. Early in 1884 he noted in his journal: "I don't see why I shouldn't do the 'self-made girl'... in a way to make her a rival to D[aisy] M[iller]."[24] At the time this note might have been intended to signify nothing more, of course, than his hope that the successful portrayal of his "self-made girl" in America, as the initial delineation of a recognizable type, could attract to her something of the attention accorded earlier to his portrayal of the young free-wheeling American Girl at her travels. The result was "Pandora."

Such hopes for his heroine Pandora Day, enhanced by the durability of Daisy's reputation, encouraged him to draw "Pandora" and *Daisy Miller* as closely as possible while keeping it clear that his two heroines constituted, after all, different types. But how could James plant the suggestion in readers' minds that Pandora Day was both like and unlike Daisy Miller? Would his audience perceive such connections and differences if he did not make them explicit? Could he make his point without resorting to excessive authorial comment? In short, his task was to dramatize, not state, the connection between the story and the novella.

One possible solution to the problem lay in a suggestion made years earlier by an American reviewer. "No American who has not been abroad can really appreciate this story," ran an anonymous notice of *Daisy Miller*. "One must have shuddered at the approach of Randolph C. Miller's type to understand the full horror of that child seen in a land of well-trained children.... We hope it [*Daisy Miller*] will be published in 'Tauchnitz,' be in the bookcases of all the ocean steamers."[25] James's notion that a copy of *Daisy Miller* could be used to link the two works seems to have had its source in this review in the *Nation*. That James knew this review is all but certain. The omnibus review containing these observations on *Daisy Miller* carried no signature at the time of publication, but the index of contributors to *The Nation* identifies the author of these remarks as Mary Eliot Parkman of Boston. Moreover, it identifies the reviewer of the last novel covered in the same catchall review (William Black's *Macleod of Dare*) as— Henry James himself.[26] Since James contributed to *The Nation* for nearly fifteen years, it would not have been at all extraordinary for him to know the identity of the fellow contributor who had commented on *Daisy Miller*.[27] In any case, just as Mrs. Parkman had hoped, *Daisy Miller* was published by Tauchnitz, making it plausible for James to equip "Pandora's" Count Vogelstein with a copy of *Daisy Miller* in the Tauchnitz edition, one ready to hand for shipboard reading.

In the early pages of "Pandora" James's young German diplomat, settling in his sea-chair, draws "from this pocket a Tauchnitz novel by an American author whose pages, he had been assured, would help to prepare him" for his first visit to the United States.[28] Later, after Miss Pandora Day, the "self-made" American girl from Utica, New York, has placed herself before this "intelligent young German," James notes: "It was the oddest coincidence in the world; the story Vogelstein had taken up treated of a flighty, forward little American girl, who plants herself in front of a young man in the garden of an hotel. Was not the conduct of this young lady a testimony to the truthfulness of the tale, and was not Vogelstein himself in the position of the young man in the garden?" (363). But Pandora's "young man" cannot then resolve these questions; he continues to compare his new American acquaintance and her family with the dramatis personae of the James novel he is reading. Pandora and Daisy have mothers who behave alike, he decides, and each does have a brother, although Pandora's is nineteen years old; while Pandora, who is not really a "Daisy Miller," he observes, does have a young sister who is "a Daisy Miller *en herbe*" (370).

From the very outset of his thinking about "Pandora" James's intention extended beyond merely studying "the self-made girl," to a treatment of his recent Washington hosts, Henry and "Clover" Adams. "[The story] must take place in New York," he started out in his journal. "Perhaps indeed Washington would do. This would give me a chance to do Washington, so far as I know it, and work in my few notes, and my very lovely memories of last winter. I might even do Henry Adams and his wife."[29] In the finished story, Henry and "Clover" Adams would emerge as Mr. and Mrs. Alfred Bonnycastle, a couple whose spacious house—"that intensely lively Washington salon," as James would later put it—becomes the dramatic social center of James's fictional Washington.[30]

Apart from this sprightly allegorical name-change, James made no effort to hide the identity of the real-life models behind his fictional characters. There was really no need to do so, of course, for he had sketched the Adamses generously with a loving, if lightly satiric, hand. Just as he had in another story from this period, "The Point of View," James infused "Pandora" with sentiments and observations characteristic of his sometimes supercilious Washington friends.[31] Here, for example, is the historical Henry Adams writing to an English friend within a year of James's first Washington visit.

> You have lost a very indifferent winter; bad weather, bad roads, bad dinners, and very indifferent talk. I never have had less enjoyment, but am rather surprised to find how much I have had, notwithstanding all draw-backs. The truth is, the thing amuses me. One should always meet in society those one hates or those one loves; indifference poisons even champagne. Abroad I have no one to hate; here I loathe my neighbor with passion. To sit at dinner next people to whom one does not bow, is a decided amusement if rightly understood; it animates wit and stimulates hatred. I can't get this sort of thing in Europe and that is why I like my own land.
>
> Little as I care about politics, I always feel a very active sentiment of personal antipathy to politicians, and rarely fail to tell them so. This results in winning their cordial aversion to a surprising degree. The resentment which mean minds often feel, is remarkable. A friend of mine, in high administrative office, said to me the other day when I recommended tact as a means of dealing with legislators: "Tact is of no use! A Congressman is a hog. You must take a big club and hit him on the snout!" Now, curiously enough, I could not tell that story to a Congressman without giving offence. I know, because I have once or twice tried. They actually look cold and are not cordial afterwards.
>
> Nevertheless I always try to say something as pleasant as that, but still I am not popular, and few politicians come to my house unless I ask them to feed. They would go anywhere to feed.[32]

This sounds rather like the fictional Alfred Bonnycastle, who thinks that for Washington, Bonnycastle "society was really a little too good" (383), and to prove the mettle of that society he bursts out with mock-enthusiasm: "Hang it, there's only a month left; let us have some fun—let us invite the President!"

(383).³³ As the historical Adams once explained, "The fact is I gravitate to a capital by a primary law of nature. This is the only place in America [Washington] where society amuses me, or where life offers variety."³⁴ This view is congruent with the Bonnycastles' attitude toward politicians and Congressmen:

> The legislative session was over, but this made little difference in the aspect of Bonnycastle's rooms, which, even at the height of the congressional season, could be said to overflow with the representatives of the people. They were garnished with an occasional senator, whose movements and utterances often appeared to be regarded with a mixture of alarm and indulgence, as if they would be disappointing if they were not rather odd, and yet might be dangerous if they were not carefully watched.... Members of the House were very rare, and when Washington was new to Vogelstein he used sometimes to mistake them, in the hall and on the staircases where he met them, for the functionaries engaged for the evening to usher in guests and wait at supper. It was only a little later that he perceived these functionaries were almost always impressive, and had a complexion which served as a livery. At present, however, such misleading figures were much less to be encountered than during the months of winter, and, indeed, they never were to be encountered at Mrs. Bonnycastle's [383–84].

James's genial satire of the Adamses works even in details. One example stands out. Vogelstein's penchant for discovering parallels and determining differences between the Day family of Utica and the Miller family of Schenectady provides James with the occasion for indulging in another 'insider' reference: "If his sister [Pandora] did not resemble the dreadful little girl in the tale I have so often mentioned," writes James, "there was, for Vogelstein, at least an analogy between young Mr. Day and a certain small brother—a candy-loving Madison, Hamilton, or Jefferson—who, in the Tauchnitz volume, was attributed to that unfortunate maid. This is what the little Madison would have grown up to at nineteen, and the improvement was greater than might have been expected" (369). Since Vogelstein has been reading *Daisy Miller* all the while, his inability to recall the name of Daisy's young brother strikes the reader as rather odd. Why does the author choose to hide Randolph's name behind this parade of famous names from early national history? There seems to be no immediately apparent thematic purpose in the German diplomat's failure to recall that Daisy's brother's name is "Randolph," not "Madison," "Hamilton," or "Jefferson." The explanation for his lapse of memory is simple, I suspect. This confusion over the Miller boy's name was aimed directly at "Clover" and Henry Adams. James wrote *Daisy Miller* in 1878, and four years later Adams published his *John Randolph* in the American Statesman Series. In addition, as James had seen in 1882, Adams was already at work on his multi-volume *History of the United States of America During the Administrations of Jefferson and Madison*. In fact, while James was visiting Washington, Adams was not only in the midst of writing about Madison, Jefferson, and, to a lesser extent, Hamilton, but he was also proofreading his Randolph biography.³⁵

"Pandora" was less than an unqualified success in its own day. Contemporary notices ranged from the observations that it was "a complete failure" and that its only contribution was to introduce us "to a highly disagreeable Daisy Miller, a trifle more honest, but not less provincial" to the grudging acknowledgment that it was "by far the cleverest thing" in what was, however, "decidedly a miscellaneous collection."[36] Clearly in the minority was the journalist and biographer Lilian Whiting, who praised James's story: "He seizes the salient points of life. How perfectly in 'Pandora' is imaged the new type of American girl, made by social evolution."[37]

Yet "Pandora," unlike so many of James's novels and tales, moreover, has never been seriously revalued.[38] Still it is interesting to learn that in "Pandora" James incorporated his personal reactions to American Presidents and Congressmen, that he played cat-and-mouse with both *Daisy Miller* and the reviews of that book, and that in 1884 he made several scarcely veiled allusions to the Adamses intended only for them and, possibly, a few friends.

Less than a year after "Clover" Adams took her life, she "reappeared" in James's fiction. "In a little tale, 'A Modern Warning [sic],'" writes the author's most assiduous biographer Leon Edel, "Henry James may have incorporated the suicide scene as he re-imagined it—his heroine taking poison while her husband and brother, to whom she is as attached as 'Clover' was to her father—are out of the house." It is true "the lady in the story," cautions Edel, "is not modeled on Clover," who is "milder, gentler, less incisive." "But the tale itself, with its sharp words between Americans and English—its dialogue between the civilizations of the Old and New World—contains echoes of talk of Henry James with Mrs. Adams."[39]

"The Modern Warning," a notebook entry at the time reveals, began with James's reading of the latest criticism of the United States by a European. Although the best European writing about America is still read—that of Mrs. Trollope, Tocqueville, Dickens, and Matthew Arnold—Sir Lepel Henry Griffin's *The Great Republic* (1884), based on a three-week visit to the United States, is now all-but-forgotten.[40] The work of an Englishman famous for his administrative successes as a member of the Indian Civil Service, *The Great Republic* launches a broad-side attack on the politics and manners of the United States. "The ideal aristocracy, or government of the best, has in America been degraded into an actual government of the worst," he writes, "in which the educated, the cultured, the honest, and even the wealthy, weigh as nothing in the balance against the scum of Europe which the Atlantic has washed up on the shores of the New World."[41]

Reviewers on both sides of the Atlantic were largely unimpressed with the ironically titled book. In the United States Griffin's work was largely dismissed as a study of "our institutions through the large lens of a telescope," while, among the English, Goldwin Smith cautioned that the book was "too rampant to produce a serious effect."[42] But *The Great Republic* struck a deep chord in Henry James, resulting ultimately in a story he would first call "Two Countries" when it ran in *Harper's Magazine* and then "The Modern Warning" when it appeared in book form.[43]

On July 9, 1884, shortly after reading *The Great Republic*, James set down his ideas for a story. He conceived of a character who is the "type of the conservative, fastidious, exclusive Englishman (in public life, clever, etc.), who hates the U.S.A. and thinks them a contamination to England, a source of *funeste* warning, etc., and an odious country socially." The plot, as the author sees it, calls for the Englishman's falling in love with "an American Girl and she with him." The complication, as "he lets her know, frankly," is that he "loathes her country as much as he adores her personally." He proposes marriage and she, surprisingly, accepts his proposal. James's thoughts continue:

> She is patriotic in a high degree—a genuine little American—and she has the sentiment of her native land. But she is in love with the Englishman, and though she resists on patriotic grounds she yields at last, accepts him and marries him. She must have a near relation—a brother, say—who is violently American, an *anglophobiste* (in public life in the U.S.A.); and of whom she is very fond. He deplores her marriage, entreats her to keep out of it, etc. He and the Englishman *loathe* each other. After the marriage the Englishman's hostility to the U.S. increases, fostered by the invasion of Americans, etc. State of mind of the wife. Depression, melancholy, remorse and shame at having married an enemy of her country. Suicide? There is a certain interest in the situation—the difficulty of choice and resignation on her part—the resentment of a rupture with the brother, etc. Of course internationalism, etc., may be found overdone, threadbare. That is to a certain extent a reason against the subject; but a weak, not a strong one. It is always enough if the *author* sees substance in it.[44]

And so it happens in James's "The Modern Warning." Of Agatha Lady Chasemore's brother, McCarthy Grice, it is said: "McCarthy's patriotism was of so intense a hue that, to his own sense, the national life and his own life flowed in an indistinguishable current."[45]

> There was indeed something, in his whole attitude, which seemed to say that it was not only from him that she [Agatha Lady Chasemore] separated herself, but from all her fellow-countrymen besides and from everything that was best and finest in American life. He regarded her marriage as an abjuration, an apostasy, a kind of moral treachery. It was of no use to say to him that she was doing nothing original or extraordinary, to ask him if he did not know that in England, at the point things had come to, American wives were as thick as blackberries, so that if she were doing wrong she was doing wrong with—well, almost the majority.[46]

Lady Chasemore finds herself hopelessly caught between loyalty to her chauvinist brother and loyalty to Sir Rufus Chasemore, her equally chauvinist husband. "I couldn't be happy with you," she tells her husband, "if you hated my country."[47] But even as she enters into this marriage she has an idea that by bringing around her husband to a favorable appreciation of her native land, she will persuade her brother that her marriage does not constitute a betrayal of her country. But Sir Rufus Chasemore, the author of *The Modern Warning*, an anti–American work like Sir Lepel Griffin's *Great Republic*, cannot be moved.[48] She has miscalculated badly.

In some sense James's story re-examines his own bold assertion, in 1878, that "to be a cosmopolite is not, I think, an ideal; the ideal should be to be a concentrated patriot."[49] Yet like many others, including Matthew Arnold, James would come to the conclusion that his countrymen's super-patriotism was a great failing. James was close in spirit to the Arnold who complained against those Americans who proclaimed "themselves at the top of their voices to be 'the greatest nation upon earth,' by assuring one another, in the language of their national historian, that 'American democracy proceeds in its ascent as uniformly and majestically as the laws of being, and is as certain as the decrees of eternity.'"[50]

But his warnings now against the excesses of super-patriotism and their possible consequences, as illustrated by the plot of "The Modern Warning," held little appeal for James's reviewers.[51] The opposition came from both camps—the British and the American. Invoking the familiar metaphor that James himself had employed in *The American* (1877)—in Christopher Newman's words is heard "the voice of the spread eagle"—the *Scottish Review* admonished:

> In "The Modern Warning," we find the American Eagle screeching anew, and disposed to wave aloft the Star Spangled Banner, while he dances on the faded worn-out Union Jack, and we feel inclined to say, "My dear bird, do not screech so loud. Nobody denies the glories of the Great American Nation! and at any rate, be logical. If Great Britain is the home of a worn-out despised nation, be not so exuberantly exultant over every American girl who contrives to get herself chosen as a wife by a son of that degenerate race."[52]

On the American side of the Atlantic, most reviewers, though less expressively so, were equally negative. The notice in *Life* magazine took the interesting and not entirely satirical position that in Lady Chasemore and her brother had failed to represent the current state of the American conscience because, during the previous decade, "the sensitive Puritan conscience" of Americans had become healthier and more robust through broad social changes brought about by great material prosperity.[53] Other reviewers thought that James had embodied his serious theme—the consequences of an uncompromising and unblinking loyalty to one's country—in a silly plot culminating, unconvincingly, in the gratuitous act of suicide. It is this last view, in fact, that has come to characterize subsequent scholarly commentary. As S. Gorley Putt puts it, "the violent dislike of a British aristocrat for the public manners of his American wife's native land will lead to a situation melodramatic to the point of farce."[54]

"The Modern Warning" concludes melodramatically with the suicide of the depressed heroine caught between loyalty to her brother and her country and the pressures brought upon her by her English husband. James was not unaware that his heroine's suicide was as melodramatic as that of Roderick Hudson, for example, or Hyacinth Robinson's in *The Princess Casamassima*. Any similar death would not be a suitable conclusion to *A London Life*, the story he was then writing, James reminded himself. "It's too rare, and I used it the other day in the Two Countries," that is, "The Modern Warning."[55] Reviewers of "The Modern Warning" had deplored the death of James's heroine as neither prepared for nor necessary. "In the name of all probability we must protest against Mr. James's needless slaughter of Lady Chasemore," complained *The Literary World*, "it is not characteristic of such women as she is described to be to poison herself under such absence of provocation; her suicide comes upon the reader with such a shock of surprise which immediately turns to indignation at the author for perpetrating such wanton murder."[56] When William Dean Howells argued that "the truthfulness of the supposed case and the supposed people" outweighed any consideration of whether, in life, an American wife "would have killed herself if her English husband had written a book against her native land," the *San Francisco Evening Bulletin* replied: "if there is a moral" to "The Modern Warning," it is "that persons of strong national sympathies ought to marry among their own kind."[57]

Yet the choice to end "The Modern Warning" with the heroine's sudden death was not entirely arbitrary. If the suicide of the heroine of "The Modern Warning" is meant as a "sacrifice" to virulent American nationalism, James had already written about the same theme. In *An International Episode*, the companion piece to *Daisy Miller*, for example, Mrs. Westgate (sounding a bit like Mrs. Henry Adams) speaks out to English nobility:

> I don't apologise, Lord Lambeth; some Americans are always apologising; you must have noticed that. We have the reputation of always boasting and bragging and waving the American flag; but I must say that what strikes me is that we are perpetually making excuses and trying to smooth things over. The American flag has quite gone out of fashion; it's very carefully folded up, like an old table-cloth. Why should we apologise? The English never apologise—do they? No, I must say I never apologise. You must take us as we come—with all our imperfections on our heads.[58]

"On she went at immense length, the pretty lady, then and later," notes Constance Rourke in *American Humor* (subtitled *A Study of the National Character*), "with a mild merciless monotony, a paucity of intonation, an impartial flatness that suggested a flowery mead scrupulously 'done over' by a steam roller that had reduced its texture to that of a drawing-room carpet."[59]

In his notebook entry in 1884 James had asked himself whether the young American wife would commit suicide. As we have seen, his final decision was that his story called for such a death for the needy Agatha Grice. Behind that fictional suicide was the dark secret of the death of the friend James had called "the incarnation of my native land."[60] The suicide of "Clover" Adams on December 6, 1885, less than eighteen months after his journal entry regarding the story that would become "The Modern Warning," seems to have confirmed in him, at least subconsciously, that his first intimations for the fitting outcome of his story were sound. So sprightly "present" as a super-patriot earlier in the decade in James's "The Point of View" and "Pandora," Marian Clover Hooper, the young Mrs. Henry Adams, is the real-life forerunner of Agatha Grice.

8

Artifice in "The Real Thing"

"I have an old servant, a butter and sugar thief—who is an artist in her way—a joy. Her feeling for hot plates and for what dear Henry James might call the real right gravy is supreme. These things are so important."[1] Katherine Mansfield's observation pokes gentle fun at James's story of appearance and reality, model and subject, character and type, painting and illustration, reality and representation in "The Real Thing." First published in the London journal *Black and White* on April 16, 1892, and collected in *The Real Thing and Other Tales* in 1893, this story is told from the first person point of view of a working painter, employed to do magazine and book illustrations. A retrospective monologue, it strives to do in prose just about what Robert Browning accomplishes in verse, particularly in poems about painters, such as "Andrea Del Sarto" and "Fra Lippo Lippi." By deciding on a characterized first-person narrator, James—like Browning—avoids the problems that might arise were he to state as the "truth" or offer "theories" in his own voice about the themes that inhere in his narrative: realism achieved through art, actuality as the basis for realism, and the opposition of character to type. The great difference between the point of Browning's major monologues and that of James's first-person narratives is that the poetic monologues serve to reveal the speaker's character while in the first-person stories the narrator's self-revelations are usually overshadowed by the story he tells. This is true of the early novel about an American artist *Roderick Hudson* (1875), told from the point of view of Rowland Mallet, who remains little more than an observer despite James's half-hearted attempts to make him into something more than that in the basic story of Roderick and Christina Light.

In "The Real Thing," published in 1892, seventeen years after *Roderick Hudson*, James rings the changes on the distinctions that are so often to be made between what is actual and what is real. The couple that comes to the artist's studio to offer themselves as models for pay, Major and Mrs. Monarch, are actually "gentlefolk," but they turn out not to be actually models, not useful even to stand for representative members of upper society. Miss Churm, a young cockney woman, is both actually and really a model, though she is not actually a member of any of the groups she is seen to typify. She seems to be really a model and really something of an actress—though she is not actually an actress. Oronte, the young Italian male who comes to the door, is actually an Italian male, no more than that, but he is a natural model (though he does not seem to know it), one capable of serving the artist in many ways. In fact, Miss Churm, the cockney, can be turned into an Italian by the artist, just as Oronte, the Italian, can be made to be, in the illustrations, an Englishman.

James rings the changes on this running discrepancy between the credentials that inspire credence and those that do not. The Monarchs have credentials that have some credence out in the world but they turn out not to have the kind of credentials that make them employable in the world of art. The young cockney woman and the young Italian male are given their credentials by the world of art—as models. Successful modeling adds to their actuality, even as it makes them useful to the artist who can use them to bring his characters and drawings to life, that is to say, to make them appear real. Certainly he cannot make a silk purse out of a sow's ear, but just who, metaphorically, is the silk purse in this case is irrelevant to the artist of the real.

The narrator of "The Real Thing" talks about an alchemy of art that will turn a cockney woman and an Italian male into virtually a plethora of figures and characters. But no alchemy of art, he suggests, can transform the Monarchs into versatile models or make the figures based on them into credible art. The artist can make his real models into something, but he can make nothing out of his genuine gentlefolk, not even, it seems, credible gentlefolk. To underline his point about what is "real" in art and what is "not real," moreover, James chooses as his artist-narrator, not a greatly talented or even a commercially important painter, but one who while aspiring to be a respectable painter, works away at what he calls his "pot-boilers." If the reader steps back from the painter's narration, he will see that when James has his narrator say that "in those days there were few serious workers in black-and-white," he is, as Robert L. Gale points out, referring to "black-and-white illustrations to accompany published prose." "On a lower level," however, James is also "taking a little poke at the contemporary London magazine *Black and White*," in which he had already published one story and for which "The Real Thing" was destined.[2] There is no doubt, of course, that James (like his artist-narrator) considered himself to be among the few serious writers contributing to *Black and White*.

It is to the narrator's credit as an artist, perhaps, that the very reputable and obviously serious landscape painter, Claude Rivet, has sent him the Monarchs as potential models. When he first sees them, he thinks that they have come as possible patrons. But he soon discovers that they wish not to commission their portraits but to hire out as models.

> It was only then that I understood the service Claude Rivet had rendered me; he had told them how I worked in black-and-white, for magazines, for story-books, for sketches of contemporary life, and consequently had frequent employment for models. These things were true, but it was not less true (I may confess it now—whether because the aspiration was to lead to everything or to nothing I leave the reader to guess), that I couldn't get the honours, to say nothing of the emoluments, of a great painter of portraits out of my head. My "illustrations" were my pot-boilers; I looked to a different branch of art (far and away the most interesting it had always seemed to me), to perpetuate my fame. There was no shame in looking to it also to make my fortune; but that fortune was by so much further from being made from the moment my visitors wished to be "done" for nothing. I was disappointed, for in the pictorial sense I had immediately seen them. I had seized their type—I had already settled what I would do with it. Something that wouldn't absolutely have pleased them, I afterwards reflected.[3]

Obviously their "type" was not the kind needed for the book illustration commissions now awaiting this particular artist's hand. As for painting the likes of the major and his wife as the "things" that they actually are, that is a theme James had already explored rather incisively elsewhere, most strikingly in "The Liar."[4] But not in "The Real Thing." As the painter-illustrator insists: "I had not the least desire my model should be discoverable in my picture."[5]

9

"The Pupil" Rejected

I

"At the beginning of the 1890s, he [Henry James] has the unusual experience of having a short story rejected by the new editor of the *Atlantic* [*Monthly*]—the tale of 'The Pupil,' which posterity has judged among his finest."[1] This statement prepares the reader for the three letters from James to Horace E. Scudder, the *Atlantic*'s editor, that Leon Edel reproduces in the third volume of his edition of *Henry James Letters* (1980). It is not surprising, given this context, that the story of James, Scudder, and "The Pupil" has always been told from James's point of view and entirely in his favor. "Scudder had rejected 'The Pupil,'" writes James's editor; "we may infer he did not want to print in the *Atlantic* a tale about a mendacious, itinerant, and drifting American family."[2]

To the best of my knowledge, Edel first offered his interpretation of what happened between James and the *Atlantic*'s new editor in 1952 when he suggested that Scudder had rejected the story, "probably fearing that the picture of a mendacious American family would not appeal to *Atlantic* readers."[3] In the intervening years Edel would on at least two other occasions restate his views, expanding on them only to include the possibility that Scudder might have had a second reason for rejecting the story. "He may have been troubled by the picture of the child's attachment to the young man," wrote Edel in 1963; but "more likely he was bothered by James's account of a mendacious American family which jumps its hotel bills and lives a hand-to-mouth existence."[4] Six years later, in the third volume of his biography of James, Edel put forth much the same reasons but at greater length:

> Scudder may have been worried by the possible hint of unconscious homosexuality in the attachment of tutor and boy. Yet there is no evidence that in the early 1890s—before the trial of Oscar Wilde—there was among readers or editors any such awareness of or alertness to deviation; friendship and affection between tutors and their charges were regarded as normal in the Victorian age. A more plausible theory is that the prosaic

Scudder was worried that the *Atlantic*'s readers would resent a story about an American family which jumped its hotel bills and behaved with such deliberate mendacity. Americans were not supposed to do such things.[5]

One wonders what meaning Edel intends to convey, in this context, by the adjective "prosaic," even if one does not want to quarrel with him over the extent to which readers and editors of the 1890s were "alert" to matters of "deviation."

Since in *Henry James Letters* Edel buttresses his speculations and inferences over the years with James's own letters in defense of his story, it is more than likely that Edel's view of the matter will continue to obtain, especially since Scudder's own words on the matter remain unknown. It is true that the original of Scudder's letter to James rejecting "The Pupil" has not yet turned up. Its contents, however, have survived in the form of a copy of the letter available in letterbooks kept by the *Atlantic*'s publisher Houghton Mifflin. When the contents of this copy, along with the contents of two other hitherto unpublished letters, are read chronologically within the sequence of James's letters, the reader is less inclined to accept Edel's explanation that Scudder's decision to turn down James's offer of "The Pupil" was based largely, if not exclusively, on his negative reaction to the mendacious, itinerant, drifting Moreen family, whose exploits would not appeal to the *Atlantic*'s readers. It is revealing and typical of James, as will be seen, that he does not answer Scudder's charges. He ignores what Scudder says about his impressions of the story's structure, imprecision, and lack of proportion.

The hard evidence for an understanding of the story of Scudder's and James's falling-out over "The Pupil" lies in their exchange of letters in 1890–1891. To allow that story to unfold in its particulars, much as it did to the correspondents themselves, it seems best to reproduce the letters exchanged during that period. There are seven such letters—three from Scudder and four from James. Three of James's letters (numbers 3, 5, and 7) are reproduced from the third volume of Edel's edition of the *Henry James Letters*: the fourth letter (number 2) is transcribed from manuscript.[6] Scudder's letters (numbers 1, 4, and 6) derive from copies in the Houghton Mifflin letterbooks.[7]

II

THE LETTERS

1.

20 August 1890

My dear Mr James

    In the September *Atlantic* you will see a brief notice of *The Tragic Muse* which I wrote. I speak of it only to emphasize the fact that the new editor of *The Atlantic* values your work highly, and wishes to know what he may look for from you the coming year.

Can you not promise me at least four single number stories before 1892? I should not mind if one of these were a double number, but I have as many serial sails set as I care to carry. Kindly let me hear from you as soon as may be as I shall be called on for my predictions soon,

Sincerely yours
Horace E. Scudder

Henry James esq.

2.

August 30th '90

34 DeVere Gardens, W.

Dear Mr. Scudder:

Your note of the 20th gives me great pleasure, especially as the September *Atlantic* coming in with it, I have been able to read the pages of charming sympathy that you have therein dedicated to the *Tragic Muse*. They have really brought tears to my eyes—giving me a luxurious sense of being understood, perceived, felt. Your words are delightful & I thank you for them with all my heart: perhaps especially for those about the reader's never being "in any eddies of conversation, but always in the current." That discovery is of a sort far beyond the compass of the usual Anglo-Saxon intelligence. Therefore I regard you as still more as an acute than as a benevolent critic. Have you not achieved the miracle of suspecting there may be a meaning in what one writes? I don't notice that any one else ever has!—As regards your proposal to send you four short stories before 1892, I embrace it with enthusiasm. I am perhaps even capable of sending you five. One of them shall be a two-number tale; the others a single number, & I will very presently dispatch you the first. I will do the very best I can for you; I appreciate the friendly quality of your hospitality, & I am very truly yours

Henry James

3.

34 DeVere Gardens

October 5th 1890

Dear Mr. Scudder.

I send you, in a heavy registered packet, by this post, a tale called *The Pupil*, which I have tried to make as short as possible. Do what I would (& I boiled it down repeatedly), it insists on being of dimensions that represent, as I measure them, about 23 & ½ pages of the *Atlantic*. This, obviously, you will regard as long for a "short" story—though it isn't very long for me; at least until, after much disuse of the practice, I succeed, with more trials, as I fully mean to do, in working myself back to an intenser brevity. At any rate 1 greatly hope you will, on looking on this performance, fancy it justifies itself sufficiently to go in as one thing—not as two. I can't but think it would suffer greatly by partition. I have given it much care, & it hangs all together—it has one long rhythm. If you will print it as one I promise you, for the next time, a thing that will take only 10 pages. I hope *The Pupil* comes in time for me to see a proof of it. Yours very truly

Henry James

4.

30 October 1890

My dear Mr. James

Shortly after writing you, I had your note and the story of *The Pupil* which I received gladly, though with a little misgiving when I discovered its length and learned from you that it was not easily divisible.

Upon reading the story I came to the same conclusion. It could not be divided, and must be read at a sitting. Of course, its length, irrespective of magazine consideration, is not such as to prevent such reading, and under some conditions I might not be greatly affected by the fact that it was a few pages longer than the conventional length of a single number story in the magazine.

There are considerations, however, which I must take into account. I have promised stories by you, with great alacrity. I do not need to tell you how much I admire your best work. The *Atlantic* has been hospitable, and its doors are wide open to you now. I am more or less under fire as the new editor and naturally I mean that the *Atlantic* shall not suffer by my accession. To publish, therefore, as the first of your contributions a story which from its length will receive special attention, but which I cannot defend as "as good as it is long" is to invite criticism both for you and for me which I wish to avoid. Frankly, my reluctant judgment insists upon regarding the story as lacking in interest, in precision and in effectiveness, and however you may temporarily regard it, I should not be surprised if you came to take the same view of it. The situation seems to me too delicate to permit quick handling, and with such a family to exploit I should suppose a volume would be necessary. At any rate I find the structure of the story so weak for carrying the sentiment that I am afraid other readers will be equally dissatisfied, and say hastily—"vague"—"unformed."

I hate to write all this, but I should hate myself still more if I didn't!

Yours faithfully
H. E. Scudder

Henry James, esq.

5.

34 DeVere Gardens W.

November 10th 1890

Dear Mr. Scudder.

I am very sorry to learn we have made such a bad start, and to this regret is added the shock of a perfectly honest surprise. I sent off *The Pupil* with a quite serene conviction that I had done a distinctly happy thing, and when I asked for indulgence for its length on the score of its probable value, I expressed a confidence which was deeply genuine, though the event now makes me smile at it. The tale, in truth, was the fruit of much labour—and I regarded it as a little masterpiece of compression (I so boiled and re-boiled it down), of the effort to give a large picture in a small compass. It was precisely this tender treatment of it that made me long in getting it off. But I have, thank heaven, no pretension at all to never making a mistake—no such uncomfortable glory, and I am very glad you have been perfectly frank in pointing out the occasion on which it seems to you that I have done so. For me, artistically, the sense of a mistake is a still more fertilizing excitement than that of a success; and I shall be perfectly ready to admit that I have gone astray with the *Pupil* if doubts of it are born to me, as is perfectly possible, on a reperusal of it in the light of your impression. But the thing I most regret is that your impression makes me feel nervous and insecure about the things I have had it in mind still to send you. I mean that if I was mistaken

about *The Pupil*—and badly mistaken, given my really exceptional confidence—I may be deluded about things produced with, after all, similar hopes. However, I shall face this risk about a shorter story (it is called The Servant), which I am just sending off to be typecopied and which when it comes back, I shall despatch you—if in reading it over with the test of the vivider surface, I am not panic-stricken in regard to its possible fate. But even in this case I shall try again—though deploring such delays. Please keep *The Pupil* in your desk for me till I can consider what I had best ask you to do with it. Perhaps I should like it sent to an address in the U.S.—I shall have the MS. recopied and study it afresh—and then perhaps ask you to destroy your copy.
Yours very truly

Henry James

[At the time Scudder was satisfied with James's response to his declining *The Pupil*. He could not have been further from the mark. He would not again hear from James until he himself wrote to complain about James's silence.]

6.

19 February 1891

My dear James

Why this deathlike silence? Has the type-writer broken down? I have looked every Monday morning, when my foreign mail usually comes, for the story which long ago was waiting only to be put into final shape for its passage across the Atlantic.

I do not know if you have paid special attention to the magazines but if you have you may have seen that I have had no single number story in it for several months. I wished both to break through the convention which calls for a short story in each number, and then when people began to notice this austerity of mine to break forth into some specially good ones, and I have hoped I might interrupt the silence with one of yours.

Sincerely yours
H. E. Scudder

Henry James, esq.

7.

Paris

March 4th 1891

Dear Mr. Scudder.

Your letter demands a frank answer. My "deathly silence" has been the result of the fact that when after last writing to you I read over *The Pupil* in the light of your remarks about it. I quite failed to see that you had treated me fairly: I could not see that it was a performance that the *Atlantic* ought to have declined—nor banish from my mind the reflection that the responsibility, in any case, as regards the readers of the magazine, the public, should, when it's a question of an old and honourable reputation, be left with the author himself. The editor, under such circumstances, may fairly leave it to him—and I should not have shrunk from any account the readers might have held me to. These impressions were distinctly chilling as regards the production of further work. I had in my hands a little story which I had meant to send to you—but there was nothing in it to assure me that it would seem to you to have a different quality from its predecessor, and I couldn't bring myself to despatch it. The pen fell out of my hand, and I took refuge in other work, which has proved fruitful and [in] which I am now immersed. I fear I shall remain so—certainly all this month—which I am spending in this place. But on my return to London on April 1st I will do my best to get back to some tales. I feel uncertain as to how I shall do them—and as if the spell, for today, were rather broken. But you shall have a couple of specimens and I will do my best to keep them really short. Please destroy the copy of *The Pupil* you have—if you still have it—in your hands. I sent the story to Longman, to which I had long promised a tale, and it presently appears. The other little thing comes out in the new Illustrated weekly London periodical *Black and White*.

Yours very truly
Henry James

III.

That four months later James was still angry over Scudder's criticism of "The Pupil" and its rejection is clear enough. He was not "treated ... fairly" by the *Atlantic*, he insists, and he would arrogate the right to be heard by the *Atlantic*'s readers, even at the expense, if need be, of the new editor himself. But James never addresses Scudder's charges that the story is "lacking in interest, in precision and in effectiveness" and that its "situation" seems to be "too delicate to permit quick handling." Nor does James choose to comment on the hint so clearly present in Scudder's suggestion that "with such a family to exploit I should suppose a volume would be necessary." He prefers to take his stand entirely on what he would see as his rights as a veteran contributor to the *Atlantic* with "an old and honorable reputation."

James's letter depressed Scudder. On March 13, a Friday, he confided to his private notebook that the mail that day had brought him "a letter from Henry James showing that he did not take my rejection of his story with the equanimity I had at first thought.... Truly the ways of an editor are not pleasant ways." Furthermore, James had undermined his confidence in his own judgment. "Perhaps I am too prone to see defects in the work brought before me," he considered, "yet the necessity for passing judgment constantly is most irksome. I do not find that I grow any more confident. Rather, I seem more liable to sudden panic over my decisions."[8] The fact that Edel had only James's angry letter and the story as published as his basis for guessing at Scudder's reasons for turning down "The Pupil" and the inadequacy of the evidence provided by those two sources suggest the interesting possibility that the version of the story James offered Scudder differed from the version he subsequently published in England and which is the version all readers know. Given Scudder's reputation for unstinting honesty, there is every reason to believe that he followed James's instructions when he told him to destroy the copy of the story in his possession. The question that can be raised legitimately is did James, stung by Scudder's decision against "The Pupil," nevertheless find enough merit in what Scudder said to compel him to rewrite or at least revise the story before placing it with Longman's. Did James attempt to answer Scudder's criticisms that the "situation" was "too delicate to permit quick handling" and that "with such a family to exploit" he would "suppose a volume would be necessary"? James's letter, as we have seen, does not address these observations. Rather James characteristically chooses to focus on the question of the story's length, a matter Scudder had put aside at the outset of his letter. Were there not other "considerations," Scudder is quick to point out, he would readily have considered printing the story in a single issue of the *Atlantic*. Surely no reader of "The Pupil" has ever called the finished product, that is to say, the story as James published it, either "vague" or "unformed." It is hardly reasonable to think that only Scudder, astute reader and highly professional editor that he was (consider James's own happy response to Scudder's review of *The Tragic Muse*), would have been so dissatisfied with the structure of "The Pupil."

As for the "second" story Scudder had hoped to get for the *Atlantic*—originally called "The Servant" but retitled "Brooksmith"—James sent it elsewhere, to *Harper's Weekly*, a competitor. Scudder apparently learned his lesson, for when, a few months later, James offered him two different stories—"The Marriages" and "The Chaperon"—the editor of the *Atlantic*, without a moment's hesitation, agreed to publish them. In the future, so long as Scudder was the *Atlantic*'s editor, James would pretty much have his own way. "Although James's best did not result in brevity" as he had promised, notes Ellen Ballou, "from now on Scudder accepted with only minor criticism whatever James submitted. He did not wish to lose an author whose writing he deeply admired and whose name had been so long associated with the *Atlantic*."[9]

10

New Christians and "The Liar"

An earlier title for this chapter—"Henry James Among the Portingales"—was intended to pay homage to T. S. Eliot. It was intended not to be entirely well-meaning. "Sweeney Among the Nightingales" was a favorite among practitioners of the New Criticism for its critic-friendly allusions and references. Accepting whole the poet's notion that poetry was an escape from personality, such critics easily dismissed the biographical basis for the poem's least attractive feature, namely Eliot's poisonous disdain for what he called the "apelike" Irish. He had looked upon the turn-of-the-century Irish poor when, as a Harvard undergraduate, he emulated the literary naturalists by scouting the so-so parts of Boston for his biological images and social metaphors.

Now Henry James—in many meaningful ways Eliot's direct cultural antecedent—came from Irish stock. But no one—not even Eliot (or Henry James, for that matter—see his hostile views of the American Irish in *The American Scene*)—seems ever to have identified James with his Hibernian countrymen. Certainly no one has linked him to Eliot's Sweeney, who peers in at the window, doubly the outsider, both to the seduction scene going on inside the house and to the great Western culture that provides the measure for condemning such low-life behavior.

> The silent man in mocha brown
> Sprawls at the window-sill and gapes;
> The waiter brings in oranges
> Bananas figs and hothouse grapes;
> The silent vertebrate in brown
> Contracts and concentrates, withdraws;
> Rachel *née* Rabinovitch
> Tears at the grapes with murderous paws[.][1]

There is an analogy here: as with T. S. Eliot and the Irish (along with the Jews—the Bleisteins and Sir Ferdinand Kleins of other poems), so with Henry James and the Portuguese (along with, once again, the Jews). The analogy is imperfect (fortunately, given Eliot's virulent racism) but it may prove useful in my attempt to trace James's attitudes within his nineteenth-century context. A closer analogy for my title—"Henry James Among the Portingales"—might have been "Eliot Among the Sweeneys."

The story of Henry James and the Portuguese can be divided into two parts. Part one considers James's references to matters or characters Portuguese in his fiction as well as in his review of a travel book about Portugal. Part two takes up James's story "The Liar," which dates from the late 1880s and which the standard James bibliography lists as one of the earliest of James's works to be translated into Portuguese. *O Mentiroso*, put into Portuguese by Januário Leite, was published by the Lisbon publisher Portugália in 1944 in its "Biblioteca de Algebeira" (Pocket Library) series, its publication preceded by that of João Gaspar Simões's translation of *The Turn of the Screw*, which appeared only a year earlier, in 1943, under the idiosyncratic title of *Calafrio* (Chill).[2] Why "The Liar," certainly not one of James's better known stories, was chosen for translation at that time went unexplained, the story appearing without preface or introduction. Of interest, though, is its illustrative cover showing a gentleman sitting in an upholstered chair, holding forth, apparently, with full assurance. He holds a lit cigarette, from which emanates a long curl of turning and twisting smoke. Fittingly, like all liars, this one too blows smoke.

1

(The Outsider)

In 1875, at the age of thirty-two, Henry James—an American citizen but no stranger to England or the Continent—left the United States once and for all, intending to set up permanent residence in Europe. He became still another American expatriate, living briefly, at the outset, in France, and then, after 1877, in England. Yet only in the last months of his life—forty years later (he died in 1916)—did he give up his American citizenship, doing so to become a British subject, principally to dramatize his support for England's participation in the Great War as well as his disappointment with the United States for not having rallied to England's side. James himself, it might be noted in passing, served as the honorary head of an American volunteer ambulance group set up by a scion of the noted Norton family (friends of James's) of Cambridge, Massachusetts.

During his four decades of expatriation, James frequently visited the Continent, preferring to spend his time, on such extended stays, in France, Switzerland, Germany, and Italy. His fiction, essays, and letters—not to mention his travel books—are replete with references to his experiences as a visitor to these countries. He wrote a travel book, *A Little Tour in France* (1884), and travel essays later collected in books such as *Italian Hours* (1909) and—even though England was now his home—*English Hours* (1905). So long had he been abroad before revisiting the United States that he even wrote a travel book about his native land, *The American Scene* (1907), based on his sojourn spent traveling in the United States in 1904–1905.

But nowhere, if recollection holds true, does the author of the early European novels, *Roderick Hudson* and *The American*, demonstrate that he has any first-hand knowledge of the Iberian peninsula countries. That James should not have paid any attention to Spain, particularly, is quite remarkable since not only was the country of Madrid and Toledo well-known to many American writers, including, for instance, Washington Irving and Henry Wadsworth Longfellow, as well as James's friends, Henry Adams and John Hay, but James himself was once seriously proposed for a position in the American legation in Madrid by the then Minister, the critic and poet James Russell Lowell. It is interesting to contemplate what might have happened to James's literary career had the Department of State acceded to Lowell's request and James had turned to a career in diplomacy, beginning with an appointment in Spain.

As for Portugal, that was always a different matter. Among Americans—unlike the English—there was no strong tradition for visiting the country. Hence, for example, since he had managed not to visit Portugal before 1875, James apparently saw no good or compelling reason to visit the country at all. That much is clear, at least, from the little he left recorded on the matter of Portugal and the Lusitanians, as her citizens are sometimes called, even by the English. In 1875, for instance, in a review of a book called *Travels in Portugal*, he writes on the eve of his departure from the United States for Paris: "Mr. [John] Latouche has made an exceptionally agreeable, in fact, a very charming book about it [Portugal]. And yet, upon his showing, it does not appear that Portugal is especially well worth seeing, or that the tourist world is greatly the loser by leaving it alone."[3] "Portugal is of course not such a terra incognita as Afghanistan," he distinguishes, "but it lies fairly well out of the beaten track of travel."

Continuing to strike James as a place that was oddly distant, and well off the familiar course, Portugal (and the Portuguese) took on a certain mildly symbolic meaning for him. Brief references to this country that he would never see surface occasionally in his fiction. In the fourth chapter of his novel *The Portrait of a Lady* (1881), for instance, there occurs the following exchange over Isabel Archer, James's young heroine from Albany, New York.

> "Well, I don't like originals; I like translations," Mr. Ludlow had more than once replied. "Isabel's written in a foreign tongue. I can't make her out. She ought to marry an Armenian or a Portuguese."

"That's just what I'm afraid she'll do!" cried Lilian, who thought Isabel capable of anything.[4]

Suffice it to say, that the author of *Washington Square* had not visited Armenia either, or, for that matter, Afghanistan.

Then there is the odd reference in James's late novel *The Ambassadors* (1903). At the social gathering held in the artist Gloriani's studio (Book 5, Chapter 1), the middle-aged Lambert Strether and his younger countryman John Little Bilham are deep in discussion. Little Bilham talks about the sort of guests one might expect to find at one of Gloriani's "Sundays at home." "There are always artists—he's beautiful and inimitable to the *cher confrère*,'" says Little Bilham, "'and then *gros bonnets* of many kinds—ambassadors, cabinet ministers, bankers, generals, what do I know? Even Jews. Above all always some awfully nice women—and not too many; sometimes an actress, an artist, a great performer—but only when they're not monsters; and in particular the right *femmes du monde*.'"[5]

This talk of women naturally piques Strether's interest. His overall task, after all—to look for the woman, as all Woollett, Massachusetts, wants to know, who is the young Chad's "virtuous attachment"—sets him wondering whether Madame de Vionnet has yet arrived so that he can judge things for himself. He attends to his companion's words and follows the "direction" of Little Bilham's "eyes." "'Are they all, this time, *femmes du monde?*'" Strether asks. "'Are there any Poles?'" His knowledgeable companion considers this question for a moment, and then answers: "'I think I make out a "Portugee." But I've seen Turks.'" Strether wonders, oddly "desiring justice": "'They seem—all the women—very harmonious.'" To which Little Bilham replies knowingly, "'Oh in closer quarters they come out!'"[6]

This "'Portuguee'"—one of Gloriani's *femmes du monde*—appears only on this occasion, a brief showing enabled by Little Bilham's recognition and identification. Since the reader learns no more about her, what might be made of this single appearance of a woman called a "Portugee" (the word itself set off from its context by being enclosed within single quotation marks)? James obviously wished to distinguish between the vulgar term "Portuguee"—"a false singular formed from the true singular ending in *s*, with the correct singular Portuguese being mistaken for a plural"[7]—and what would have been and is the socially correct and linguistically more acceptable term "Portuguese." (After all, as we have seen, when in *The Portrait of a Lady* James wished to refer to a citizen or national of Portugal he called that person, quite properly, "Portuguese," and he did so without placing the term within quotation marks.) Are we to infer, moreover, that those quotation marks around "Portugee" indicate that this particular *femme du monde* at Gloriani's soiree, is not really a Portuguese national or native but a foreign type, perhaps even Parisian, of an unidentified national origin, though sufficiently recognizable to Little Bilham to warrant the author's use of those signifying quotation marks? Surely, Little Bilham uses the term in a common enough way, one that, similarly, the *Oxford English Dictionary* attributes to vulgar users, notably sailors, but the quotation marks he uses alert us to the fact that the author wants the reader to know that he is undoubtedly well aware that the term is both common and colloquial.[8] What it is meant to suggest to the reader, if not to Strether (at least, perhaps, not immediately to Mrs. Newsome's ambassador from Woollett), is that something of Little Bilham's *savoir faire* lies in his easy but perhaps mildly cynical commerce with the *femme du monde* of the type that Gloriani brings to the entertainment at one of his Sundays at home. There are still other possibilities, however, namely, that the term "Portuguese" had become generically associated with "the subject of love," especially in its literary form since the appearance of the so-called *Portuguese Letters* in the eighteenth century.[9] If Little Bilham knew that much, then it follows that he is playing ironically with the notion of "Portuguese" before the rather innocent and culturally naive American who is Lambert Strether. And finally, it might be suggested, there is the possibility that "Portuguese" passes for a code name in James's world for the Jew. As James himself had written, a quarter of a century earlier in his review of Latouche's *Travels in Portugal*, "It was formerly thought safe to call any Jew of a certain type a Portuguese."[10]

None of this tells us much, however, about James's overall attitude toward Portugal and the Portuguese. For that, we must look elsewhere. To begin with we can return to James's unsigned review of Latouche's *Travels*, which appeared in the New York weekly, *The Nation*, just as he was about to depart for Europe. Although it appears to be the only review that James wrote of a book devoted to Portugal or matters Portuguese, he does note, in passing that Latouche's *Travels* complements *Fair Lusitania*, a title published in London, in 1874, by Catherine Charlotte (Lady) Jackson—an observation implying that James was familiar with the earlier book.

Of particular interest in James's review of Latouche's book are his emphases, beyond those on the author's observations regarding the presence of Jews in Portugal (which anticipate, as shall be seen, James's later difficulty with the Sephardic community when he used the name "Capadose" in the 1888 story "The Liar"), on his assertion that "there never was a Portuguese school of art," and his approving notation that Latouche found "the people of the Southern provinces a quite different race from the mountaineers of Beira—the great province north of the Tagus—and an inferior one, being lazy, dirty, and shiftless."

Oddly, two of these last three adjectives, "lazy" and "shiftless," applied here to the "Beirense" (inhabitants and natives of the Beira area in continental Portugal), echo Mark Twain's pejorative characterization of the Azorean Portuguese in *The Innocents Abroad*, published first as newspaper letters and in book form in 1869. In Chapter Six of that account, Mark Twain applies these adjectives to the Azoreans, but in so doing he finds that "the community is eminently Portuguese—that is to say, it is slow, poor, shiftless, sleepy, and lazy."[11] It is possible that James had read Twain's feisty book, even though, at first blush, it would seem unlikely that someone as cosmopolitan as James had already become by the time he emigrated to Europe, would find *The Innocents Abroad*, to be appropriate reading fare. It will be recalled, however, that Twain subtitled his book *The New Pilgrims' Progress*, a choice that might have held some initial appeal to the Henry James who would call his first book, a collection of stories, *A Passionate Pilgrim* (1875).

When James reviewed Latouche's travel book, he had already decided to make his home in Europe, a move that would put to an end his own notion of himself as pilgrim. Whether or not he could actually make a life for himself in Paris (as he then hoped to do) he did not know for sure. But what was certain to him was that there was no desirable future for him in the United States. A few years later, echoing Nathaniel Hawthorne, the future author of that great American-European moral fable, *The Golden Bowl*, would lament that his native land offered little historical or legendary substance to the would-be novelist. "One might enumerate the items of high civilization, as it exists in other countries, which are absent from the texture of American life, until it should become a wonder to know what was left," wrote James in *Hawthorne*, the subject of which was his much admired predecessor, in 1879. He rattled off his litany of the items putatively "missing" in America: "No sovereign, no court, no personal loyalty, no aristocracy, no church, no clergy, no army, no diplomatic service, no country gentlemen, no palaces, no castles, nor manors, nor old country-houses, nor parsonages, nor thatched cottages, nor ivied ruins; no cathedrals, nor abbeys nor little Norman churches; no great Universities nor public schools—no Oxford, nor Eton, nor Harrow; no literature, no novels, no museums, no pictures, no political society, no sporting class—no Epsom nor Ascot."[12]

In similar fashion, in his review of *Travels in Portugal*, James had set down a list of what was absent from Portugal, though, it will be recalled, he had no first-hand knowledge of the country. His list on this occasion is shorter, to be sure, than his American bill of complaints, but it is offered in the same reproving spirit. "The best scenery is not first-rate, and what remains apparently not even second-rate," writes James. "There are no inns (to call inns), no architecture, no painting, no monuments, no local customs of a striking nature." In fact, Portugal is as un-picturesquely provincial as, the novelist-critic would soon decide, his own, now abandoned, country.

The notion of an America marked by its provincialism became a matter of some contention between James and his editor, friend and benefactor, the formidable novelist and literary arbiter William Dean Howells. In his review of James's critical study of Hawthorne, Howells zeros in on James's complaints. He essays to refute his countryman's charges by taking to a higher road, writing in the *Atlantic Monthly*: "After leaving out all those novelistic 'properties,' as sovereign, courts, aristocracy, gentry, castles, cottages, cathedrals, abbeys, universities, museums, political class, Epsoms, and Ascots, by the absence of which Mr. James suggests our poverty to the English conception, we have the whole of human life remaining, and a social structure presenting the only fresh and novel opportunities left to fiction, opportunities manifold and inexhaustible."[13]

James felt the necessity to reply in return, but he chose to forego Howells's public forum. In his letter to Howells, dated January 31, 1880, he chose to focus on his own use of the term "provincial" to describe the societies of Salem and Concord that were available to Hawthorne as a writer, a use that Howells had found excessive. "It is quite true I use the word provincial too many times—I hated myself for't, even while I did it," begins James.

> But I don't at all agree with you in thinking that "if it is not provincial for an Englishman to be English, a Frenchman French, etc., so it is not provincial for an American to be American." So it is not provincial for a Russian, an Australian, a Portuguese, a Dane, a Laplander, to savor of their respective countries: that would be where this argument would land you. I think it is extremely provincial for a Russian to be very Russian, a Portuguese very Portuguese; for the simple reason that certain national types are essentially and intrinsically provincial.[14]

So there it is. Like the Russians, the Australians, the Danes, the Laplanders, the Armenians (recall that James will link the Armenians with the Portuguese in *The Portrait of a Lady*), and the Americans themselves, the Portuguese are "essentially and intrinsically provincial." Small wonder that James, an inveterate traveler, never bothered to venture into Portugal. It is in the context of the judgment he had made in his little book on Hawthorne regarding his and his subject's own native land, that the issues raised in James's 1875 review of Latouche's *Travels* can be best understood. It is not surprising, therefore, that the author of *The American* and *The Europeans* concludes rather flippantly, as he does in reviewing Latouche's book, that "Portugal is a good country to visit after one has been everywhere else."

2

("The Liar")

In his journal on June 19, 1884, James sketched out an outline for a story. "One might write a tale (very short) about a woman married to a man of the most amiable character who is a tremendous, though harmless, liar," he begins.

> She is very intelligent, a fine, quiet, high, pure nature, and she has to sit by and hear him romance—mainly out of vanity, the desire to be interesting, and a peculiar irresistible impulse. He is good, kind, personally very attractive, very handsome, etc.: it is almost his only fault though of course he is increasingly very light. What she suffers—what she goes through—generally she tries to rectify, to remove any bad effect by toning down a little, etc. But there comes a day when he tells a very big lie which she has—for reasons to be related—to adopt, to reinforce. To save him from exposure, in a word, she has to lie herself. The struggle, etc.; she lies—but after that she hates him. (*Numa Roumestan*.)[15]

James did write the story, as he almost always did when he thought things out in his journals. "The Liar" appeared in the *Century Magazine* over the course of two issues—May and June 1888—and was collected in book form in *A London Life*, published in London and New York in 1889. Twenty years after its first publication, "The Liar" was included in the twelfth volume of the New York Edition of James's work, a volume that opened with *The Aspern Papers*, followed, in order, by *The Turn of the Screw*, "The Liar," and "The Two Faces." In the preface James wrote for this volume—the writing of which was an act largely, as he calls it, of "backward consciousness"—James writes of the origins—the *donée*—of his narrative of the circumstances and effects of a military officer's penchant for "romancing."

> For by what else in the world but by fatal design had I been placed at dinner one autumn evening of old London days face to face with a gentleman, met for the first time, though favourably known to me by name and face, in whom I recognised the most unbridled colloquial romancer the "joy of life" had ever found occasion to envy? Under what other conceivable coercion had I been invited to reckon, through the evening, with the type, with the character, with the countenance, of this magnificent master's wife, who, veracious, serene and charming, yet not once meeting straight the eyes of one of us, did her duty by each, and by her husband most of all, without so much as, in the vulgar phrase, turning a hair? It was long ago, but I have never, to this hour, forgotten the evening itself—embalmed for me now in an old-time sweetness beyond any aspect of my reproduction. I made but a fifth person, the other couple our host and hostess; between whom and one of the company, while we listened to the woven wonders of a summer holiday, the exploits of a salamander, among Mediterranean isles, were exchanged, dimly and discreetly, ever so guardedly, but all expressively, imperceptible lingering looks. It was exquisite, it could but become, inevitably, some "short story" or other, which it clearly pre-fitted as the hand the glove.[16]

When one considers this typically over-elaborated account of the origins of the "The Liar" against the by-now largely forgotten germinal note in James's notebooks in 1884, two things stand out. One is that nowhere in the earlier account does James mention the fortuitous dinner which found him in the presence of this great "romancer." And too, nowhere in the 1908 preface does James mention, as he had in 1884, his tale's similarity to *Numa Roumestan*, Alphonse Daudet's novel about a lying politician and his supportive wife.

And there is another interesting matter that James does not mention in the preface (or, understandably, in his early notebook entry). That is, the circumstances surrounding the choice he made in naming his "romancer" Clement Capadose. In 1896, eight years before James wrote his preface and eight years after he had first published "The Liar" in the *Century*, he received a letter from one Antonius Everdinus Capadose regarding the real-life identity of the character James had called Capadose. With his customary grace and tact (and not a little smoke), James replied to Mr. Capadose on October 13, 1896:

> My dear Sir,
> You may be very sure that if I had ever had the pleasure of meeting a person of your striking name I wouldn't have used the name, especially for the purpose of the tale you allude to.
> It was exactly because I had no personal or private association with it that I felt free to do so. But I am afraid that (in answer to your amiable inquiry) it is late in the day for me to tell you how I came by it.
> The Liar was written (originally published in the Century Magazine) 10 years ago—and I simply don't remember.
> Fiction-mongers collect proper names, surnames &c.—make notes and lists of any odd or unusual, as handsome or ugly ones they see or hear—in newspapers (columns of births, deaths, marriages, &c.) or in directories and signs of shops or elsewhere; fishing out of these memoranda in time of need the one that strikes them as good for a particular case.
> 'Capadose' must be in one of my old note-books. I have a dim recollection of having found it originally in the first columns of The Times, where I find almost all the names I store up for my puppets. It was picturesque and rare and so I took possession of it. I wish—if you care at all—that I had applied it to a more exemplary individual! But my romancing Colonel was a charming man, in spite of his little weakness.
> I congratulate you on your bearing a name that is at once particularly individualizing and not ungraceful (as so many rare names are).
> I am, my dear Sir,
> Yours very truly
> (Sgd.) Henry James[17]

James's letter to Capadose was eventually put to good use by the family. It was presented as supporting evidence in Bertram Brewster's 1936 account of the Capadose family in England for the assertion that the "Colonel Capadose [who] died unmarried in Jamaica, 29 February 1848, his next of kin being Captain Henry Capadose, son of his brother Jacob, who (Henry) died at Malines, Belgium, 29 September 1862," was "not to be identified with the novelist Henry James's romancing Colonel who figures in his story of "The Liar." "As to that personage," Brewster explains, "we have the authority of the author, who in a letter to Anton Capadose states in effect that his sole reason for appropriating the name was its picturesque rarity."[18]

Of course, the Capadose and their family chronicler had, in James's letter, the very thing they deemed necessary and sufficient to scotch once and for all the notion that the lying Colonel in James's story had anything to do with the actual Capadose family—living or dead. Understandably, if any of the Capadose ever examined either James's story or his letter more closely than Brewster's report of both seems to indicate, they kept their conclusions to themselves. But having available both James's notebook entry (which does not mention the name "Capadose") and the preface (which not only does not mention the name "Capadose" but which supplies, interestingly, an autobiographical account of the "germ" for the story (missing in the notebook of 1884), one might look a bit more skeptically into James's denial to Anton Capadose that he had knowingly borrowed the name directly from the Capadose family.

Now, among the prominent members of the Capadose family was one Colonel Henry Capadose (a fortuitous first name for the ever-alert novelist), a member of the 1st West India Regiment, Governor of Trinidad, author of *Sixteen Years in the West Indies* [in two volumes, published by T. C. Newby in London in 1845], *Travels in India* [which is not listed in the British Museum's General Catalogue], and other works"—among them translations of *Organs of the Brain, A Comedy* (1838) and *Kindred, A Comedy* (1837), plays by A. F. F. von Kotzebue.[19] If the novelist James did not have in mind this military officer named Capadose, who died in 1848, he might have had in mind the Captain Capadose, son of Jacob Capadose, who was "more than forty years a member of the London Stock Exchange, and held property at 6 Epping and Somers Town, also the Manor Avon Estate, Llandillo, Carmarthenshire,"[20] for imbedded in James's story is the information that Colonel Clement Capadose's father, a general, was "a rather smart soldier, but in private life of too speculative a turn—always sneaking into the city to put his money into some rotten thing."[21] Moreover, besides having for a father a General who dabbles in shady business deals, James's Colonel Capadose has a clergyman brother, the Dean of Rockingham. To go along with their several career military officers, the Capadose family had also produced several clergymen and church workers, various in stripe, including, in James's own time, one Dr. Isaac Capadose, who, beginning in 1876, "served many years ... as a Coadjutor to the Apostles in the 'Catholic Apostolic Church.'"[22]

Two or three, more or less salient, points. One, it may be recalled that the fictional Capadose, like the historical Henry Capadose, also tells stories about service in India. And two, the fictional Colonel's wife, the narrator's erstwhile friend, is named Everina. An uncommon name, to say the least, and one that James appears not to have used anywhere else in his fiction, "Everina" echoes the middle name of the Anton Capadose who wrote to James in inquiry about his use of the name "Capadose." His "Everdinus" inevitably recalls "Everina," a name that, in James's artist's economy, fits rather closely a wife whose constancy to her lying husband meets successfully every challenge put to it by James's scheming portrait-painter narrator.

The point of all this, of course, as will be readily surmised, it that the Capadose, Sephardic Jews all, were originally Portuguese. If the author of *Travels in Portugal* too readily thought "it safe to call any Portuguese a Jew," as James quotes in his 1875 review, the American novelist might have continued to think it safe, as "it was formerly thought," to call "any Jew of a certain type a Portuguese."[23] In the case of the Capadose, moreover, it was literally true. The family traced itself back with full certainty to one Aaron Israel Capadose, "born at Oporto 1614," "being the first who made proper records, and from whom," testified Dr. Abraham Capadose, "I descend in the direct line, being born of parents who most likely ... were expelled by the Inquisition from Portugal during the reign of King Emmanuel, and probably lived formerly under another name as New Christians in that country."[24] To what extent James's use of "Capadose" as his liar's family name constitutes an act of anti–Portuguese sentiment or one of anti–Semitism (or both) defies precise and, surely, final measurement. But given James's evasions—in his 1908 preface and, earlier, in his 1896 letter to Anton Capadose—it is not unreasonable to suspect that under that smoke lies some largely undetected fire. Yet that this is so should not be entirely surprising, for it was, beginning in the 1880s after all, that James had introduced in his fiction (usually) disdainful references to the Jews, notably, in the stories "The Pupil" (1891), "Glasses" (1896), and "Covering End" (1898), and the novels *The Tragic Muse* (1889), *The Spoils of Poynton* (1896), *What Maisie Knew* (1897), *The Awkward Age* (1899), *The Ambassadors* (1903), and *The Golden Bowl* (1904).[25]

Needless to say, there was much history behind James's fictional Capadose. Yet, curiously, the origin of the name "Capadose" itself has not been determined. "In my voluminous notes and ample literary collection devoted to the Marranos and their history," writes Cecil Roth, "I have not been able to trace any family bearing the name other than that with which we are here concerned. It is possible nevertheless to hazard a conjecture as to its derivation. At the time of the Forced Conversion of the Jews of Portugal in 1497 the vast majority of the victims assumed the surnames of those who stood their sponsors at baptism. Is it possible that the godfather of the first member of the family was titular Bishop of Capadocia in partibus infidelium? That would at least explain the exotic name for which so transparent a heraldic derivation (Capa-dulce) was afterwards given."[26]

Broadening the historical context will enable us to draw out even more interesting implications of what it meant for any "New Christian" family of Portuguese Jews to adopt a Christian name. The following passage is drawn from the introduction to a modern translation of Francisco Machado's *Espelho de Cristãos Novos* (*The Mirror of the New Christians*), the original of which dates from 1531.

> Following the expulsion of the Jews from Spain in 1492, many of the exiles settled among their coreligionists in the neighboring Kingdom of Portugal. Throughout the Middle Ages, the Jews in that country had led a comparatively irenic existence and it appeared that Portugal might offer a safe place of refuge. Their hopes were short-lived. King Manuel, wishing to secure a political and dynastic alliance with Spain through his marriage with Isabel, daughter of the Catholic Monarchs, agreed to her demand that the Jews be expelled from his realm as well. Manuel, however, had no desire to follow the precedent of Spain and lose whatever material benefits the Jews provided. He therefore decided upon an alternative approach. Rather than expel the Jews, he would expel Judaism. On December 24, 1496, he enacted an Edict of Expulsion according to which all Jews were to vacate the kingdom by the end of October, 1497. Yet when the fateful day came, the entire Jewish community of Portugal—with literally only a handful of exceptions—were baptized by force. In this way, the class of the New Christians (Marranos, conversos)—Christians of Jewish origin—was created.
>
> Manuel's policy toward the new converts was relatively moderate. They were left unmolested in order to allow them sufficient time to become assimilated to their new social and religious status. In 1497, he granted them a twenty year immunity from investigation and persecution and renewed this pledge in 1512. When Manuel's son, John III, ascended to the throne in 1521, he continued the policy established by his father. However, subjected as he was to various political and ecclesiastical pressures and inspired by religious zeal, he initiated proceedings to establish an inquisition after the fashion of that in Spain. After five years of opposition and hindrance, the Inquisition was established in 1536, with John's brother, the youthful Prince Henry, assuming the office of Grand Inquisitor in 1537. On September 20, 1540, exactly one year to the day before the completion of the *Mirror of the New Christians*, the first auto-de-fé was held in Lisbon. Thus began the long and intricate history of the Portuguese Inquisition and its efforts to purge the Lusitanian monarchy of its heresies—especially the alleged judaizing of the New Christians.[27]

One of the historical results—still argued over by historians—is the question of whether or not—or, if so, to what extent—the New Christians, forced to convert to Christianity, continued to practice their religion clandestinely, that is, to engage in so-called judaizing.[28]

If Henry James knew something about the history of the Marranos—the New Christians—of Portugal and knew, further, that the Capadose, behind their Portuguese surname, were actually Sephardic Jews, what, then, might "The Liar" yield? What might one find, then, to be the sub-text of James's letter to Anton Capadose almost a decade after the publication of his story about Colonel Henry Capadose, the first among the tale's three liars? It might well be said that the Capadose family, in taking on a new name, effectively masked their Jewish origins. When their late fifteenth-century forebears, facing the Inquisition, repudiated the Jewish religion for Christianity, might they, too, as did so many others, have acted expediently rather than in conviction? Were they not perforce compelled to live the great lie, over centuries, of a new and inherently inauthentic identity? It seems to me that James's reply to Anton Capadose's letter of inquiry regarding his use of the family name of Capadose deserves another look. The name had appealed to him, insisted the author, because it was "picturesque" and "rare"; and if, thinking about it at this later date, he might rather have "applied it to a more exemplary individual," he did find his "romancing Colonel" to be "a charming man, in spite of his little weakness." And then, rather disingenuously it seems, James closes out his letter with an observation the possible implications of which could not have been entirely lost on a descendant of "New Christians": "I congratulate you on bearing a name that is at once particularly individualizing and not ungraceful (as so many rare names are)."[29] Not entirely irrelevant are the lines of a seventeenth-century epithalamium regarding Abraham Capadose, who had written an account of his conversion to Christianity,

> Graceful Abraham Capadose,
> Gallant of the blessed Law,
> Courts science with grace and gallantry.[30]

The lying in "The Liar" begins with Colonel Capadose, turns to his wife Everina, née Brant, and finally to the narrator, the portrait painter Oliver Lyons. Indeed, the story has been read as a portrait of the artist as liar, a reading that depends upon one's recognizing that the narrator is unreliable.[31] It was Colonel Capadose as "romancer" that most contemporary readers saw as the subject of James's tale. But at least one of James's friends read the story as a revelation about a type of woman exemplified by the Colonel's loyal wife. "Please read Harry James's Liar in the May *Century*," wrote Henry Adams to a confidante. "He has hit on a nice study of femi-nature. I have known such men, and have pondered in like perplexity about their wives."[32] James's narrator insists on Everina Brant's Englishness. "[T]here's something in her face—a sort of nobleness of the Roman type, in spite of her having such English eyes," he writes. "In fact she's English down to the ground; but her complexion, her low forehead and that beautiful close little wave in her dark hair make her look like a transfigured Trasteverina"—that is to say, a denizen of that proud section of Rome called Trastevere (Across the Tiber), a second source for her given name.[33] In supporting her husband's lies to the last, she reenacts in a connubial way the entire English propensity for historically accepting at face value the masking English identities of the "New Christians" in their midst, not the least of whom in the nineteenth-century was the First Earl of Beaconsfield—the author of several so-called "silver-spoon" novels, the politician who twice was Queen Victoria's prime minister, Benjamin Disraeli—who just might have provided an historical parallel in James's view for the fictional (lying) politician of Daudet's *Numa Roumestan*.

In 1936, with Jews under virulent attack in Nazi Germany, it was vital to define English Jews as both Jews and Englishmen. As Cecil Roth observes of the Capadose family, "True, they have for a century and more been severed from the Jewish community. Yet one cannot but recall with pride how, when sympathy with Judaism was a capital offence, they nurtured it in their hearts, returning after many generations to the faith of their fathers and playing thereafter a notable part in Jewish life."[34] Forgotten here, perhaps, was that such necessary dissimulation about one's beliefs and convictions had degenerated, in the English military officer bearing the Sephardic name of Capadose, into downright plain out-and-out lying about just about everything.

Yet it was precisely this truth about Colonel Capadose that James's painter had wanted to capture in his portrait of the so-called "liar platonic."[35] And that he succeeded in so doing is the point of the Colonel's English wife's reaction to the painting. "'It's too cruel—oh it's too cruel!'" she cries out. "It's all there—it's all there!' 'Everything there ought n't to be—everything he has seen. It's too dreadful!'"[36] One student of James's story has taken pains to argue that it is improbable to believe that any painter—including James's fictional one—could have conveyed in a portrait just exactly the mendacity at the heart of the Colonel's character.[37] Perhaps this is true for the generic liar, but when it is considered that James is dealing with a "new Christian," that difficulty disappears. Here is one last quotation from Brewster's essay on "The Capadose Family":

> In the invariably pleasing physiognomy of this brown-eyed- Sephardic family I noted nothing markedly Semitic for the most part; the mother (a van Hoytema), it is true, and also the paternal grandmother (a van der Houven) being of the purest Dutch ancestry. Dr. Capadose [Dr. Isaac Capadose, James's contemporary] was himself an exception, but in this case the finely chiselled features seemed suggestive of some blending of Hellenistic culture. With the nose sharply aquiline, the mouth firm, but of a peculiar sweetness, he seemed the physiognomical expression of the family motto: De Fuerte salió Dulce ["Out of the strong came forth sweetness"—Judges xiv.14].[38]

James's narrator-painter paints Colonel Capadose but never describes his (inferentially Semitic) features. To do so would have been to give away too much of James's figure in the carpet in this tale—too much of the truth hidden within the heart of his Sephardic "liar." James's story may not be mainly one of plot invented "purely to be an exposition of an impression," as Ezra Pound asserted, but it is undoubtedly an allegory—perhaps even, as Pound also insisted, "the best of the allegories."[39]

11

The Poynton Marbles

Marbles—as (false) transl. of F. *meubles*: furniture, movables, personal effects; "the goods" (*slang*). (*OED*)

Edgar Allan Poe's master detective explains the principle of ratiocination that enables him to locate the letter that the prefect of police cannot find. "It is merely," says Monsieur C. Auguste Dupin, "an identification of the reasoner's intellect with that of his opponent"—a principle that enables the schoolboy playing at the game of "even and odd" to win "all the marbles of the school."[1] It is not far-fetched, I think, to consider some of Henry James's detective-like characters as somehow related to Dupin—Hugh Vereker's readers in "The Figure in the Carpet," the governess in "The Turn of the Screw," the narrator in *The Sacred Fount* or Lambert Strether in *The Ambassadors*. Each of them works, with varying degrees of success—not to win a game per se—but to establish pertinent facts, fit pieces to a puzzle, or search out the mystery at the center of some web of relationships. The efforts of Mrs. Gereth of *The Spoils of Poynton*, however, are of a different sort. She is more like Poe's schoolboy, intending to win all the marbles. To win she must not lose the furnishings she and her late husband have so assiduously assembled and that, at her husband's death, must now go to their son and the wife he chooses.

In an account of James's use of French words and phrases in his fiction, Edwin Sill Fussell writes of *The Spoils of Poynton* that even though the action of the novel is "purely English and its language nearly as insular," the novel contains significant French touches: "former Parisian art student [Fleda Vetch] obligingly gives us *morceau de musée* and *bibelot*, the former continental antique hunter [Mrs. Gereth] adds her *n'en parlons plus*, and narrative authority chimes in with *endimanché*, *flair* (italicized as if French), *objets d'art*, *cachet*, and 'entrée.' Louis Seize furniture is spoken of and Marie Antoinette in the Conciergerie."[2] Missing from James's novel, oddly enough, are *meuble* and *meubles*, words that appear in French translations of *The Spoils of Poynton* as the equivalents for "furniture" and "furnishings" and that James employs elsewhere—*The Golden Bowl*, for example.

The Spoils of Poynton is "a story of cabinets and chairs and tables," James recalled. Its germ—another case of "clumsy Life again at her stupid work," he said—was an anecdote about how "a good lady in the north, always well looked on, was at daggers drawn with her only son, ever hitherto exemplary, over the ownership of the valuable furniture of a fine old house just accruing to the young man by his father's death."[3] The novel cannot be reduced to a "damned fuss about furniture," as Ezra Pound would have it.[4] There is more to it than the irony that it is an early morning fire that "inherits" the Poynton collection, foiling, once and for all, Mrs. Gereth's one-sided game and its high-stakes gamble. No one is a match for her, but the laws of inheritance are another matter. The lawful outcome of disestablishment at her husband's death she has not circumvented. Mrs. Gereth will be out-matched not by any of her opponents but by the insensitive and undiscriminating law of the land. Only by weaning her son away from Mona Brigstock and steering him in the direction of the acceptable and more deserving Fleda Vetch, Mrs. Gereth reasons, can she "save" her "Things," the "rare French furniture and oriental china" in place at Poynton—her own "Imperial Garde Meuble."[5] Indeed, Fleda, too, will be "a bit of furniture," as Mrs. Gereth says to Fleda, "for that, a little, you know, I've always taken you—quite one of my best finds" (245). And Fleda does not object, for "the position of a scrap of furniture was one that Fleda could conscientiously accept" (245).

When James published the novel in book form, he changed its title from *The Old Things*, as it was called during its serialization in the *Atlantic Monthly*, to *The Spoils of Poynton*. Some of his readers lamented the change. "We prefer the original title," wrote one reviewer, "for really these 'old things'—namely, a collection of rare and choice objects of art—furnish the motive and center of action of the novel."[6] A second reviewer went so far as to declare "that the real Personage of the book is … none other than 'The Old Things'"—not any of its characters.[7]

In re-titling his story, however, James effected a significant shift in emphasis from the "things" themselves—the connoisseur's furnishings collected at Poynton—to a "war" over those furnishings as spoils. That there was a joke in all this fuss, I think, was indicated by the reviewer who concluded that "the reader remains calmly indifferent, as to what becomes of either the *meubles* or the *dramatis personae*."[8] When he identifies the Poynton "spoils" as *meubles*, James's reviewer points to the pun that goes to the heart of what matters in *The Spoils of Poynton*.

12

The Caretaker

It is a commonplace among his readers that Henry James often named his characters for their suggestive, even allegorical significance. Examples abound: Rowland Mallet, Christopher Newman, Winterbourne, Gilbert Osmond, Dr. Prance, Miss Birdseye, Maria Gostray, and Fanny Assingham, to name a few.[1] My proposal is that Juliana, the aged lover of Jeffrey Aspern, by virtue of her surname—Bordereau, which *Webster's New World Dictionary* defines as "a memorandum, especially one that gives a list of documents"—belongs on that list.[2] James's use of "bordereau," anticipating by a decade or so the appearance of the most famous "bordereau" in French history, the (forged) list of documents entered in evidence against Alfred Dreyfus—is subtle and nuanced.

In his preface to the volume in the New York Edition that includes *The Aspern Papers*, James reveals that the situation in his novella was suggested to him by the recent death, after long residence in Florence, of Jane Clairmont.[3] The half-sister of Mary Godwin and the mother of Lord Byron's daughter Allegra, Clairmont becomes the model for Juliana Bordereau in James's novella, while Byron gives way to a fictional American poet, Jeffrey Aspern. James's plot does not reflect the more sensational aspects of the relationship between Byron and his wife's half-sister, as another writer's might have done, but works through the notion that the American poet's lover has in her possession letters from the poet and, possibly, manuscripts of his poetry. Since such material is greatly desired by the literary scholar, James chooses to focus on the ethics of scholarly behavior and literary exploitation rather than, for example, the moral issue of incest considered to be paramount in the Clairmont—Byron story in Byron's day and long after. Or, perhaps, on the rumors of Byron's homosexuality, circulated throughout the nineteenth century.[4]

Since the unnamed "publishing scoundrel" of *The Aspern Papers* sees himself as a keeper of the Jeffrey Aspern flame, it is only natural that for him "there hovered about" the name of the poet's ancient lover "a perfume of impenitent passion."[5] Juliana Bordereau's name is a spur to this covetous suitor who thinks he will stop at nothing to get his hands on the "box full" (13) of the poet's letters in her possession. But Juliana herself, apparently the only living memory of Aspern, turns out to be a stubborn and immovable gatekeeper, unsympathetic to anyone else's interest in the Aspern letters, and steadfast in her determination to frustrate the scoundrel in his quest.

Acting within her rights as the proprietor of documents that others think they treasure more than she does, Juliana wills the papers to her niece Tina. When Juliana dies, Tina is free to strike a bargain for them. In a meeting with the "scoundrel" the niece fumbles her way to an explanation: if she were to release the papers to "a relation," (133) their fate—that is, publication—would no longer be her responsibility. Marriage in return for possession of Jeffrey Aspern's papers—the editor realizes, recoiling with something close to horror—is the one price he will not pay. But overnight his resolve on this score weakens and, although he is still unsure as to whether he will meet the price or somehow find another way to get his prize, he meets again with Tina, only to be surprised a second time. He's too late. She has burned the Aspern papers. Nothing remains; the "deal" is now moot. And even Juliana, who while alive was herself a "bordereau"—a memorandum—of the contents of Jeffrey Aspern's letters—is no more. The narrator of James's story, the "publishing scoundrel," tells us that "there hovered about her name a perfume of impenitent passion" (118). But it will come as no surprise to any sympathetic reader of *The Aspern Papers* that scheming every which way to obtain the "box full" of the late poet Jeffrey Aspern's letters believed to be in the possession of Juliana Bordereau, he has both forgotten that "perfume" and, it may be said, "objectified" her. No matter how sympathetically he claims to see her, she holds interest for him only because she possesses the thing he so obsessively and desperately desires.

Willing to pay any price for the documents (or so he thinks), the editor nevertheless balks at the price Aspern's now aged lover sets for the papers—Tina's long-term security. Acting as merely the long-term holder of what others see as documents, Juliana will release the papers to the outside world if her price is met. She is not "witchlike," as she has been called[6]; she is merely the possessor of some of Aspern's papers. She is not the keeper of the poet Aspern's flame, whose keeper, if it has one, is "the publishing scoundrel" himself. Juliana has herself become a "bordereau," more or less, the list of documents and other things associated with the long dead poet, things that are much sought after, but nothing more than objects. In choosing to name Jeffrey Aspern's paramour "Bordereau," James himself participates in his publishing scoundrel's transgressions against the woman, reducing her to an object, the thing she has allowed herself at the last to become. While "there's nothing the matter with objects, so long as they're not used to replace people," it can be seen that in this case Juliana has not been replaced by "the papers" but that she herself has been transformed into merely a "container" for those papers.[7]

Not unexpectedly, the American editor's frustration at the loss of the Aspern letters spilled over to some of James's first readers. "The way in which the man, so to speak, sinks the biographer, actually in part, is delightful; though it is disappointing to lose in consequence all knowledge of what the papers contained," complained the *Scottish Review*.[8] Not so the biographical James, however, who in 1910 chose to reveal that he had destroyed the vast correspondence of which he himself, was the "bordereau." "I kept almost all letters for years—till my receptacles would no longer hold them," he said; "then I made a gigantic bonfire and have been easier in mind since."[9] Of course, his dramatic gesture in the direction of privacy may have protected his correspondents but it did not protect him from future "publishing scoundrels," who would ferret out the letters he wrote—no one, it seems, destroyed those—to make their content known to the world.

13

Figure in the Carpet

Among the correspondence awaiting Henry James's return to London in early summer 1899 after a stay in France and Italy was a letter from Ford Madox Hueffer, along with a copy of a recent issue of *The Outlook*. Neither Hueffer's letter nor James's copy of the magazine seems to have survived. But James's reply has, providing us with useful information and leads that are worth pursuing. The letter sheds some light on the disciple-master relationship that Hueffer envisioned between himself and James. One senses the eagerness with which he brought to James's attention what he saw as a favorable review by Edward Garnett. But the letter's true import lies elsewhere. It can be read as one of the motivating sources for Hueffer's own later assessment of James's achievement after fifty years of writing. It introduces to scholarship on James the name of one of the most respected literary critics of the day. And James's letter encourages us to consider the long-range effect that Edward Garnett's ruminations had on James's theorizing about *The Awkward Age*.

> Lamb House, Rye
> July 9th 1899.
>
> Dear F. M. Huefer [sic].
>
> I returned on Friday (7th) night from a long absence—4 months abroad—to find your good note of a good many weeks ago, together with the copy of *The Outlook* containing the charming notice of *The Awkward Age*. These things had awaited my return, as I had had no periodicals sent after me, & your letter was folded into the journal. Many thanks at last for each. I had not seen Mr. Garnett's very responsive review—which gives me great pleasure & in fact greatly touches me. Please tell him so for me. I am not pampered by the press, I believe—but the press seems to me, in general, on literary matters, infantile. There is a figure in the carpet of *The A. A.* which I think Mr. G. hasn't quite made out—but I am not the less yours & his most truly
>
> Henry James[1]

Garnett's review of *The Awkward Age* appeared unsigned under the title "As Subtle as Life" in *The Outlook* for 10 June 1899.[2] Unlisted in secondary bibliographies on James, the review constitutes the single example of Garnett's magazine writing on James that has surfaced. James's identification of Garnett as the author of the review derives, it seems safe to assume, from Hueffer's telling him so in his own letter.

James's reference to "the figure in the carpet" recalls, of course, the title and theme of the story he had published in *Cosmopolis* in 1896 and collected in *Embarrassments* the same year. Employing the phrase in a letter and applying it to one of his novels, almost a decade before writing the preface in the New York Edition of his collective works that discusses the story bearing the phrase as its title, James offers the reader ample assurance that he took seriously his own notion that his well-written stories and novels did have such "figures in the carpet." The phrase was not a ploy used to take in the reader who would too zealously inquire after principles of structure and strictures of meaning in James's fiction. That this phrase appears in James's letter to Hueffer takes on additional interest when one notices that it is not used in *The Awkward Age* or, understandably, in Garnett's review.

James's famous phrase does surface in Hueffer's critical book on James in 1914, although *The Awkward Age* is not mentioned, suggesting the possibility that Hueffer never got around to reading the novel.[3] He also neglects to mention Garnett's 1899 review. Yet his study tackles a large matter—the question of James's "greatness"—originally proposed by Garnett. James is "the only modern English novelist who is as subtle as life," Garnett insisted. "The chief question we have to determine is—how *great* is he?" In his search for an answer, Garnett rehearses the strengths and weaknesses of James's novel as he sees them, to arrive at this inconclusive final paragraph:

> The last pages in the book almost supply the answer to our question—Is it great? These last pages are diabolically clever, because in them the author suggests that the modern ideal of Society's life is. justified; that to know both good and evil transcends the old-fashioned ideal of ignorance and purity. The life depicted is so inevitable that criticism on it, in which the author has led us to indulge all along, is knocked suddenly out by one's realisation that even progress downhill is necessary to life. And this sudden stoppage of the book's tendency shows how amazingly *strong* is the life it brings before us, how remorseless and mysterious, how absolutely baffling, is the life when all is said and done. Nanda beats Mr. Longdon in the end, beats criticism, beats the reader and author too! She is life, and we remain paralysed with admiration. The sense of time elapsing, too, and of the gliding and receding of the past, of the present giving place and becoming past—all this is most admirably conveyed. In this respect a certain poetical feeling of the vastness of human life is given to the reader, and if Mr. Henry James can only present *that*, well! then he is great. And has he not presented us with that feeling already in "The Altars of the Dead" [sic]? And yet, and yet—is *The Awkward Age* simple enough in *form* to be great?

While James had insisted to Hueffer that Garnett had not detected the figure in the carpet in *The Awkward Age*, a later complaint that the novel had been generally misunderstood seems to take its cue from Garnett's review."Your bewilderment over *The Awkward Age* doesn't on the whole surprise me," James wrote to a friend in November 1899,"for that ingenious volume appears to have excited little but bewilderment."[4] James was reluctant to explain his work—"a work of art that one has to *explain* fails in so far, I suppose, of its mission"—but decided to do so anyway:"I had in view a certain special social (highly 'modern' and actual) London group and type and tone, which seemed to me to se prêter à merveille to an ironic—lightly and simply ironic!—treatment, and that clever people at least would know who, in general, and what, one meant. But here, at least, it appears there are very few clever people! One must point with fingerposts—one must label with *pancartes*—one must explain with *conférences!*"

Yet the problem was less with the subject he had chosen for his "picture" than with the form that brought the picture into being. James had suggested as much in his letter to Hueffer, but now he spoke with quiet exasperation and, possibly, regret: "The *form*, doubtless, of my picture is against it—a form all dramatic and scenic—of presented episodes, architecturally combined and each making a piece of the building; with no going behind, no *telling about* the figures save by their own appearance and action and with explanations reduced to the explanation of everything by all the other things *in* the picture."

Garnett had observed in passing that "in any age less insensible to drama Mr. Henry James would have been a rare and fine dramatist," but he had also decided, as has been seen, that the "greatness" of the specific novel under review depended on whether it was "simple enough in form." In his preface to the New York Edition of *The Awkward Age* James summarizes the views of those who disdain "contemporary drama":"'Remember,' they say to the dramatist,'that you have to be, supremely, three things: you have to be true to your form, you have to be interesting, you have to be clear.'"[5] What matters in such instances if making things clear diminishes the importance of what is originally intended? James resumes his summary of views critical of "contemporary drama":

> Make the thing you have to convey, make the picture you have to paint, at all rich and complex, and you cease to be clear. Remain clear—and with the clearness required by the infantine intelligence of any public consenting to see a play—and what becomes of the "importance" of your subject? If it's important by any other critical measure than the little foot-rule the "produced" piece has to conform to, it is predestined to be a muddle. When it has escaped being a muddle the note it has succeeded in striking at the furthest will be recognised as one of those that are called high but by the courtesy, by the intellectual provinciality, of theatrical criticism, which, as we can see for ourselves any morning, is—well, an abyss even deeper than the theatre itself [xviii].

The best dramatists, "in their poor theatrical straight-jacket ... have *had* to renounce the finer thing for the coarser, the thick, in short, for the thin and the curious for the self-evident," the "disdainers of the contemporary drama" continue. Take Ibsen, for example, "since from the moment he's clear, from the moment he's 'amusing,' it's on the footing of a thesis as simple and superficial as that of 'A Doll's House'—while from the moment he's by apparent intention comprehensive and searching it's on the footing of an effect as confused and obscure as 'The Wild Duck.' From which you easily see *all* the conditions can't be met. The dramatist has to choose but those he's most capable of, and by that choice he's known" (xviii-xix).

But James, who admits to "getting launched in 'The Awkward Age,' as if I were in fact constructing a play" (p. xx), has a high view of dramatic form, unlike those critics who deprecated the drama of his time. He took the existence of such general disdain as a challenge to the writer of fiction. In writing *The Awkward Age* James had, he admitted, "tasted to the full the bitter-sweetness of his [the playwright's] draught—the beauty and the difficulty ... of escaping poverty even though the references in one's action can only be, with intensity, to each other, to things exactly on the same plane of exhibition with themselves" (xx).

James then evokes obliquely his own figure of "the figure in the carpet" to describe how the novel must ultimately differ from the play and how that difference leads in *The Awkward Age* to an "over-treatment" of its subject:

> Exhibition may mean in a "story" twenty different ways, fifty excursions, alternatives, excrescences, and the novel, as largely practised in English, is the perfect paradise of the loose end. The play consents to the logic of but one way, mathematically right, and with the loose end as gross an impertinence on its surface, and as grave a dishonour, as the dangle of a snippet of silk or wool on the right side of a tapestry. We are shut up wholly to cross-relations, relations all within the action itself; no part of which is related to anything but some other part—save of course by the relation of the total to life. And, after invoking the protection of Gyp [the pseudonym of the French writer of the *roman dialogué*] I saw the point of my game all in the problem of keeping these conditioned relations crystalline at the same time that I should, in emulation of life, consent to their being numerous and fine and characteristic of the London world (as the London world was in this quarter and that to be deciphered). All of which was to make in the event for complications [xx].

James admitted that his "complications" had taken him far from the example of Gyp's novels of dialogue that he had started out with, but his plan for the book had determined its more complicated course. He recognized "with a waking vibration of that interest in which," as he said, "the plan of the book is embalmed for me, that my subject was probably condemned in advance to appreciable, or more exactly perhaps to almost preposterously appreciative, over-treatment" (xx-xxi). James's admission lays a basis for suggesting that he had not only indeed attended to Garnett's notions in his review of *The Awkward Age* but had absorbed its argument, along with its speculation over whether James's otherwise admirable novel was "simple enough in form to be great." Garnett's review had called for an answer; the need for a preface gave James the opportunity to provide one. Garnett's failure to detect James's figure in the carpet of *The Awkward Age* evokes an explanation in the form of the novelist-as-critic's detailed account of how the novelist-as-artist brought his own controlling figure into being. James recalled "sketching my project for the conductors" of *Harper's Weekly*, which serialized the novel.

> I drew on a sheet of paper—and possibly with an effect of the cabalistic, it now comes over me, that even anxious amplification may have but vainly attenuated—the neat figure of a circle consisting of a number of small rounds disposed at equal distance about a central object. The central object was my situation, my subject in itself, to which the thing would owe its title, and the small rounds represented so many distinct lamps, as I liked to call them, the function of each of which would be to light with all due intensity one of its aspects. I had divided it, didn't they see? into aspects—uncanny as the little term might sound (though not for a moment did I suggest we should use it for the public), and by that sign we would conquer....
> The beauty of the conception was in this approximation of the respective divisions of my form to the successive Acts of a Play—as to which it was more than ever a case for charmed capitals. The divine distinction of the act of a play—and a greater than any other it easily succeeds in arriving at—was, I reasoned, in its special, its guarded objectivity. This objectivity, in turn, when achieving its ideal, came from the imposed absence of that "going behind," to compass explanations and amplifications, to drag out odds and ends from the "mere" storyteller's great property-shop of aids to illusion: a resource under denial of which it was equally perplexing and delightful, for a change, to proceed [xvi-xvii].[6]

James's preface, published in 1908, was of course available to Hueffer when he undertook what was and remains, in a few important ways, a useful pioneering study. Yet it was not to James's hint regarding "the figure in the carpet" in *The Awkward Age* that Hueffer was attracted but to Garnett's original concern as to whether James's novel was "great." Unlike Garnett, however, Hueffer asks not whether a given novel is "great" but argues, more grandly and simply: "Mr. James is the greatest of living writers and in consequence, for me, the greatest of living men" (9). Hueffer acknowledges the Master's commitment to form and method but finds, remarkably (especially given Hueffer's long-standing primary interest in fictional "method"), that James's technique is in high service to his largest intentions as a novelist. James's greatness lies, simply, in his being *the* historian of his times: "He, more than anybody, has observed human society as it now is," writes Hueffer, "and more than anybody has faithfully rendered his observations for us" (48). It is true that James "has preferred to enquire into the habits of the comfortable classes and of their dependants," he will admit, but "no other human being has made the serious attempt to enquire with an unbiased mind into the habits and necessities of any other class or race of the habitable globe as it is" (49). Hueffer echoes here, significantly, what Garnett had already said of James's work: "Long ago he set himself this task (shirked, or rather not divined, by novelists of less subtle brains), to be true to the spirit of modern life, by analysing the finest shades of people's wavering relations, by criticising the progressively vulgar tangle of our hopelessly mixed caste and cash social system; and to look back upon his work from the days of *The Portrait of a Lady* is to recognise that without him English society of the "eighties and nineties would not have had its chronicler at all."

Hueffer refashioned Garnett's characterization of James as chronicler of English society into an assessment of James's largest intentions over fifty years of writing:

> If Mr. James, then, has given us a truthful picture of the leisured life that is founded upon the labours of all this stuff that fills graveyards, then he, more than any other person now living, has afforded matter upon which the sociologist of the future may build—or may commence his destructions.
>
> For, given that he has achieved this, the problem which will then present itself to the sociologist is no more and no less than this—are the prizes of life, is the leisured life which our author has depicted for us, worth the striving for? If, in short, this life is not worth having—this life of the West End, of the country-house, of the drawing-room, possibly of the studio, and of the garden party—if this life, which is the best that our civilisation has to show, is not worth the living; if it is not pleasant, cultivated, civilised, cleanly and instinct with reasonably high ideals, then, indeed, Western civilisation is not worth going on with, and we had better scrap the whole of it so as to begin again [62–63].

Little did Hueffer or James know, when this was written, what lay in store for the Western civilization they thought they knew. Eight months after the publication of his brave study of the Master as historian and fifteen years after the publication of the Master's story of Nanda Brookenham and the Buckingham Crescent at the end of the century, the Archduke Ferdinand was assassinated in Sarajevo. For James it was the opening of the abyss and for Hueffer it brought about the rupture in his life that eventuated in his remaking himself.

But to return one last time to the "figure in the carpet" in *The Awkward Age* that Garnett, according to James, had not "quite made out," and specifically to Garnett's concluding question ("And yet, and yet—is *The Awkward Age* simple enough in form to be great?"), James's preface offers an answer to this question of form. It is simply, he writes, "the neat figure of a circle consisting of a number of small rounds disposed at equal distance about a central object" (xvi). To this description James might have added the theory of informational and impressional flow from those "small rounds" implicit in the metaphors exchanged by Nanda and Mitchy that go to make up that "central object." "Doesn't one become a sort of a little drain-pipe with everything flowing through?" questions Nanda. "'Why don't you call it more gracefully,' Mitchy asked, freshly struck, 'a little aeolian-harp set in the drawing-room window and vibrating in the breeze of conversation?'" Nanda refuses Mitchy's Romantic trope "because the harp gives out a sound, and we—at least we try to—give out none."[7] Yet Nanda's objection breaks down, for it is by means of "a circle of free talk"[8]—information conveyed directly by such "drainpipes," along with information mediated by those "aeolian-harps," which make new sounds with the air that passes through them—that the "central object" (expressed most succinctly as "the awkward age") is brought into being, developed, shaped, and, at the last, sustained.

James's notion of the "figure in the carpet" has long intrigued critics and scholars of the English and American novels, often constructing elaborate theories around James's mysterious phrase. But it was St. John Hankin (1869–1909), who knew James and was a champion of his work, who structured a play around the concept. *The Charity that Began a Home (A Comedy for Philanthropists)*, in three acts, premiered on October 23, 1906. Since James was then on his famous American tour that resulted in the publication of the essays collected in *The American Scene* in 1907. it is unlikely that he ever attended the play or, perhaps, that he knew much about it. It seems likely that James did attend a performance at the Haymarket Theatre of Hankin's play *The Last of the De Mullins* in 1908, though we do not know what he thought of it.[9] James's biographer also notes that Hankin was in contact with James on at least one occasion. When James's play *The Saloon* was not used as a curtain-raiser for *The High Bid*, as James had hoped, he was "induced by St. John Hankin to submit it to the Incorporated Stage Society which gave subscription performances of non-commercial plays. The script was read by the board members and rejected by them."[10]

In *The Charity that Began a Home (A Comedy for Philanthropists)* the playwright has one character employ the phrase "figure in the carpet," and another define it to explain on what basis the hostess of this weekend stay at a country house has assembled his strange mélange of guests. As Lady Denison explains to her sister Mrs. Eversleigh [a perfect Jamesian name], "False hospitality is inviting people because you like them. True hospitality is inviting them because they'd like to be asked." She has gathered her guests accordingly, not caring whether they will get along or provide an interesting or amusing mix, whether to the hostess or themselves. The mystery of why they have been invited then, though explained to the audience, becomes the "figure in the carpet" to the invited guests. Therein the play departs for good from James's story revolving on the mystery of "the figure in the carpet" in the writer Hugh Vereker's work, going on, of course, to take up other, less directly Jamesian, matters. But did I mention that the central character of St. John Hankin's play bears the very name of James's writer in "The Figure in the Carpet"—Hugh Vereker?

14

Identity Theft

"The theme of his tale of 'A Round of Visits' and of [the unfinished novel] *The Ivory Tower* is of Americans who inherit great wealth, only to have it stolen by other Americans," writes the Henry James biographer Leon Edel.[1] But that theme was not in James's mind when he first thought about his story. As early as 1894, he set down the idea for the story he would not write until fifteen years had passed: "There came to me a night or two ago the notion of a young man (young, presumably), who has something—some secret sorrow, trouble, fault—to *tell* and can't find the *recipient*."[2] Four years later, he reminds himself that he is yet to write the story of "The young man who can't get rid of his secret—his oppressive knowledge—with solution of his *taking* one—HAVING to, from some one else—to keep it company."[3] The next year he returns to his still unwritten "story," this time in more detail:

> Don't lose, after this, the tail of the little *concetto* of the poor young man with the burden of his personal sorrow or secret on his mind that he longs to work off on some one, roams restlessly, nervously, in depression, about London, trying for a *recipient*, and finding in the great heartless preoccupied city and society, every one taken up with quite other matters than the occasion for listening to *him*. I had thought, for the point of this, of his being suddenly approached by some one who demands his attention for some dreadful complication or trouble—a trouble so much greater than his own, a distress so extreme, that he sees the moral: the balm for his woe residing not in the sympathy of some one else, but in the coercion of giving it—the sympathy—to some one else. I see this, however, somehow, as obvious and banal, *n'est-ce pas?*—"goody" and calculable beforehand. There glimmers out some better alternative, in the form of his making some one *tide over* some awful crisis by listening to him. He learns afterwards what it has been—I mean the crisis, the *other* preoccupation, danger, anguish. [The thing needs working out—*maturing*.][4]

It was not until 1910, in the *New Review*, that he finally published his story about the man who itches to tell his secret but cannot find anyone to tell it to. And now, for the first time (the germ of "A Round of Visits" dates from 1894, it will be recalled), James reveals the secret his young man, Mark Monteith, is so eager to tell: he, an American living abroad, has been swindled by his friend in America. What he wishes to say is that Phil Bloodgood's the problem:

Oh, *he's* what's the matter with me—that, looking after some of my poor dividends, as he for the ten years of my absence had served me by doing, he has simply jockeyed me out of the whole little collection, such as it was, and taken the opportunity of my return, inevitably at last bewildered and uneasy, to "sail," ten days ago, for parts unknown and as yet unguessable. It isn't the beastly values themselves, however; that's only awkward and I can still live, though I don't quite know how I shall turn around; it's the horror of his having done it, and done it to *me*—without a mitigation or, so to speak, a warning or an excuse.[5]

How had James come upon the idea of having an American-based American "swindling" of a London-based American as the "secret" that motivates a "round of visits"? It is not coincidental, I think, that the long-germinating story was not actually written until three or four years after James had returned from his lengthy visit to his native land in 1904–1905. "One does not need the resolution" of "A Round of Visits," explains Leon Edel, "to recognize its inner statement. Henry James had been robbed and betrayed; his patrimony was gone; he had lived in a treacherous world."[6] Of course, the word "robbed" in this context is used figuratively. James, however, might well have found "robbed" to be closer to the literal truth in his own case: while in America he had fallen victim to what is now known as identity theft. Identifying himself as the renowned novelist Henry James, a thief had swindled an optician out of the price of a costly pair of glasses. Like the swindled Mark Monteith of "A Round of Visits," James, too, was victimized by a "swindler" or "desperado" or "absconder" (the words come from "A Round of Visits")[7] though in James's case it was not his money that he had lost to the swindler but his identity. Here are the details as reported in 1905, while James was still in America:

> Henry James' Double
> Since Henry James' return to America, a well-dressed perpetrator of frauds has been trading on a superficial resemblance he bears to the famous author. Not long ago he swindled a down-town optician out of an expensive pair of glasses.
> "Send the bill," he said, "to Henry James, in care of Harper & Brothers." The optician, who was familiar with Mr. James' portrait, never doubted and now bemoans his loss for Mr. James writes his publishers: "I should never thought of having a bill of mine so unceremoniously sent you. I never heard of the people nor ordered nor saw the glasses. I am sorry you should have been troubled. It is either a gross mistake or an attempt at some thing worse."[8]

Besides the "swindling" and his own victimization, the defrauding incident may have recalled, even earlier, the idea of the "double" to James. The idea of the dual nature of the individual was not new to James's fiction, of course—in "The Private Life" (1892), a fantasy based on his acquaintance with the poet Robert Browning, he had allegorized the two-person writer, the one free to live a full social life because the other, his "double," does all the writing—but here he was faced with the fact that a confidence man swindling an optician—had usurped his very "Self." It is interesting that he will exonerate himself with his publishers (who were sent the bill) by appealing less to common ethics or morality than to his own high sense of personal manners. One imagines him mulling the matter over until it emerged in "The Jolly Corner" as a fantasized search for the self he might have been had he lived out his life in America and in "A Round of Visitors" as the betrayed and swindled American of a "finer-grain"[9] who—too trusting of his friend in charge of his finances in America—is swindled.

15

Great White Hunter

> Above all, the Labyrinth was the center of activities concerned with those greatest mysteries, Life and Death. There men tried by every means known to them to overcome death and to renew life.... The Labyrinth was the centre of all the strongest emotions of the people—joy, fear and grief were there given the most intense forms of expression.
> —C. N. Deedes, *The Labyrinth* (1935)[1]

> There can by nothing else so intricate, unless it were the brain of a man like Daedalus, who planned it, or the heart of any ordinary man; which last, to be sure, is ten times as great a mystery as the labyrinth of Crete.
> —Nathaniel Hawthorne, "The Minotaur" (1852)[2]

Over the years, the November 1882 issue of the *Century Magazine* proved to be particularly memorable for Henry James, and not principally, not at first at least, because his travel piece on "Venice," occupying twenty-one pages, was its lead.[3] Of course, that the essay was well received by readers (despite its "hideous misprints," as he wrote to an admirer[4]) must have been a source of considerable pleasure. His fellow writer, Constance Fenimore Woolson, for instance, wrote to him with an intimate's knowledge of "the beautiful old water-city."[5] When, shortly after the publication of his essay, James asked Constance for "a picture" of Venice to keep him "going," she replied with grace and generosity: "But what can I say to you—in reality—of all the enchantment,—all the delicious, rich, lovable beauty of this sweet place, when you know it all so well,—when you have written out your feeling about it in those exquisite pages I love so much myself—whose every word I know, almost by heart. The magazine containing them lies on this table as I write—the copy you sent me in Paris. And I care so very much for it that—like the Old Indulgences—you may sin a good deal, on the strength of it."[6]

Yet welcome and comforting as such a response must have been to James, there were other things about the November 1882 *Century* that made that issue uncommonly memorable for the author of "Venice." For one, it carried as well William Dean Howells's appreciative essay, "Henry James, Jr."—a piece that quickly achieved notoriety on both sides of the Atlantic.[7] As early as 27 November 1882, a week after his arrival in Boston, James would write to Howells, who was then abroad, about the "little breeze produced ... by the November *Century*."[8] That breeze would soon turn into a storm as detractors of James and Howells persisted in misreading the purport of Howells's observations on the development of fiction in English. "The art of fiction has, in fact, become a finer art in our day than it was with Dickens and Thackeray," ventured Howells. "We could not suffer the confidential attitude of the latter now, nor the mannerism of the former, any more than we could endure the prolixity of Richardson or the coarseness of Fielding."[9] To Howells, James explained, still quoting from the letter of 27 November 1882, "You are accused of having sacrificed—in your patriotic passion for the works of H. J. Jr.—*Vanity Fair* and *Henry Esmond* to *Daisy Miller* and *Poor Richard*! The indictment is rubbish—all your text says is that the 'confidential' manner of Thackeray would not be tolerable today in a younger school, which should attempt to reproduce it. Such at least is all I see in it and all you ever meant to put."[10]

This I rehearse here not to begin to retell still again a familiar story, one told and retold in much more detail by students of James and Howells alike, but to call attention to the importance the November 1882 *Century* took on for James, for its publication of his "Venice" and the publication of Howells's "Henry James, Jr." And for a third reason: the same issue of the *Century* carried a short story that became one of the sensations of the day and would prove to be the most famous of its author's stories. The full aesthetic significance Frank R. Stockton's "The Lady, or the Tiger?" held for James would not emerge until two decades after he had encountered it in the pages of the *Century*.[11] On 26 February 1903, Methuen in London and Scribner's in New York simultaneously published James's *The Better Sort*, a collection of stories. The ninth story, which achieved print for the first time in that volume, was "The Beast in the Jungle." James could just as readily have appropriated, I would suggest, Stockton's title, for are not James's John Marcher's own never fully realized alternatives conveyed in the question: The Lady or the Beast? I shall come back to Marcher's inability to define his situation, but first, some other matters. It has been speculated that James got his title from a passage in Nathaniel Hawthorne's *Blithedale Romance*, one he quoted in his own critical study, *Hawthorne*, in 1880: "Hollingsworth scarcely said a word, unless when repeatedly and pertinaciously addressed. Then, indeed, he would glare upon us from the thick shrubbery of his meditations, like a tiger out of a jungle, make the briefest reply possible, and betake himself back into the solitude of his heart and mind."[12] If James did draw his title from this passage in Hawthorne, it is noteworthy that his title reads "Beast" rather than "Tiger," although on one occasion James does refer to Marcher's notion that "a man of feeling didn't cause himself to be accompanied by a *lady* on a *tiger-hunt*."[13] I have italicized the two words to call attention to the imbedded allusion in James's clause to Stockton's story (and its title), but I should have italicized hunt as well, for James was also familiar with Francis Marion Crawford's novel *Mr. Isaacs: A Tale of Modern India*. This work, published in 1882, not only features a lengthy account of a tiger-hunt but contains a brief exchange on the question of whether or not a young woman should be allowed to go on a tiger-hunt. Drawing on these three sources, then, I would suggest another title for James's story: "The Lady, or the Tiger in the Jungle?" The substitution of "Beast" for "Tiger," however, does serve to lead the reader (and the scholar) away from James's sources, away, at least, from Hawthorne and especially Stockton. It is entirely understandable that above all things James would not want to invite comparison with Stockton and Crawford and their great popular successes. At the same time, however, James's substitution does take us in the direction of myth. That, too, will be taken up later.

To say that in "The Beast in the Jungle" James levied extensively on "The Lady, or the Tiger?" is not to suggest that Stockton's story is as powerfully realized (in Jamesian terms) as James's modem parable. But there is critical purpose in reading James's story against the background of "The Lady, or the Tiger?" Stockton's story employs the structure of the folk tale ending with a riddle that has no predetermined solution because the events of the story stop just short of the outcome—what follows the opening of the door—that would "solve" the riddle. The story takes place in a "very olden time" in the realm of a "semi-barbaric king" who has devised a system of justice for his subjects in which guilt or innocence was decided in the arena not by combat but by "the decrees of an impartial and incorruptible chance."[14] This is how it worked.

> When all the people had assembled in the galleries, and the king, surrounded by his court, sat high up on his throne of royal state on one side of the arena, he gave a signal, a door beneath him opened, and the accused subject stepped out into the amphitheatre. Directly opposite him, on the other side of the enclosed space, were two doors, exactly alike and side by side. It was the duty and the privilege of the person on trial to walk directly to these doors and open one of them. He could open either door he pleased. He was subject to no guidance or influence but that of the aforementioned impartial and incorruptible chance. If he opened the one, there came out of it a hungry tiger, the fiercest and most cruel that could be procured, which immediately sprang upon him, and tore him to pieces as a punishment for his guilt. The moment that the case of the criminal was thus decided, doleful iron bells were clanged, great wails went up from the hired mourners posted on the outer rim of the arena, and the vast audience, with bowed heads and downcast hearts, wended slowly their homeward way, mourning greatly that one so young and fair, or so old and respected, should have merited so dire a fate.

> But if the accused person opened the other door, there came forth from it a lady the most suitable to his years and station that his Majesty could select among his fair subjects; and to this lady he was immediately married, as a reward of his innocence. It mattered not that he might already possess a wife and family, or that his affections might be engaged upon an object of his own selection. The king allowed no such subordinate arrangements to interfere with his great scheme of retribution and reward. The exercises, as in the other instance, took place immediately, and in the arena. Another door opened beneath the king, and a priest, followed by a band of choristers, and dancing maidens blowing joyous airs on golden horns and treading an epithalamic measure, advanced to where the pair stood side by side, and the wedding was promptly and cheerily solemnized. Then the gay brass bells rang forth their merry peals, the people shouted glad hurrahs, and the innocent man, preceded by children strewing flowers on his path, led his bride to his home [L, 4–5].

This generalized explanation precedes the event dramatized in which a young man, who has dared to love the King's daughter, is brought to trial. He, too, will, on public display, have to choose between the Lady and the Tiger. For him it is a choice between life and death, between the beautiful young woman he would be compelled to marry or the tiger that would tear him to pieces. In either case, the king would have disposed of the young man and his love for the princess. And at this point it becomes apparent that the story belongs to the princess, for it is she who, after discovering just who or what lies behind each door—"Gold, and the power of a woman's will, had brought the secret to the princess" (L, 9)—must decide by signal to the young man, who apparently trusts that she will act in his best interest, whether to send him to his death or to the other woman. So, the princess possesses the secret and at the climactic moment she signals her lover by raising her hand and making "a slight, quick movement toward the right" (L, 10) a signal no one but her lover sees. "Without the slightest hesitation, he went to the door on the right, and opened it" (L, 10). At this moment, the narrator becomes self-reflexive: "Now, the point of the story is this: Did the tiger come out of that door, or did the lady?" (L, 10). He then turns to an analysis of the princess's possible fears, motives, and fantasies, all of which might have contributed to her choice, a choice which, of course, takes the element of chance out of the trial. At the outset, the narrator admits: "The more we reflect upon this question, the harder it is to answer. It involves a study of the human heart which leads us through devious mazes of passion, out of which it is difficult to find our way" (L, 10). For the princess it all added up to: "She had lost him, but who should have him?" (L, 10). The narrator will not answer the question. "It is not for me to presume to set up myself as the one person able to answer it," he insists, "so I leave it with all of you: Which came out of the opened door—the lady or the tiger?" (L, 12).[15]

In "The Beast in the Jungle" James did not set out, of course, to rewrite Stockton's conundrum tale. Working more like Hawthorne, who also filled his notebooks with ideas, themes, and motifs for stories and novels, James began first to think of an idea for fiction. As early as 5 February 1895, James turned to his notebook:

> What is there in the idea of *Too late*—of some friendship or passion or bond—some affection long desired and waited for, that is formed too late?—I mean too late in life altogether.... It's a passion that *might* have been. I seem to be coinciding simply with the idea of the married person encountering the real mate, etc.; but that is not what I mean. Married or not—the marriage is a detail. Or rather, I fancy, there would have been no marriage conceivable for either. Haven't they waited—waited too long—till something else has happened? The only other "something else" than marriage must have been, doubtless, the wasting of life. And the wasting of life is the implication of death. There may be the germ of a situation in this; but it obviously requires digging out.[16]

As late as 27 August 1901, James was still turning this notion around in his head. He begins his notebook entry for that date: "Meanwhile there is something else—a very tiny *fantaisie* probably—in small notion that comes to me of a man haunted by the fear, more and more, throughout life, *that something will happen to him*: he doesn't quite know what. His life *seems* safe and ordered, his liabilities and exposures (as a *result* of the fear) a good deal curtailed and cut down, so that the years go by and the stroke doesn't fall. Yet 'It *will* come, it will still come,' he finds himself believing—and indeed saying to some one, some second-consciousness in the anecdote. 'It will come before death; I shan't die without it.'"[17]

The entry continues, but this—the opening—suffices for our purposes. While the first excerpt quoted could have led to either or both "The Beast in the Jungle" and *The Ambassadors*, the second excerpt led only to the former. What neither excerpt (nor the unquoted portions of either entry) points to is the style, broadly conceived, that James would employ for the pictures, scenes and episodes that would dramatize the unlived life of John Marcher, as well as the story's overall structure. One can't reconstruct with any finality just how an artist imagines and re-imagines his theme into the substance of fiction. That he does not invent everything out of whole cloth encourages us to follow some clues as to those sources that enable borrowings and inspire adaptations.

Stockton's tale, as we have seen, is structured around an unanswerable riddle. Indeed, the only one who knows the answer to the riddle before the closure of the incident can take place, namely the emergence of the lady or the tiger from the doorway on the right, is the princess. The answer to the riddle, because the narrator insists that he cannot know it, remains hidden in, as the author calls them, the "devious mazes of human passions" (L, 11). In a more complex way the answer to the riddle of Marcher's "catastrophe" (B, 508)—"the superstition of the Beast" (B, 527)—remains imbedded in May Bartram. She teases him with hints first as to the nature of the secret and then, increasingly, as to whether or not the beast has already come. Here James ingeniously swings his thematic and narrative focus away from the impending event—the spring of the beast—to Marcher's confusion as to whether or not he has been "sold" (B, 512). For if we are to pose the riddle for Marcher as (in Stockton's terms) "the Lady or the Tiger?" the answer is obvious rather early on, certainly no later than Marcher's April visit to the dying May Bartram. Marcher has chosen the tiger. The riddle now is whether there has been or there will be a "beast" that will spring at him. That James does not want anyone to miss the notion that the story is structured around a riddle is apparently behind his decision to depict the dying May as a sphinx:

> Almost as white as wax, with the marks and signs in her face as numerous and as fine as if they had been etched by a needle, with soft white draperies relieved by a faded green scarf on the delicate tone of which the years had further refined, she was the picture of a serene and exquisite but impenetrable sphinx, whose head, or indeed all whose person, might have been powdered with silver. She was a sphinx, yet with her white petals and green fronds she might have been a lily too—only an artificial lily, wonderfully imitated and constantly kept, without dust or stain, though not exempt from a slight droop and a complexity of faint creases, under some clear glass bell. The perfection of household care, of high polish and finish, always reigned in her rooms, but they now looked most as if everything had been wound up, tucked in, put away, so that she might sit with folded hands and with nothing more to do. She was "out of it," to Marcher's vision; her work was over; she communicated with him as across some gulf or from some island of rest that she had already reached, and it made him feel strangely abandoned [B, 513–514].

Marcher is no Oedipus, however, and he cannot solve the riddle posed by the May Bartram / Sphinx. All he knows is that May has aged and is dying and that he is even older than she. But in this scene May is also an Ariadne abandoned on an island by Theseus, who was to love her. This is not the first time that James has hinted at the Ariadne / Theseus parallel to the May / Marcher affair.

It was on an October afternoon many years earlier that John Marcher had met May Bartram for the second time. "It was his theory, as always, that he was lost in the crowd," in the "great rooms" that "caused so much poetry and history to press upon him" (B, 482–483). May Bartram's face, which would accompany him on much of his life's journey from that day on, is, at the moment, "a reminder, yet not quite a remembrance" (B, 483). He is troubled, albeit "rather pleasantly," for he sees it "as the sequel of something of which he had lost the beginning" (B, 483). But "the young woman herself hadn't lost the thread" (B, 483) of their search for the memories of their first meeting in Naples ten years earlier, when he was twenty-five and she twenty. It had even happened that at Pompeii, a violent thunderstorm had driven them to seek refuge in an excavation, "on an occasion when they had been present there at an important find" (B, 485). It is no wonder, then, in a story about a man who figures his life under the image of a springing beast, the author should have metaphorically crossed Hawthorne's and Stockton's jungle tigers with the beast in the labyrinth. There are several instances in which the jungle and the labyrinth, along with the tiger and the beast, become interchangeable. I quote three examples.

> Something or other lay in wait for him, amid the twists and the turns of the months and the years, like a crouching beast in the jungle. It signified little whether the crouching beast were destined to slay him or to be slain. The definite point was the inevitable spring of the creature; and the definite lesson from that was that a man of feeling didn't cause himself to be accompanied by a lady on a tiger-hunt [B, 497].
>
> ["Of the imagination always with them"] it had always had its-incalculable moments of glaring out, quite as with the very eyes of the very Beast, and, used as he was to them, they could still draw from him the tribute of a sigh that rose from the depths of his being [B, 503–504].
>
> When the possibilities themselves accordingly turned stale, when the secret of the gods had grown faint, had perhaps even quite evaporated, that, and that only, was failure. It wouldn't have been failure to be bankrupt, dishonoured, pilloried, hanged; it was failure not to be anything. And so, in the dark valley into which his path had taken its unlooked-for twist, he wondered not a little as he groped. He didn't care what awful crash might overtake him, with what ignominy or what monstrosity he might yet be associated ... [B, 511–512].

It is no wonder that on the April visit May, "frail and ancient and charming," looked "as if she had lost the thread" (B, 515). Marcher has already lost his guide to his labyrinth, the seat of his "secret," the arena of his potential encounter with his Beast, his Minotaur.

Neither Hawthorne nor Stockton levies on the Ariadne / Minotaur / Labyrinth myth for imagery of elements of structure. But such myth and imagery, along with historical and archeological excavation, appear to have been very much on James's mind when he composed "The Beast in the Jungle." And small wonder, for in the early months of 1900 occurred the discovery of the existence of the Minoan civilization at the site of Knossos in Crete. Its importance was equaled only by Schliemann's discovery of Troy in 1871. Here in actual life was the evidence for linking "poetry and history," for beneath the Palace at Knossos, legend had it, Daedalus built the labyrinth to contain the dreaded Minotaur. Moreover, this great discovery, as every Londoner knew, was the work of an otherwise undistinguished individual, who was known to his contemporaries as "Little Evans, son of John Evans the Great."[18] Arthur Evans's most recent biographer describes him in 1900: "Everything about the discovery contributed to its drama, and not the least the man himself. Nothing in his outward appearance betrayed the mettle, the panache within. He was insignificant in stature, barely five feet two inches tall. He was myopic, middle-age, and unabashedly Victorian from his polished boots to his homburg."[19] Had it not been for his find on Crete, it might be asked, would Arthur Evans's contemporaries have ever seen the evidence for his "mettle" and his "panache"?—even as no one, other than May, was in on

> the secret of the difference between the forms he [Marcher] went through—those of his little office under Government, those of caring for his modest patrimony, for his library,

> for his garden in the country, for the people in London whose invitations he accepted and repaid—and the detachment that reigned beneath them and that made of all behaviour, all that could in the least be called behaviour, a long act of dissimulation. What it had come to was that he wore a mask painted with the social simper, out of the eyeholes of which there looked eyes of an expression not in the least matching the other features. This the stupid world, even after years, had never more than half-discovered [B, 499].

But there were crucial differences between the historical Arthur Evans and the fictional John Marcher: Evans was always a doer and a risk-taker, while Marcher is imagined as passive, as receptive only to impressions and nuances. For all of his involvement with the dust and dirt of quotidian archeology, Evans was something of an aesthete, a collector of objets d'art. Marcher, however, is too narcissistic even to be a collector of any thing. And yet Marcher is ironically imagined right out of the ethics of aestheticism championed by Walter Pater.

James knew about Pater's work at least as early as 1873, with the appearance of *The Renaissance*, Pater's major collection of studies. The book interested him enough to encourage him to prepare an unsolicited review, which he sent off to America for possible publication.[20] The review, if published, has never been located, and since no manuscript appears to have survived, we do not know what specifically interested James. Yet, judging from James's strong interest in the theme of aestheticism as it leached out of art into the quotidian life itself, we can safely surmise that Pater's brave and challenging conclusion caught his full attention. Indeed, it seems to have stung, stimulated, and haunted him for the rest of his creative life.

> One of the most beautiful passages of Rousseau is that in the sixth book of the *Confessions*, where he describes the awakening in him of the literary sense. An undefinable taint of death had clung always about him, and now in early manhood he believed himself smitten by mortal disease. He asked himself how he might make as much as possible of the interval that remained; and he was not biassed by anything in his previous life when he decided that it must be by intellectual excitement, which he found just then in the clear, fresh writings of Voltaire. Well! we are all *condamnés*, as Victor Hugo says: we are all under sentence of death but with a sort of indefinite reprieve—*les hommes sont tous condamnés à mort avec de sursis indéfinis*: we have an interval, and then our place knows us no more. Some spend this interval in listlessness, some in high passions, the wisest, at least among "the children of this world," in art and song. For our one chance lies in expanding that interval, in getting as many pulsations as possible into the given time. Great passions may give us this quickened sense of life, ecstasy and sorrow of love, the various forms of enthusiastic activity, disinterested or otherwise, which come naturally to many of us. Only be sure it is passion—that it does yield you this fruit of a quickened, multiplied consciousness. Of such wisdom, the poetic passion, the desire of beauty, the love of art for its own sake, has most. For art comes to you proposing frankly to give nothing but the highest quality to your moments as they pass, and simply for those moments' sake.[21]

It will be recalled that in his 1895 notebooks, in the entry that started him thinking about the "idea of *Too late*" there is already much talk about passion. What finally emerged in the finished tale eight years later, however, was the story of a man who cannot feel passion, whose ego demands experience—at least one extraordinary, unique experience—commensurate with his singular conception of his fate. Focusing on his secret, his fate, the "thing," Marcher tacitly sacrifices Pater's notion that "art comes to you proposing frankly to give nothing but the highest quality to your moments as they pass, and *simply for those moments' sake*" (emphasis added). He will keep himself prepared for, and sensitized to, the spring of the Beast, his great fate.

There is a third notebook entry relating to "The Beast in the Jungle." That one focuses, as does the passage from Pater just quoted, on the theme of death and the self: "What I fancied … was that this Dead Self of the poor man's lives for him in some indirect way, in the sympathy, the fidelity (the relation of some kind) of another.… [My] little note contained the fancy of his *recovering* a little of the lost joy, of the Dead Self, in his intercourse with some person, some woman, who knows what that self was, in whom it still lives a little.… *She is his Dead Self: he is alive in her and dead in himself*—."[22]

It is not to be wondered at that Pater's ethic of aestheticism should have emerged in this story about a man who has tried to turn his life into a work of Pater inspired perception. It is even Pater's language and imagery that, as elsewhere (most notably in "The Altar of the Dead"), James takes over. In the picture with which James leaves us at the end—Marcher having seen the "other" mourner, who displayed "the deep ravage" (B, 533, 534) of passion—it is Pater's references to light and passion that predominate. The incident at the cemetery on an autumn day, James tells us, had put "the match to the train laid of old by his misery" (B, 532). "With the light before him," he is able to "come round of himself to the light" (B, 532) as "in letters of quick flame" (B, 534). The stranger's face "flared" for Marcher as "a smoky torch" (B, 534). When the illumination had at last begun, it "blazed to the zenith," but what it showed forth, for him, was "the sounded void of his life" (B, 535). The image of "scarred passion" (B, 534) before him enabled his discovery that "no passion ever touched him, for this was what passion meant; he had survived and maundered and pined, but where had been *his* deep ravage?" (B, 534). If "success in life" was "to burn always with this hard, gemlike flame, to maintain this ecstasy"—to quote from the most famous sentence in all of Pater's writings—"The Beast in the Jungle" can be read as a trenchant critique of Pater's ethic of aesthetics.[23] It was in similar terms, in fact, that James remembered the story when he returned to it in his preface to *The Altar of the Dead* volume of the New York Edition. He writes there of John Marcher in terms that come close to parodying Pater:

> His career thus resolves itself into a great negative adventure, my report of which presents for its centre, the fine ease that has caused him most tormentedly to "*burn*," and then most unprofitably to stray. He is afraid to recognise what he incidentally misses, since

what his high belief amounts to is not that he shall have felt and vibrated less than any one else, but that he shall have felt and vibrated more; which no acknowledgement of the minor loss must conflict with. Such a course of existence naturally involves a climax—the final flash of light under which he reads his lifelong riddle and sees his conviction proved [emphasis added].[24]

Yet "The Beast in the Jungle" had its sentimental side as well. "James had known a woman and taken her friendship, and never allowed himself to know her feelings," writes Leon Edel. "She was kind and interested—and he had never imagined an interest beyond friendship. In the end she had taken her life, one winter's morning in Venice, in great loneliness and melancholy. All this had happened a decade earlier, and out of these sombre memories James seems to have distilled the essence of 'The Beast in the Jungle.'"[25] The woman, as Edel had identified her earlier, was Constance Fenimore Woolson.[26] A writer, she too was, perhaps only coincidentally, very much enamored of Egypt and the Ionian Islands, having written about them enthusiastically toward the end of her life, in essays in *Harper's Monthly*.[27] Her deep passion for the Near East, particularly Egypt, however, comes through best in her letters. We do not have her letters to James, except for four of them written in the early 1880s,[28] but we do have her letter to a mutual friend. On 20 December 1890, Woolson wrote to John Hay:

> I ordered the other day a small volume of Milton in order to reread the Hymn on the Nativity at this Xmas season. What brought it to my mind was the sailing past Paxo (south of Corfu) a year ago: for it was here, you know, that the sailors heard the voices crying "Great Pan is dead." Milton puts it in: "The lonely mountains o'er [/] And the resounding shore—" &c. I see there is a sketch of your life in the last Sunday Tribune. But it does not say whether *you* have been to the East, &, en route thither, to the Ionian Islands & Greece? Did I write you from any of those points last winter? I think I did not. But if I did, I know the letter was fairly lyrical! I wo'nt [sic] burst forth again (though longing to): but I will just say that now at last I know my own land: it is Egypt. There must be Egyptian blood in me somehow. Nothing that I have ever seen or imagined can approach the reality of Egypt, as it was to my eyes. (I mark "my," because my sister hated it.) I have never seen anything so solemn as the ancient temples, &c. And never anything to beautiful as the Arabian architecture at Cairo. I understand now why Venice has fascinated me so strongly: it was simply the oriental tinge there. You may say: "And not Greece?" And I answer, "No; not Greece." Grecian things are too perfect for me. Possibly if I had a classic nose myself, I should enjoy them more. I ought to add that I was not long enough in Athens (only two weeks) to really appreciate the things in the museums. The Parthenon I did appreciate. But in Egypt I stayed long months. I returned thither alone, after the Holy Land, and had a second long stay. You know Arabian architecture &c, having seen it in Spain.[29]

Unlike Constance Woolson or John Marcher, James never did visit Egypt, although he had a singular opportunity to do so. In 1897, three years after Woolson's death in Venice, a probable suicide, James turned down an offer by no one other than John Hay to accompany him, Mrs. Hay, and Henry Adams on a month's voyage down the Nile. After May Bartram's death, however, John Marcher leaves London for a year, visiting "the depths of Asia" (B, 530), only to find that "the state of mind in which he had lived for so many years shone out to him, in reflexion, as a light beside which the glow of the East was garish and cheap and thin" (B, 530). Nor are his "impressions of Egypt" any better, for "the past glories of the Pharaohs were nothing to him" (B, 30). Did James, in 1897, fear that he could not yet handle a visit to Woolson's beloved Egypt? In any case, on 1 December 1897, to his sister-in-law, Alice James, he explained his reasons for not taking up Hay's offer:

> I have no positive plan save that of just ticking the winter swiftly away on this most secure basis. There are, however, little doors ajar into a possible brief absence. I fear I have just closed one of them rather ungraciously indeed, in pleading a "non possumus" to a most genial invitation from John Hay to accompany him and his family, shortly after the new year, upon a run to Egypt and a month up the Nile part—in which he offers me the said month's entertainment. It is a very charming opportunity, and I almost blush at not coming up to the scratch; especially as I shall probably never have the like again. But it isn't so simple as it sounds; one has on one's hands the journey to Cairo and back, with whatever seeing and doing by the way two or three irresistible other things, to which one would feel one might never again be so near, would amount to. (I mean, of course, then or never, on the return, Athens, Corfu, Sicily the never-seen, etc., etc.)[30]

The never-seen Egypt and Athens and Corfu, combined with his memories of the always constant Constance, took their place in the artist's subconscious, along with Stockton's "The Lady, or the Tiger?," Walter Pater's ethics of aestheticism, and the accounts of Sir Arthur Evans and his discovery of the Minoans, to emerge as the whole that is "The Beast in the Jungle," a mordant tale in which one of James's "poor sensitive gentlemen"[31] thinks he chooses, in answer to the riddle, the Tiger over the Lady, much as the writer himself had chosen art—for "the beast in the jungle" please read "the figure in the carpet"—over, however subconsciously until her death, the love of the woman, proffered or not proffered, who once wrote to him: "only now and then do I wonder how I shall ever be able to get away from Venice; whether the end of the riddle of my existence may not be, after all, to live here, and die here, and be buried on that plateau in the lagoon."[32] When Constance Woolson died in Venice in 1894, she was buried not in Venice but in Rome, the city in which John Marcher first locates, but mistakenly, his first meeting with the young May Bartram.

And finally there was William Dean Howells. It will be recalled that the first notebook entry, that of 5 February 1895, introduced the theme of "*Too late*," which could have led to either "The Beast in the Jungle" or *The Ambassadors* or both. Another entry in the same year, on 31 October, records James's recognition of a subject for fiction in a conversation he had held the evening before with Jonathan Sturges:

> We were talking of W.D.H. and of his having seen him during a short and interrupted stay H. had made 18 months ago in Paris—called away—back to America, when he had just come—at the end of 10 days by the news of the death—or illness—of his father, he had scarcely been in Paris, ever, in former days, and he had come there to see his domi-

ciled and initiated son, who was at the Beaux Arts. Virtually, in the evening, as it were, of life, it was all new to him: all, all, all. Sturges said he seemed sad—rather brooding; and 1 asked him what gave him (Sturges) that impression. "Oh—somewhere—1 forget when I was with him—he laid his hand on my shoulder and said à propos of some remark of mine: "Oh, you are young, you are young—be glad of it: be glad of it and live. Live all you can: it's a mistake not to. It doesn't so much matter what you do—but live. This place makes it all come over one. I see it now. I haven't done so—and now I'm old. It's too late. It has gone past me—I've lost it. You have time. You are young. Live!'"[33]

This entry, of course, provided the germ for *The Ambassadors*, with Howells's brave speech to Sturges recast in the form of Lambert Strether's advice to Little Bilham. Upon finishing the novel in the summer of 1901, just about the time, possibly, he was writing "The Beast in the Jungle," James wrote to Howells about Sturges's repetition of "five words you had said to him one day on his meeting you during a call at Whistler's."[34]

If Howells—at least the Howells temporarily in Paris in 1894—was the first model for Strether, was he also a model for John Marcher? In 1899 Howells had published *Their Silver Wedding Journey*, a novel detailing the European stay of Howells's autobiographical couple, who had also figured in *Their Wedding Journey* (1871) and *A Hazard of New Fortunes* (1889): the Marches. (If Howells's hero's given name is Basil, it will be recalled that the "initiated" son Howells was visiting in Paris in 1894 was called, as James knew, John.[35] It is of more than passing interest, moreover, that the recipient of Strether's Howellsian advice, Little Bilham, is also named John and his last name doubles down as "Bil," so strong was James's writer's logic in associating Strether, Little Bilham, and Marcher with Howells's germinating words.)

The Ambassadors, James had assured Howells, "had long before—it had in the very act of striking me as a *germ*—got away from you or from anything like! had become impersonal and independent."[36] The same can be said for the presence of Howells in "The Beast in the Jungle." Yet the riddle remains: why, in this late, partly autobiographical tale, did James take over for his personage the name of his friend Howells's most closely autobiographical hero, changing it only to indicate a comparison? Was there perhaps revealed, in Howells's "five words" to Sturges, something confessional, something along the lines of 'The Lady, or the Tiger,' in Howells's life as well? Had Howells, unlike James, chosen both the Lady and the Tiger, only to come out in the same place as March(er)? "Poor March, my dear Howells—what tricks you play him," James once pitied, "—even worse than those you play Mrs. March!'"[37]

16

The Example of Late James

By early 1877, the thirty-three-year-old Henry James had settled into quarters at 3 Bolton Street, Piccadilly, in what would be the beginning of his long siege of London. Having abandoned his original plan of living his European life in Paris (he had tried it for a year), he was now ready to stretch his social wings in a London that hardly knew of his existence. His friend Henry Adams, now living in America and finding himself temporarily in Boston, had had a lengthy stay in London in the 1860s while serving as his father's private secretary during the latter's troubled term as Minister to the Court of St. James. In the intervening years Henry Adams had kept up his London friendships, and was in position, therefore, to outfit his friend from Cambridge (Massachusetts) with letters of introduction. He provided several, the most important of which (for James's fiction, at least) turned out to be the letter to Sir Charles Milnes Gaskell of Wenlock Abbey, which ultimately led to what was probably James's first weekend stay at a British country-house.

James was most grateful for Adams's letters, which he characterized civilly as being "beyond my expectations or my merits." In his brief note acknowledging the receipt of this "packet," however, James, flush with the high expectations and exuberant spirits attending his fresh start in a new country, turns at the end to a most interesting thought: "Your picture of Boston with its gorgeous Turners and its frescoed churches, is really glowing, and I feel like hurrying home, to become the Vasari of such a Florence, where indeed I advise you to remain and become the Machiavelli."[1]

Of course James did not rush home to Boston to become its Vasari, nor for that matter, did Adams plant himself in Boston to become its Machiavelli. In neither case (the evidence is superabundant) could Boston have been conceived as large enough, important enough, or interesting enough by either of these writers to attract his not inconsiderable talent. Boston was not yet Florence, nor was it about to become Florence enough to satisfy a not-so-budding

Vasari. Over a lengthy career, James would write art criticism whenever and wherever the occasion permitted him to do so, but art criticism would never be his métier. As for politics, James seemed generally to have been more interested, as a writer, in those who had politics in them than, with a few exceptions, those who were in politics. Adams, on the other hand, would turn out to be something of a Machiavelli—though not of Boston. If, like the Alfred Bonnycastle of James's own tale "Pandora," he was not exactly in politics, politics were in him, for politics and literature—as he would insist in *The Education of Henry Adams*— were early and late his major interests. Like Machiavelli, Adams would write a guide for those who would understand power though not, necessarily, wield it. Is not *The Education* comparable, in certain subtle senses, to Machiavelli's *The Prince*? Were not both Adams and Machiavelli historians who understood fiction well enough to write it? If James did not become as much of a Vasari as he might have, Adams—who made no claim for the comparison—replicated, in some respects, the essence if not the career of the redoubtable Machiavelli.[2]

After James had presented the letters Adams had provided for him, he would again write. In May 1877, some five months after his first letter, James reported to Adams on his social experience in London, along with conveying his impressions of some of the friends Adams's letters had made available to him. He had seen a good deal of Sir Robert Cunliffe and his wife, he wrote, "a capital couple" whose "friendliness and attentiveness have been more than fraternal." Lord Houghton had become, he reported, his "guide, philosopher and friend—he has breakfasted me, dined me, conversatzioned me, absolutely caressed me." He had met the artist Woolner—"a very honest, vigorous fellow and, for a Englishman, quite a handsome sculptor"—and Sir Francis Palgrave, the historian and father of the critic and anthologist famous for the *Golden Treasury of Songs and Lyrics*, with whom James, on one occasion, talked "*de manibus rebus.*"[3] James does not yet mention Milnes Gaskell. He would soon do so. On July 15, 1877, James wrote to Adams from Wenlock Abbey, which he was then visiting. Indeed, to accept the Gilkes's invitation to go down to Shropshire, he had at the last moment deferred his impending departure for the Continent.

Up to that point James had seen "next to nothing of Gaskell and his wife in town," not having been able to accept their one invitation to dinner, but this invitation to a weekend at a country-estate was not to be missed. Of his host he wrote, "Gaskell I find an excellent fellow, an entertaining companion and the pearl of hosts. We have talked together as people talk in an English country-house when, during the three days of a visit, two, alas, turned out too brutally pluvial." Regarding "Lady Catherine G.," as he referred to her, he wrote:

> I can't give you a trustworthy one [description], for 1 really think I am in love with her. She is a singularly charming creature—a perfect English beauty of the finest type. She is,

> as I suppose you know, very young, girlish, childish: she strikes me as having taken a long step straight from the governess-world into a particularly luxurious form of matrimony. She is very tall, rather awkward and not well made, wonderfully fresh and fair, expensively and picturesquely ill-dressed, charmingly mannered, and, I should say, intensely in love with her husband. She would not in the least strike you at first as a beauty (save for complexion); but presently you would agree with me that her face is a remarkable example of the classic English sweetness and tenderness.... She says very good things, smiles adorably and appeals to her husband with beautiful inveteracy and naturalness. There is something very charming in seeing a woman in her pretty "position" so perfectly fresh and girlish. She will doubtless, some day, become more of a British matron or of a fine lady; but I suspect she will never lose (not after twenty London seasons) a certain bloom of shyness and softness.

Then James pulls up short to say, "But I am drawing not only a full-length, but a colossal, portrait."[4] Just how much of James's first impressions of Lady Catherine went into the composition of his portrait just three years later of the fictional Isabel Archer—of what Isabel is to start out with and what she might have become had she married Lord Warburton—is a matter for speculation. But not for Henry Adams, who made no mention of any such resemblance when he picked up his friend's novel, only to put it down without finishing it, as he wrote to Lady Catherine's husband on January 29, 1882: "I frankly own that I broke down on *The Portrait of a Lady*, but some of my friends, of whose judgment I think highly, admire it warmly, and find it deeply interesting. I hope you may be of their opinion."[5]

In his July 15, 1877 letter, James had also described his first experiences at Wenlock. "This is a Sunday morning, with a great raw rain-storm howling outside," he wrote; "but though this unpleasantness has lasted forty-eight hours it has really not put me out of humour with Wenlock."

> The morning after my arrival, luckily, Gaskell and I started off and made an heroic day of it—a day I shall always remember most tenderly. We went to Ludlow, to Stokesay and to Shrewsbury and we saw them all in perfection. You spoke of Stokesay, and I found it of course a gem. We lay there on the grass in the delicious little *préau*, beside the well, with every feature of the old place still solid and vivid around us, and I don't think that, as a sensation, I ever dropped back, for an hour, more effectually into the past.[6]

Adams broke down on *The Portrait of a Lady*, as we know, and he generally would not read his friends' books, he said at the time; but he did pay attention to this friend's letters. In this case he not only attended to what James was saying but paid him the honor, I suspect, of long remembering what James said about his day with Gaskell, for Adams echoed it decades later in his account of his "own favorite Abbey on Wenlock Edge." In "Darwinism (1867–1868)," Chapter XV of *The Education*, Adams, too, takes his leave and loafs on the grass:

> By this time, in 1867, Adams had learned to know Shropshire familiarly, and it was the part of his diplomatic education which he loved best. Like Catherine Olney in *Northanger Abbey*, he yearned for nothing so keenly as to feel at home in a thirteenth-century Abbey, unless it were to haunt a fifteenth-century Prior's House, and both these

joys were his at Wenlock.... He rode about the Wrekin, or visited all the historical haunts from Ludlow Castle and Stokesay to Boscobel and Uriconium ... but perhaps he liked best to ramble over the Edge on a summer afternoon and look across the Marches to the mountains of Wales.... As one lay on the slope of the Edge, looking sleepily through the summer haze towards Shrewsbury ... nothing suggested sequence.... The shepherds ... had they approached where he lay in the grass, would have taken him only for another and tamer variety of Welsh thief.[7]

What Adams had been looking for in 1867 (although he did not, perhaps, yet know it as potentially contributing to his "accidental" education) was evidence of sequence and evolution. The theme, his own, is nowhere to be found in James's letter, but the pose of the studious observer, lying there in the grass and losing himself in thoughts of times past, is already present in James's epistolary account. It would also crop up in a travel piece James published shortly thereafter. Again drawing on his first impressions of Wenlock Abbey, James would write, "I have rarely had, for a couple of hours, the sensation of dropping back personally into the past in a higher degree than while I lay on the grass beside the well in the little sunny court of this small castle, and idly appreciated the still definite details of mediaeval life."[8]

If Adams knew this particular essay by James or, indeed, if he read much of James's extensive work in this vein, the record is largely silent. Certainly Adams was not particularly taken with James's fiction in the 1870s and 1880s. We know what he thought of James's *Portrait of a Lady*, of course, and when in 1878, he had read *Daisy Miller*, he claimed (as he wrote, again in a letter to Gaskell) that he had been "induced" to do so, but had found it to be only "really clever."[9] Yet there is no mention anywhere of his having read *The Bostonians* or *The Princess Casamassima, Washington Square, The American, Roderick Hudson* or *The Europeans*. He knew something of James's highly referenced stories of the 1880s—"The Point of View," for example, which draws on James's conversations with the Adamses in Washington, or "Pandora," which portrays Henry and Marian "Clover" Adams as the Alfred Bonnycastles—but it is possible that that knowledge came to him at second hand, from his wife's reading of the stories rather than his own. When he did react directly to James it was to disapprove of what he considered back-scratching and tub-thumping by James and William Dean Howells—what he considered the regrettable actions of a two-man mutual admiration society in which the principals were out to aggrandize themselves by denigrating the artistry of the English Masters, Dickens and Thackeray. "I venture to say, openly and confidently," Adams wrote to John Hay in 1883, "that in my opinion both Shakespeare and Thackeray wrote as well as Harry James.... I venture to think that Desdemona was *felt* by a genius of considerable purity, though to my own mind her conduct was such as I can never approve. Shakespeare evidently did not feel my objections."[10] What it was exactly about Desdemona's conduct that earned Adams's disapproval is a matter for speculation, but that Shakespeare had, in his genius, felt her to be what she was (unlike James, perhaps, in the case of Daisy Miller or Isabel Archer) showed him to be, like Thackeray, a great writer. That James's deficiencies as a novelist were much in Adams's mind at this time may be indicated in two ways: (1) his use of the term "felt" in this context suggests (indeed anticipates) James's notion in the preface to *The Portrait of a Lady* that the novelist's task is to create the "felt" sense of life; and (2) his own earlier letter to John Hay, written in his feigned role as friend to the anonymous author of *The Bread-Winners*, considers the subject of the knowledge of women displayed by recent novelists, to wit, the author of *The Bread-Winners*, William Dean Howells, and Henry James. On September 24, 1883, while Hay's *Bread-Winners* was running in the *Century*, Adams wrote to Hay,

> As a work of art, I should not hesitate to put the *Breadwinners* so far as the story has gone, quite at the head of our Howell's-and-Jame's [sic] epoch for certain technical qualities, such as skill in construction, vivacity in narration, and breadth of *motif*. It has also one curious and surprising quality, least to be expected from an unknown western writer. Howells cannot deal with gentlemen or ladies; he always slips up. James knows almost nothing of women but the mere outside; he never had a wife. This new writer not only knows women, but knows *ladies*; the rarest of literary gifts.[11]

Obviously, judging from what he said and left unsaid, Adams did not consider Desdemona to be a lady. But no matter. Howells, of course, would remain married to his wife until her death and would not remarry, and James would not marry at all. But James, as well as Howells, would continue to provide readers with portraits of women, some of whom were ladies, some of whom were not. After his initial complaint Adams did not much care. He paid very little attention to what James was writing and publishing—until, perhaps, that day in 1888 when he suggested to Elizabeth Cameron that she read James's latest story: "Please read Harry James's Liar in the May *Century*. He has hit on a nice study of femi-nature. I have known such men, and have pondered in like perplexity about their wives."[12]

This brief encomium—delivered when Adams was fifty, and coming three years after the death of his own wife—is the first indication given by Adams that he might learn something from James's work. It was a beginning, as Adams might say, one that would lead right into *The Education*, nearly two decades later. But Adams did not know that then. What he did know, to take up his hint, was that James had seen below the surface of what Adams called femi-nature in this story about the varieties of lying. The title character, a rather straightforward embellisher of actuality who invents left and right to amuse and mislead, is an habitual liar; but because it does not take much to catch him out, the game of tripping him up is not worth anyone's candle. James's narrator is no exception in this, but he is interested in just what this liar's wife knows about her husband's behavior and to what extent she will tolerate his lying before standing forth publicly on principle and for the sake of common decency.

"The Liar" opens with the narrator's account of his journeying to a weekend at a country-house belonging to the Ashmores. On at least two occasions the narrator, a painter named Oliver Lyon (he is the "Liar's"—Colonel Capadose's—alter ego), refers to Stayes as an "asylum." There he learns that the Colonel, whom he has just met for the first time, is married to a model (the former Everina Brant, to whom Lyon himself had once unsuccessfully proposed marriage), and he meets the Colonel's young wife. What motivates the story is the mystery that the narrator weaves around his former lover, a mystery he thinks he must solve, for its solution will determine his judgment of the woman's character and morals. Does she also lie, he asks, and if so how far will she go before she balks at any further lying? Early on, the painter's ruminations are formulated this way:

> He watched her with an interest deeply quickened when he mingled with the company; he had had his own troubles in life, but he had rarely been so anxious about anything as he was now to see what the loyalty of a wife and the infection of an example would have made of an absolutely truthful mind. Oh, he held it as immutably established that whatever other women might be prone to do she, of old, had been perfectly incapable of a deviation. Even if she had not been too simple to deceive she would have been too proud; and if she had not had too much conscience she would have had too little eagerness. It was the last thing she would have endured or condoned—the particular thing she would not have forgiven. Did she sit in torment while her husband turned his somersaults, or was she now too so perverse that she thought it a fine thing to be striking at the expense of one's honour? It would have taken a wondrous alchemy—working backwards, as it were—to produce this latter result.[13]

Adams at the time of "The Liar," it seems to me, could reveal to his close friend Mrs. Cameron no more than that he was still learning about "femi-nature." But the "accidental" education he ultimately derived from James's "Liar" had less to do, as it turned out, with *femi*-nature than with *human*-nature. When in *The Education*, Adams would write, "knowledge of human nature is the beginning and end of political education," he was only capping off a chapter on the British political mind as he had come to know it, first in the 1860s and then as a result of later revelations about the English politicians he had known.[14] Indeed, it was in 1889, in the year following his reading of James's story, with the publication of the biography of Earl Russell, a key English official of the 1860s, that Adams realized that he had totally misunderstood the complex attitudes and web of untruths behind British policy toward the Union and its opponent, the Confederacy. In 1907, writing about Palmerston, Gladstone, Russell, and Delane, Adams lays out a story of men with, in his words, an *idée fixe*, one which accounted for each aspect of their behavior toward the Union. In 1907 the

Henry Adams who narrates the story of the young man, his earlier self, serving his father as personal secretary can only look back on the young man he was with considerable distance, not to say condescension. The Minister's secretary had focused on Russell, with the same intensity and just as obsessively, I would suggest, as James's painter had focused on the Liar's wife.

> Young Adams thought Earl Russell a statesman of the old school, clear about his objects and unscrupulous in his methods—dishonest but strong. Russell ardently asserted that he had no objects, and that though he might be weak he was above all else honest. Minister Adams leaned to Russell personally and thought him true, but officially, in practice, treated him as false. *Punch*, before 1862, commonly drew Russell as a schoolboy telling lies, and afterwards as prematurely senile, at seventy. Education stopped there. No one, either in or out of England, ever offered a rational explanation of Earl Russell.[15]

The mystery, as Adams saw it, was one of character. "The true issue lay not in the question of his fault [that is to say, Earl Russell's fault, for it was his fault], but of his intent," wrote Adams. "To a young man, getting an education in politics, there could be no sense in history unless a constant course of faults implied a constant motive."[16] Substitute in this sentence the word *femi-nature* for *politics* and the result is a formulation that will be useful to an understanding of any number of James's texts, including the one in 1888 that had taught Adams something about women. Change the word *politics* to *nature* and you have a key to the motives Adams chooses for his own quest for what lies behind faults, lies, truths, and hypothesis.

Twice in Chapter XVIII ("The Battle of The Rams [1863]") Adams refers to the notion of the *idée fixe*. He talks about Russell, whose obsession is "the nullity or fatuity of the Washington Government," or about Delane, who possesses a "thick cortex of fixed ideas."[17] In the next major instance of accidental education Adams received from reading James, Adams uses the term *idée fixe* to describe both himself and James, thereby linking the two not merely as persons but as writers. It was John Hay who called Adams's attention to James's *The Sacred Fount*. Unlike the earlier occasions on which Hay and Adams had discussed James's work, Hay was now alarmed. Adams, on his side, also admitted to being unsettled. To Elizabeth Cameron, on May 6, 1901, he wrote,

> Harry James has upset me. John Hay has been greatly troubled by Harry's last volume, the *Sacred Fount*. He cannot resist the suspicion that it is very close on extravagance. His alarm made me read it, and I recognized at once that Harry and I had the same disease, the obsession of *idée fixe*. Harry illustrates it by the trivial figure of an English country-house party, which could only drive one mad by boring one into it, but if he had chosen another back-ground, his treatment of it would have been wonderfully keen. All the same it is insanity, and I think Harry must soon take a vacation, with most of the rest of us, in a cheery asylum.[18]

If Adams, unlike James's fictional Oliver Lyon, who saw Staves as "an asylum," or the narrator of *The Sacred Fount*, who saw Newmarch as "the great asylum of the finer wit," had another kind of institution in mind for James and himself, he nevertheless saw the logic of what James was after in this first-person narration.[19] How could the soon-to-be author of the not-yet-begun account of his own education not respond to the dramatization of a quest for facts and truth that seemingly ends in failure, an exploration undertaken sometimes directly, sometimes haphazardly, in which signs are taken and mistaken? How could the Adams, young or old, who wanted from the education furnished him by Earl Russell the sense that "a constant course of faults implied a constant motive," not have seen a kindred spirit in the narrator who could observe himself and write about himself: "I was on the scent.... I was just conscious, vaguely, of being on the track of a law, a law that would fit, that would strike me as governing the delicate phenomena—delicate though so marked—that my imagination found itself playing with. A part of the amusement they yielded came I dare say, from my exaggerating them—grouping them into a larger mystery (and thereby a larger 'law') than the facts, as observed, yet warranted; but that is the common fault of minds for which the vision of life is an obsession."[20]

Just how much James's 1877 description of his stay at Wenlock Abbey had to do with Adams's *Education*, one cannot finally say. But certainly, that early experience, some of it recorded and some of it, obviously, not recorded, remained a reservoir of images and impressions for James's fictionalizing mind. As for James's obsessed narrators, whether they look for the figure in the carpet or for the pattern of faults indicating a constancy of motive, it can be suggested that—sensitive gentlemen or not—they continued to provide a literary/artistic example both for the "Uncle" who speaks the whole of *Mont-Saint-Michel and Chartres* and the narrator who looks back on the manikin he sees himself as having been in the course of his lifelong quest for education.

It is small wonder, then, that Adams chose to see his *Education* as a literary experiment—a Jamesian experiment at that. When in 1907 William James heard about Adams's privately printed "autobiography" circulating among mutual friends in Cambridge and elsewhere, he appealed to the author to send him a copy. Adams did so. Promptly, James criticized the book (as he had been invited to do), and Adams reacted in turn: "As for the volume [*The Education*], it interests me chiefly as a literary experiment, hitherto, as far as I know, never tried or never successful"—adding in the next sentence, "your brother Harry tries such experiments in literary art daily, and would know instantly what I mean."[21] To Henry James himself, on May 6, 1908, Adams repeated the claim that *The Education* was the work of a literary artist. Admitting that the volume was "a mere shield of protection in the grave" and advising James to take his "own life in the same way, in order to prevent biographers from taking it in theirs," Adams warned him: "you being a literary artist, and therefore worth the trouble of fore-warning—I note for your exclusive use the intent of the literary artist—*c'est moi!*—to make this volume a completion and mathematical conclusion from the previous volume about the Thirteenth Century,—the three concluding chapters of this being only a working out to Q.E.D. of the three concluding chapters of that. This is only for my own horizon; not for your confusion."[22]

James acknowledged receipt of his copy of *The Education* two days later with typically Jamesian exuberance. "I am kept here in gilded chains, in gorgeous bondage, in breathless attendance and luxurious *asservoissement*," he begins his letter, "otherwise I should have acknowledged sooner your magnificent and magnanimous bounty. I am deeply and proudly grateful—and I promise myself an experience of the rarest quality as soon as I sit down to you in calmer conditions than these or than those I shall *immediately* find on my return (tomorrow) to England." For William will be there, lecturing at Oxford, he notes, and there will be "a good deal of a social and other hurly-burly." But he "shall defy the Fates, all the same," he promises, "to keep me from getting at you more or less—and I foresee that I shall be borne aloft on billows of ecstatic comment. But of these things you shall hear from yours all constantly and gratefully Henry James."[23] Unfortunately, this promissory mention of *The Education* seems to be unique. What Henry James actually thought of Adams's literary experiment has, so far as I know, escaped the written record. How would he have couched his reaction to work in some ways so much like his own work—"The Beast in the Jungle," for example, and *The Ambassadors*? How would he have "reviewed" a book in which its author plants the clue as to the ethics of reading *The Education* (in the same chapter, incidentally, in which he takes up the cases of Palmerston, Gladstone, and Russell) in terms such as these: "Henry James had not yet taught the world to read a volume for the pleasure of seeing the lights of his burning-glass turned on alternate sides of the same figure"?[24] And what would he have made of Adams's explanation of *The Education* as something of what amounted to literary experiment or sort of novel: "If you can imagine a centipede moving along in twenty little sections (each with a mathematical formula carefully concealed in its stomach) to the bottom of a hill; and then laboriously climbing in fifteen sections (each with a new mathematical problem carefully concealed in its stomach) if it can get up on a hill an inch or two high, so as to see ahead a half inch, or, so, you will understand in advance all that the 'Education' has to say."[25]

One could just drop the matter right there. But a guess is possible. James would have said something like this, having forgotten that he had already resorted to this particular ploy in responding to an earlier work by Adams. After all due apologies over his not having written to him sooner, he might say, "I have of late, alter much frustration, been reading you with the baited breath of wonder, sympathy and applause. May I say, all unworthy and incompetent, what honour I think the beautiful volume does you and of how exquisite and distinguished an interest I have found it, with its easy lucidity, its saturation with its subject, its charmingly taken and kept *tone*. Even more than I congratulate you on the book I envy you your relation to the subject."[26] James had been reading *Mont-Saint-Michel and Chartres*. It is doubtful that by this time James could have learned anything new, by way of either direct or accidental education, from his friend Henry Adams. Nor was Adams about to learn anything further from James. Consequently, when James got around to "taking" his own life—in two autobiographical volumes, *A Small Boy and Others* and *Notes of a Son and Brother*—Adams saw cause only for discomfit and unhappiness in what he called, tellingly, James's "last bundle of memories."[27] To understand the gravity of Adams's charge, we need only recall that of himself, at low ebb, he had written in *The Education*: "His identity, if one could call a bundle of disconnected memories an identity, seemed to remain; but his life was once more broken into separate pieces."[28] In 1914, for both of them, education was long since over.

17

Quest for Truth

The conference papers in question—Henry Wasser's "Henry Adams, Intellectual" and William Merrill Decker's "A Martyr to the Disease of Omniscience"—focus on an essentially problematic Henry Adams.[1] Wasser takes up the question: just, precisely, what kind of intellectual was Adams. Was he, for instance, what is now called a public intellectual? It can be said that in the 1860s and 70s he was something of the sort, although he often shunned attention by remaining anonymous. Throughout it all, however, Adams's inquiring mind and Baconlike reach for all knowledge, especially after the publication in the years 1891–96 of his nine-volume *History of the United States of America during the administrations of Jefferson and Madison*—to recall Decker—resulted in several books that Adams was in no hurry to share with the public at large. If "Adams perceived the life of the mind as the highest form of human endeavor," as Decker says, it is also so that "knowledge per se receives from Adams less attention than the effort to know, as ideas for him are seldom more interesting than the people who produce them under specific personal and historical conditions."

Wasser's and Decker's papers encourage me to formulate the basic question of how to take Adams. If we are to understand his mind and achievement, should he be seen as an intellectual, an artist, or, perhaps, something else? Now we are all well aware that an intellectual can be an artist, as Wasser all but states, in the case of Adams, and that an artist, as Decker, Louis Auchincloss, and J. C. Levenson have made clear in their work, can be an intellectual. What I would like to know is how Adams takes himself (to adopt Robert Frost's definition of "style"). I am also well aware that that if the question were put to him, Adams himself would probably deny being either an intellectual or an artist. It is, of course, the fact that he left behind a vast body of historical and literary writings (not to mention his wonderful letters) that makes this a significant matter. What one decides, finally—whether Adams is primarily an intellectual or an artist—will matter relatively little to most readers of the Adams canon. The works are the works, after all, and they will remain what they are.

Yet this question seems to me to be an important subtext of Wasser's paper, and it actually breaks out, in its last pages, into a quotation from Henry James's famous reply of March 21, 1914, to Adams's (lost) letter of March 7, 1914, registering his reaction to Notes of a Son and Brother, James's second autobiographical volume. We do know something about how Adams reacted to this work, however, for on March 8, 1914, he wrote to his confidant Elizabeth Cameron: "I've read Henry James's last bundle of memories which have reduced me to dreary pulp. Why did we live? Was that all? Why was I not born in Central Africa and died young. Poor Henry James thinks it all real, I believe, and actually still lives in that dreamy, stuffy Newport and Cambridge, with papa James and Charles Norton—and me! Yet, why! It is a terrible dream, but not so weird as this here which is quite loony. Never mind!"[2] Now here is James's letter in its entirety, a letter that has been in print since Percy Lubbock's two-volume edition of James's letters in 1920.

> I have your melancholy outpouring of the 7th, & I know not how to acknowledge it than by the full recognition of its unmitigated blackness. Of course we are lone survivors, of course the past that was our lives is at the bottom of an abyss—if the abyss has any bottom; of course too there's no use talking unless one particularly wants to. But the purpose, almost, of my printed divagations was to show you that one can, strange to say, still want to—or at least can behave as if one did. Behold me therefore so behaving—& apparently capable of continuing to do so. I still find my consciousness interesting—under cultivation of the interest. Cultivate it with me, dear Henry—that's what I hoped to make you do; to cultivate yours for all that it has in common with mine. Why mine yields an interest I don't know that I can tell you, but I don't challenge or quarrel with it—I encourage it with a ghastly grin. You see I still, in presence of life (or of what you deny to be such,) have reactions—as many as possible—& the book I sent you is a proof of them. It's, I suppose, because I am that queer monster the artist, an obstinate finality, an inexhaustible sensibility. Hence the reactions—appearances, memories, many things go on playing upon it with consequences that I note & "enjoy" (grim word!) noting. It all takes doing—& I do. I believe I shall do yet again—it is still an act of life. But you perform them still yourself—& I don't know what keeps me from calling your letter a charming one! There we are, & it's a blessing that you understand—I admit indeed alone—[3]

Adams's reply, and surely there was one, has also been lost. So we cannot know whether Adams took the hint and considered the possibility (as James set it out) that Adams, too, was an artist, one who must continue to cultivate his consciousness. It was an old notion with James, moreover, for he had reacted to Adams's *Mont-Saint-Michel and Chartres* (1904) with one artist's praise for another artist: "May I say, all unworthy & incompetent, what honour I think the beautiful volume does you & of how exquisite & distinguished an interest I have found it, with its easy lucidity, its saturation with its subject, its charmingly taken and kept, *tone*. Even more than I congratulate you on the book I envy you your relation to the subject."[4] That this is meaningful praise (from a master, to be sure, of the "gracious twaddle of praise") I infer from his recognition that Adams has established a "relation" to his subject and, even more importantly, his decision to emphasize the word *tone* (always very important matters, for James, in his consideration of any writer's artistry). In a sense, of course, James was preaching to the choir, teaching a priest his message. Yet, in another sense, James has struck straight through Adams's affectation of world-weariness and cosmic despair.

James himself shared Adams's obsession to know. Yet, it was a remarkable insight on T. S. Eliot's part (he called James "the most intelligent man of his generation"), when in memorializing James in 1917 he ventured famously that James had "a mind so fine that no idea could violate it."[5] Because the salient implications of the word "violate" in this context were long (and conveniently) ignored (or misread) Eliot's dictum became a familiar and much abused shibboleth, especially in anti–James criticism. Had Eliot applied the notion to Adams, however, (and he could have) its meaning would have been lucid and (I think) unsusceptible to ironic dismissal. And here Wasser quotes R. P. Blackmur, often a gray eminence in discussions of the Adams–James relationship: "If we may quote T. S. Eliot's remark that Henry James had a mind—a sensibility—so fine that no mere idea could ever violate it, then we should say that Henry Adams had an intellect so fine—so energized—that no mere item of sensibility could ever violate that."[6]

An intellectual temperament, if I may use the phrase, receives ideas. An artistic temperament records or creates order out of experience. If Adams had a mind more capacious than that of James—at least for the reception of ideas, his rage for order was no less essential to him than James's cultivation of his consciousness. For if James is interested in the dramatics of thinking, Adams thought dramatically. To put it (too) bluntly, perhaps, James conceived of things (external or in the mind) as inherently dramatic, while Adams sought always to dramatize his conceptions. Therein, to me, lies the main difference between Adams's novel *Democracy* (1880) and James's *The Portrait of a Lady* (serialized in 1880–81) as well as *The Education of Henry Adams* (1907) and James's *The Ambassadors* (1903). Mutatis mutandis, it could be well said of James, as Decker says of Adams: "[He] perceived the life of the mind as the highest form of human endeavor and his narratives bear regular witness to the drama of intellection."

Now I would return for a moment to James's compliment, after reading *Mont-Saint-Michel and Chartres*, on Adams's authorial tone. Theodore Roosevelt found the great failing of John Hay, his Secretary of State, to have been

> his temptation ... to associate as far as possible only with men of refined and cultivated tastes, who lived apart from the world of affairs, and who, if Americans, were wholly lacking in robustness of fiber. His close intimacy with Henry James and Henry Adams—

> charming men, but exceedingly undesirable companions for any man not of strong nature—and the tone of satirical cynicism which they admired, and which he [John Hay] always affected in writing [to] them, marked that phase of his character which so impaired his usefulness as a public man.[7]

Surely the sweeping, general description—"satirical cynicism"—misses the mark. Yet, limiting myself now only to Adams, I would say that it is precisely "tone," always the key to intention, that is the most elusive quality in Adams's late writings especially. Take, for example, Adams's "A Letter to American Teachers of History" (1910). If Adams has "arrive[d] at his final position" in the "Letter," as Decker so argues, is that work a more or less direct statement of Adams's final theory about history and meaning or is it, as has been argued, something of a *blague*, a more or less serious put-on, as has also been argued, one intended to stimulate his professional readers to come up with something of their own that would be more satisfactory than the second law of thermodynamics?

It is not as poets that we commonly (if ever) *think* of James and Adams (despite Adams's secretive poems "Prayer to the Virgin of Chartres" and "Buddha and Brahma"), but to both of them it may be appropriate to apply Wallace Stevens's resonant adage in "Of Modern Poetry": a poet's desire to write "the poem of the mind in the act of finding what will suffice." If the thought is sufficient, we need no more. Or is it that we, for whatever reason, out of weariness or frustration, will sadly settle for what we have come up with, even though there might well be more to know or that the "truth" might lie elsewhere?

18

The Spirited Daisy

First published in London in the *Cornhill Magazine* in June-July 1878, "Daisy Miller" immediately prompted a controversy over the character of the story's heroine. Had Henry James offered readers a fair and judicious portrait of the young "American girl"? By March 1879, even *Lippincott's Magazine*, which had originally passed on the story, had its say. "Miss Daisy Miller, in almost any circle of society in any city here, would be looked upon with a pity akin to contempt," it announced. Daisy exemplified those young American girls who "have fine social gifts," to be sure, but whose "cleverness is too much for them, and if allowed any influence their folly runs away with them, like horses with the bits between their teeth."[1] The figure—the spirited American girl as a runaway horse—hints at what might be the *Lippincott* writer's little joke. Let me explain.

Annie is the diminutive form of the given name of James's young American heroine, but everyone knows her as "Daisy," the nickname reflected in the title of this "study" of the "American Girl Abroad," as James's subject soon came to be known. In his preface to the volume in the New York Edition that includes "Daisy Miller," written thirty years after the story's first appearance in print, James comments on the name he chose for his heroine. "It qualified itself in that publication and afterwards as 'a Study,'" he wrote, "for reasons which I confess I fail to recapture unless they may have taken account simply of a certain flatness in my poor little heroine's literal denomination. Flatness indeed, one must have felt, was the very sum of her story."[2] To James's idea of flatness, F. W. Dupee adds that of the "generic." "Like that of the field flower she [Daisy] is named for," he writes, "her very prettiness is more generic than individual."[3]

It so happens, however, that James's heroine shares the "flatness" of her name (if not her "generic" prettiness) with another creature whose name was bruited about in newspapers just when James was settling in to write "Daisy Miller." It will be recalled that in *Hawthorne* James ends his academically celebrated list of those "items of high civilization" lacking in America that militated against the possibilities for the creation of an American novel with the lament that, unfortunately, his homeland had "no sporting class—no Epsom nor Ascot!"[4] True enough, but America did have its flat racing in the Kentucky Derby (beginning in 1875), as well as the Iron City Jockey Club Day at Friendship Park in Pittsburgh, Pennsylvania, where, two years before James published his story about Annie P. Miller's social failures in Switzerland and Italy, horses were off and running in a "one-mile dash." Not coincidentally, I think, entered in the race was a filly named "Daisy Miller."[5]

19

The Wings of Doves

The author of *The Complex Fate* (1952) traces James's title for his last-phase novel *The Wings of the Dove* (1902) to a passage in Nathaniel Hawthorne's last completed novel *The Marble Faun; Or, the Romance of Monte Beni* (1860):

> Here she dwelt, in her tower, possessing a friend or two in Rome, but no home companion except the flock of doves, whose cote was in a ruinous chamber contiguous to her own. They soon became as familiar with the fair-haired Saxon girl as if she were a born sister of their brood; and her customary white robe bore such an analogy to their snowy plumage that the confraternity of artists called Hilda the Dove, and recognize her aerial apartment as the Dove-cote. And while the other doves flew far and wide in quest of what was good for them, Hilda likewise spread her wings, and sought such ethereal and imaginative sustenance as God ordains for creatures of her kind.[1]

One can readily grant Marius Bewley the probability of the connection he makes, though it is possible that James, like Hawthorne, has drawn directly from Scripture.[2] But more useful to the reader who would understand James's novel, I would suggest, is the following passage from *Hawthorne* (1879), James's contribution to the English Men of Letters series:

> This pure and somewhat rigid New England girl [Hilda], following the vocation of a copyist of pictures in Rome, unacquainted with evil and untouched by impurity, has been accidentally the witness, unknown and unsuspected, of the dark deed by which her friends, Miriam and Donatello, are knit together. This is her revelation of evil, her loss of perfect innocence. She has done no wrong, and yet wrongdoing has become part of her experience, and she carries it a long time, saddened and oppressed by it, till at last she can bear it no longer.[3]

If in *The Marble Faun* Hilda's watching Miriam and Donatello commit a crime forces upon her the recognition of their falling into sin, in *The Wings of the Dove* it is Milly Theale's virtue and implied acts of forgiveness that will bring Merton Densher to virtue—a purer virtue, one that will demand of him renunciation as its price. In *The Marble Faun* it is Hilda who has qualified her morality and who remains at the end to go on living after Miriam's death. In *The Wings of the Dove* Milly dies, but her death brings to the fore the sea change in Densher's character that makes it possible, in the long run, for him to decide to live in a moral state of renewed integrity—a sort of re-acquired innocence, if you will, when he refuses to accept Milly's fortune (the false legacy) and with that refusal the prospect of marriage to Kate Croy. His life will now be different. The renunciation has forever changed the course of his life.

While in Hawthorne's romance, Hilda will not live in the acceptance of any semblance of corruption or sin, in James's novel, Milly's illness transforms her gradual dying into a preparation for her final act of charity. It's as if everything in her case is to be seen, logically, as the natural material of her life. Even the knowledge, if Milly has it, of Kate Croy's and Densher's plotted defection— they rationalize that their "lie" will not hurt Milly in any way and may even be viewed as a kindness—contributes to Milly's acceptance of her fate. Not only can she endure the sight of corruption, she can act as a moral balance. If *The Wings of the Dove* is her story, who can say that she did not somehow know that Densher would renounce his material fortune? He is a monument to her virtue. He is, in fact, the product of her moral sense. That both Kate and Densher are under the shadow of the wings of the dove tells us much about the relationship Milly holds to them. The central concern in James's early books, in *The Europeans* or even *The American*, say, is what has been perceived by many as the "social entity." But James worked away from that early interest, until in the work of his so-called late phase, preeminently in *The Wings of the Dove*, he focuses not on the historicity of the "social entity," but on the virtues of pursuing a "moral entity." It is just this distinction between "moral entity" and "social entity" that divides James's late work from much of his earlier, in its own way, meritorious work, which often seems to stop short of delving into the deeper morality, as it does, for example in *The Europeans* or *The American*. In the latter, Claire de Cintré is unexplored by James, while Christopher Newman's renunciation strikes the reader as an act of western bravado, and thus shallow, not convincingly motivated. It is far from certain the whole unpleasant thing with its rather finagled upshot has mattered all that much to him.

But questions of morality in personal behavior abound in *The Wings of the Dove*. Can Milly be used for their joint purposes with impunity by Kate and her secretly betrothed Densher? Legally, yes. Socially, yes. It will be recalled that Lord Mark's action results from a desire for revenge and occurs as a instance of spleen—it is not be construed as indicative of a social comment. Remember, too, that Kate uses Milly in exactly the same manner in which her sister and her father want her to use her aunt, Mrs. Lowder, and almost in the way in which Mrs. Lowder wants to use Kate: as a finished, marketable product of her social and economic art. The moral problem is that of manipulation. It occurs everywhere. The variations in the moral possibilities in relationships among individuals as they play out over time become the most dramatic lines in the work.

This observation now seems to take us far afield from Hawthorne. There is no pattern of egregious manipulation in *The Marble Faun*. And this lack signals the fact that Hilda will not be used, not even by Miriam, who, after all, wants mainly sympathy. Hilda will be humble; she will be the recipient of benevolent power rather than the user of power. No one wishes to use anyone else. But then again Hilda does not want to hold any compelling moral relationship to Miriam that will entail moral complicity or even just a mutual moral awareness. It is not because she fears manipulation or otherwise that Hilda breaks off, but through an unwillingness to draw closer to Miriam in an hour of need.

The Wings of the Dove, at least in part, is concerned with the morals of human beings, manipulation and the effects of the close moral interrelationships that arise from such situations. Morally, Densher gets much closer to Milly, than he ever does to Kate, except, perhaps, in the final scene—in which, it is noticed, he himself engages in a little manipulation in a test of Kate, in Kate's ordeal by money. *The Marble Faun* is concerned with the moral relationship concerns that arise from a human denial of aid or sympathy manifested in personal isolation—almost an oblique denial of manipulation in principle. Hilda will not remain in the position whereby she can either hurt or aid Miriam. Her knowledge could be used for any purpose—even if the motive can only be that of satisfying an overbearingly self-righteous mind—but she will blot out the matter and blot out Miriam in the process. She will do her best by Miriam by denying anything that was ever between them. And what does this moral washing-of-hands signify? It is a repudiation of the human relationship between them just as it is growing into a "moral sense." Kate herself repudiates Densher at the shock of receiving "new" knowledge, that Densher has refused the "blood" money that constitutes the powerful darker aspect of the shadow of her wings Milly has left him. This fortune is what Densher must renounce in order to be free to accept the Milly's true legacy. Densher's moral sense has, so to speak, appropriated hers through his acceptance of the unspoken forgiveness granted to him by her death. In *The Marble Faun* instead of sympathy on moral grounds there is repudiation. But it costs Hilda nothing, for her morality is egregious—her virtue untested—her innocence an authorial given. She suffers from pride—but more importantly she has no real moral sense because she denies the possibility of the situation which could give rise to the achievement of a higher "morality"—the deepening moral fate possible in any human relationship under any condition. The wings of Hilda's dove cast no shadow. There is nothing to accept, nothing to repudiate. There is no moral interrelationship, no (blood) money. Poor Kenyon, deserving of his fate or not, is ultimately more alone than is Densher.

In short, what Hawthorne and James are concerned with here are moral problems—the significance of interrelationships between individuals in the establishment, refinement, and deepening of the moral sense. If Hawthorne emphasizes that the conscious isolation of an individual will affect that person's moral sense, he fails to follow through, for his attention soon wanders over to the Miriam-Donatello theme that, of course, he had originally seen in counterpoint to the Miriam-Hilda theme. In James, however, the thrust of his narrative does not veer from an interest in the effect upon the individual moral sense that the abuse of a human relationship has upon that moral sense, especially when even abuse becomes the means of deepening (or even creating) that moral sense in a sinner.

James said of his notable predecessor that "the fine thing in Hawthorne is that he cared for the deeper psychology, and that, in his way, he tried to become familiar with it."[4] Exchange for the moment the word "morality" for "psychology" and you will have the key to James's own primary intention, having taken his hint from Hawthorne, in the splendid novel he named *The Wings of the Dove*.

20

Innocence or Experience

> Longfellow wrote a charming little poem, called "The Children's Hour," but he ought to have called it "The Children's Century."
> —Henry James, "The Point of View" (1882)

In the English-speaking world the literary child derives from that revolution in poetry and fiction dating from the late eighteenth century, with the appearance in England of William Blake's *Songs of Innocence and Experience*, that we now know as the period of English Romanticism. That revolution, insofar as it brought about an entirely new way of looking at the child in its essence, was in reaction to the eighteenth-century's way of seeing the child in its subservient place, that is, seeing that the child kept its appointed place. The Age of Enlightenment saw the child as an incomplete adult. There was nothing at all resembling the perfect child, because by definition the child's only aspiration was to be an adult. Children were imperfect adults and on a smaller scale in stature. And what was most desired was that such children would grow, as soon as possible, to maturity. The process of socialization was desirable precisely because it was civilizing. Socialization took the child from the state of un-housebroken innocence to one of maturity and decency. Behind this view of the child lay, if one can so simplify as to see the primacy of one set of ideas, the philosopher John Locke's view of the infant's beginnings. The Infant was totally receptive to experience because its mind was a clean slate, that is, a *tabula rasa*. Just how experience works on that slate is described by Locke: "Let us then suppose the mind to be, as we say, white paper, void of all characters, without any Ideas: How comes It to be furnished? Whence comes it by that vast store which the busy and boundless fancy of man has painted on it with an almost endless variety? Which has it all the materials of reason and knowledge? To this I answer, in one word, from *Experience*."[1] The initial source of those materials of reason and knowledge were, of course, the mother and the attentive family and then, to take a large jump, society at large.

The Romantic poets reversed the eighteenth-century's view of the child. Increasingly distraught at their rapidly industrializing society with its concomitant ills, social and economic, these poets, Blake, Samuel Taylor Coleridge, and particularly William Wordsworth, denied that the child's mind was a *tabula rasa*. Rather, they insisted, socialization was detrimental to the purity and the completeness of vision which the child already possessed. "Growing up," they contended, did not lead to a desirable maturity as an adult but to the tragedy attending the loss of the child's poetic vision.

The child is father to the man, insisted Wordsworth, and, unfortunately, that man would never be half the child that the child was. "Growing up" necessarily meant, for the Romantics, socialization. In his seminal poem "Ode: Intimations of Immortality from Recollections of Early Childhood," Wordsworth announces that "Heaven lies about us in our infancy; / Shades of the prison-house begin to close / Upon the growing Boy." The roads leading to that "prison-house" are several:

> Behold the Child among his new-born blisses,
> A six-years' Darling of a pygmy size!
> See, where 'mid work of his own hand he lies,
> Fretted by sallies of his mother's kisses,
> With light upon him from his Father's eyes!
> See, at his feet, some little plan or chart,
> Some fragment from his dream of human life,
> Shaped by himself with newly-learned art;
>   A wedding or a festival,
>   A mourning or a funeral;
>   And this hath now his heart,
>   And unto this he frames his song:
>   Then will he fit his tongue
> To dialogues of business, love, or strife;
>   But it will not be long
>   Ere this be thrown aside,
>   And with new joy and pride
> The little Actor cons another part;
> Filling from time to time his "humorous stage"
> With all the Persons, down to palsied Age,
> That life brings with her in her equipage;
>   As if his whole vocation
>   Were endless imitation.[2]

Wordsworth radically transvalues the role of socialization in the development of the child. For Wordsworth, socialization meant imitation, that is to say, it was fostered on a kind of rote (and false) learning: "the little Actor cons another part." And as a latter-day American romantic, E. E. Cummings, would complain about children: "and down they forgot as up they grew."[3]

In time—and not too much time at that—this new view led to a cult of the child, and one of the forms that the cult took was to view the child as the source of considerable wisdom. The child, like the child in the sanative poem, "The Emperor's New Clothes," saw things as they really were and called those things as it saw them.

It took at least two generations for these views to take on a distinctive American coloration. That is not to deny that children of the eighteenth and nineteenth centuries, in one form or other, made periodic appearances in American literature. Hawthorne, for one, was fond of the child as "conscience" (Pearl in *The Scarlet Letter*), the child as "victim" ("The Gentle Boy"), the adolescent as shrewdly instinctive being ("My Kinsman, Major Molineux"). But it was not until Henry James and Mark Twain turned to the child that the American accent was sensed strongly enough to be deemed distinctive.

With almost no exceptions Mark Twain was at the top of his form when he drew upon the boyhood experiences of Samuel Langhorne Clemens for the substance of his fiction. From *Roughing It* (1872) and *The Adventures of Tom Sawyer* (1876) to *The Mysterious Stranger* (published posthumously, 1916) Mark Twain wrote best about children and adolescents. But it was in *Adventures of Huckleberry Finn* (1884), of course, that he broke away clearly from the heavily nostalgic cast of much nineteenth-century American writing about childhood—an adult's memory of childhood from the adult's superior point of view, as it manifests itself in Thomas Bailey Aldrich's *The Story of a Bad Boy* (1870), for example, and in Louisa May Alcott's *Little Women* (1868) and *Little Men* (1871).

In *Huck Finn*, however, Mark Twain discovered one of the enduring voices of the American child—one that reaches, in our day, into the fiction of J. D. Salinger, Truman Capote, Flannery O'Connor, and Carson McCullers. That voice, a special legacy of the Romantic's cult of the child, is that of the child as society's victim and as the critic of the society that victimizes him. It is not so much that the child is innately good—for it isn't—or that its vision is complete—for it isn't by any means—or even that, as Wordsworth insisted, the child is a visionary; rather it is that the child can still cut through the shams and deceits of his society. The consequence is that the adolescent Huck, a marginal member of society who accepts his marginality and whose survival depends upon his ability to fend for himself, is able to see through to the destructive substratum of civilization as he knows it. He can in his own naive way see through the charades of a drunkard's reformation—his father's—interpreted by a clergyman as tantamount to a religious conversion. It's a charade because Huck's father's game is that of the confidence man. Huck can see through the corrosive sentimentality of a backwoods society that prizes all things patriotic, religious, and, in the bad sense of the term, "poetic." Here are some of the household furnishings in the Grangerford household, as Huck sees them.

> Well, there was a big outlandish parrot on each side of the clock, made out of something like chalk, and painted up gaudy. By one of the parrots was a cat made of crockery, and a crockery dog by the other; and when you pressed down on them they squeaked, but didn't open their mouths nor look different nor interested. They squeaked through underneath. There was a couple of big wild-turkey-wing fans spread out behind those things. On the table in the middle of the room was a kind of a lovely crockery basket that had apples and oranges and peaches and grapes piled up in it which was much redder and yellower and prettier than real ones is, but they warn't real because you could see where pieces had got chipped off and showed the white chalk or whatever it was, underneath.[4]

Huck, the perceptive child who always sees the falseness at the heart of the society—where things "warn't real because you could see where pieces had got chipped off and showed the white chalk or whatever it was, underneath"—this child goes on to point to aspect after aspect of the society in which it must make his way. To survive, it must use the putative values of that very society against itself. To survive in a society that lies, cheats, bullies, and kills—one can only lie, cheat, bully, and, if necessary, kill. Huck never does kill, but in what is one of the most harrowing episodes in America's literature he stands through a long night facing a loaded gun at his sleeping, drunken father. Notably, in Mark Twain's fiction it is the child alone who maintains integrity, even as it defeats society at its own corrupt game by following its own unstatable rules. We can conclude, if we oversimplify, of course, but only by a little, that for Mark Twain the child is the only bearer of those values espoused (if not practiced) by its society: honesty of perception and expression, and loyalty to one's friends.

No matter what the context, Mark Twain's contemporary and countryman, Henry James, is invariably set up as his opposite. Mark Twain wrote about the American West. Henry James wrote about Europe. Mark Twain was, to use the formulations of Philip Rahv, a Redskin; James a Paleface. Mark Twain was a "low-brow," to use the designation of Van Wyck Brooks; James was a "high-brow." Regardless of their differences, however, they did share a deep interest in the child as a subject for fiction.

James, too, started out using children as the vehicles of social commentary. Randolph Miller, the young brother of the famous and notorious Daisy Miller, makes his acid remarks about a Europe he ranks several notches below Schenectady, New York, where his father earns the considerable sums necessary to support Mrs. Miller and her progeny's prolonged European stay. From the beginning James was impressed by one large truth about children: whether they were boisterous, reticent, shy, sensitive, brilliant, vulnerable, weak, assertive, aggressive, or downright plain, children were always, with no exception, burdensome to adults.

The American poet Henry Wadsworth Longfellow had solved that problem. Much as he cared for children, he allowed them only a set hour for the expressions of endearment and love. Indeed, each day had its appointed time for children. His poem on the subject he entitled, simply, "The Children's Hour."

> Between the dark and the daylight.
> When the night is beginning to lower,
> Comes a pause in the day's occupations,
> That is known as The Children's Hour.[5]

For Henry James, however, who was neither a father nor a husband, no such strategies were needed. Consequently, he was able to portray children as he saw them: intelligent, sentient, receptive beings working constantly at the task of survival. "Education," in the broadest sense of the term, was one of James's great themes, perhaps his central theme. It is natural, then, to see that education—what to tell a child, what to allow that child to read, how to act in that child's presence—links James's numerous tales and novels about children, from Dolcino, the child of a woman who disapproves of the aesthetics (and, she insists, the prurience) of her husband's books ("The Author of *Beltraffio*"), to "The Pupil," a boy who cajoles, entrances, badgers, shames, and subtly coerces his well-meaning tutor into staying on even though the family will no longer pay him for his services, and to the famous children of "The Turn of the Screw," Miles and Flora, who either through revenants or delusions are initiated into indescribable sexuality.

Henry James's classic work on pre-adolescent and adolescent sexuality, however, is the novel *What Maisie Knew* (1897). James's argument in that novel is tightly dramatized through a series of meetings, liaisons, and encounters of every sort. Young Maisie, the daughter of divorced parents, each of whom has taken up with a new significant other and soon marries. Thus Maisie is shunted back and forth between these new pairs of parents, the result of a sort of marital mitosis. When it is Maisie's young nurse that her father marries, it is necessary to hire a replacement. Enter the older and benign if querulous Mrs. Wix. Over time, Maisie is exposed to the ever-changing and (to Maisie) complicated, seemingly inexplicable marital and extramarital adventures and misadventures of her natal parents. Throughout it all, Maisie is comforted with lies and puzzled with prevarications. Ultimately, Mrs. Wix is compelled to inform Maisie that what her elders are engaged in is sinful. At long last, decides the author, Maisie acquires what might be called a moral sense, thus completing that portion of her socialization.

Maisie's moral sense, full-blown, has been acquired at an astonishingly early age. She "grows up" in a hurry, precisely because she has been exposed to the reality at the heart of all the relationships within her family—immediate and extended—that is, the fact that sexual needs and sexual adventures dictate the course of Maisie's own life, but they do so—James's final point—only as long as Maisie is unaware of them. Maisie's socialization is sexual in nature, not overtly her own sexuality but certainly that of her mother and father and their respective lovers. Coming close to the end of what historians and literary critics call the Victorian era, *What Maisie Knew* bravely traces the process by which the naive, innocent child is so turned and buffeted by her bettors—the adults who care for her—that her psychic survival depends upon her discovery that she has the capacity for moral choice and that, further, she is wholly responsible for making such choices.

21

Fathers and Daughters

The *New York Times* review of *The Literary Remains of the Late Henry James* in 1885 starts out with these sentences: "It seems advisable to say at the outset that the Henry James who wrote the contents of this volume is not the author of the Daisy Miller story, and further he is not the English jurist who had sat in Cabinets constructed by Mr. Gladstone. He is, indeed, quite another and more interesting personality than either his son, the novelist, or his namesake of England."[1] The thrust at the novelist was mild and a loving son would have passed it off as an attempt at what the younger Henry James was wont to call an instance of "mere twaddle." He would have noticed, however, that even beyond his father's grave he had to put up with what he perceived to be the inferior status his father granted him.

Yet it is true that the younger of Henry James, Sr.'s two elder sons was never one to complain about the father's preferences, let alone openly confront him regarding the vexation between them. But, of course, as writer of fiction, he had other ways of dealing with any or all of the autobiographical situations that vexed him. And he did so rather early on by drawing on his relations with the immediate members of his family—his father, his elder brother, and his sister. He cast them as the principals of the 1880 melodramatic story he called *Washington Square*, a choice of title that linked the story to that "village" that had once been home to the James family.

Interestingly, two James scholars discuss probable sources for the plot of the story that James tells. These discussions occur in chapter sub-sections they name, respectively, "Fathers and Daughters" and "Free White Males and Free White Females."[2] In both cases, it is pointed out that James was influenced by accounts of instances when a father has interceded in the life of a young daughter who is being courted by, as the father thinks, an inappropriate suitor. The father thinks he knows that the young man will take advantage of his daughter. In London the actress Fanny Kemble told the young writer such a story of parental meddling in a daughter's prospective marriage, echoing in a curious way a story with similar characteristics, one in which the novelist's grandfather had "steamed down the Hudson to grill his prospective son-in-law" and to make his parental demands.[3] In the latter instance, like Catherine Sloper, the heroine of *Washington Square*, the novelist's aunt "did not question her father's authority to supervise her courtship."[4] And like Catherine, so, too, Henry, Jr., in all parental matters pertaining to him kept his own counsel and remained quiet and outwardly docile. In many ways, of course, Catherine is a surrogate for Henry, Jr. There is no doubt that when the author sided with anyone in his story, it was Catherine Sloper, just as he sympathized with his sister Alice, especially in her difficult relationship with her father, closely indicated in an incident described by Henry James, Sr.'s biographer. The elder James's "new theory of evil," he writes, "had nothing to say about what might be called relational evil, or the damage one person can do to another—as when a parent, even without ill intentions, injures his or her offspring." In the 1860s, he continues, "Alice began to realize that, contrary to what Father said, suffering was not invariably sanatory. There were times, as she sat beside him in his library trying to read, when she felt like 'throwing [her]self out of the window, or knocking off the head of the benignant pater as he sat with his silver locks, writing at his table.' The daughter's very muscles seemed to be invaded by 'waves of violent inclination.' She dared not 'let [her]self go for a moment.' There was nothing to do but sit 'immovable.' It seemed that 'the only difference between me and the insane was that I had not only all the horrors and suffering of insanity but the duties of doctor, nurse, and strait-jacket imposed upon me, too.'"[5]

It is difficult not to hear an echo of the relationship of the elder James and his daughter Alice in the observation made by the narrator of *Washington Square*: "You would have surprised him [Dr. Sloper] if you had told him so; but it is a literal fact that he almost never addressed his daughter save in the ironical form."[6]

Of course, it would be a stretch to say that the fictional Catherine is entirely drawn from the biographical Alice. It might be said, however, that in Catherine the novelist has downsized his sister's psychological complexities, her intelligence, and her quick wit, authorial sacrifices made for the sake of narrative plausibility in his portrayal of the obdurate, unforgiving relationship between a father and a daughter, one in which the father ultimately succeeds in winning her over to his cold and inflexible side when, at the last, she dismisses once and for all the suitor who would marry her for her inheritance. Curiously, the novelist's brother, William, was quick to see something of himself in Catherine's suitor, a notion that Henry immediately denied—"the young man in Washington Square is not a portrait—he is sketched from the outside merely and not *feuillé*—" adding, curiously, "the only good thing in the story is the girl."[7] James does not say whether he refers to Catherine's "goodness" or to the effectiveness of her fictional portrayal.

In any case, not all of the book's reviewers agreed with James regarding the "girl." One review is particularly interesting. While acknowledging that Catherine is "very well done," it reserves its highest praise for Dr. Sloper, who, it notes, is "capital, as any of his brother physicians will recognize."[8] Though some may find the tone in which this is said suspect, there the notion that his "brother physicians" would recognize Dr. Sloper as one of them is richly suggestive. Like the members of his professional cohort, he spends his life "estimating people" as "part of the medical trade" (104). He, too, exemplifies the medical model of those who deal with all others as types, evoking a crude version of "statistics" by insisting that he is right nineteen times out of twenty.

If James's deepest sympathies involve Catherine, his critical (and satirical) eye begins with Dr. Sloper's back story. Here is the opening paragraph of *Washington Square*:

> During a portion of the first half of the present century, and more particularly during the latter part of it, there flourished and practised in the city of New York a physician who enjoyed perhaps an exceptional share of the consideration which, in the United States, has always been bestowed upon distinguished members of the medical profession. This profession in America has constantly been held in honor, and more successfully than elsewhere has put forward a claim to the epithet of "liberal." In a country in which, to play a social part, you must either earn your income or make believe that you earn it, the healing art has appeared in a high degree to combine two recognized sources of credit. It belongs to the realm of the practical, which in the United States is a great recommendation; and it is touched by the light of science—a merit appreciated in a community in which the love of knowledge has not always been accompanied by leisure and opportunity [3–4].

James then narrows in to focus on Dr. Sloper, Catherine's father:

> It was an element in Doctor Sloper's reputation that his learning and his skill were very evenly balanced; he was what you might call a scholarly doctor, and yet there was nothing abstract in his remedies—he always ordered you to take something. Though he was felt to be extremely thorough, he was not uncomfortably theoretic; and if he sometimes explained matters rather more minutely than might seem of use to the patient, he never went so far (like some practitioners one had heard of) as to trust to the explanation alone, but always left behind him an inscrutable prescription. There were some doctors that left the prescription without offering any explanation at all; and he did not belong to that class either, which was after all the most vulgar. It will be seen that I am describing a clever man; and this is really the reason why Doctor Sloper had become a local celebrity [4].

In fact, his local celebrity was such that when calamity befell him he was given a pass. He was not held accountable for the losses suffered in his immediate family. "For a man whose trade was to keep people alive he had certainly done poorly in his own family, and a bright doctor who within three years loses his wife and his little boy should perhaps be prepared to see either his skill or his affection impugned. Our friend, however, escaped criticism; that is, he escaped all criticism but his own, which was much the most competent and most formidable" (7).

As for the remaining member of his reduced immediate family, he had a duty to protect her and a plan by which to carry out that duty.

> His little girl remained to him; and though she was not what he desired, he proposed to himself to make the best of her. He had on hand a stock of unexpended authority, by which the child, in its early years, profited largely. She had been named, as a matter of course, after her poor mother, and even in her most diminutive babyhood the Doctor never called her anything but Catherine. She grew up a very robust and healthy child, and her father, as he looked at her, often said to himself that, such as she was, he at least need have no fear of losing her. I say "such as she was," because, to tell the truth—But this is a truth of which I will defer the telling [8].

Thus ends Chapter One. The story of how the sure- and single-minded Dr. Sloper will work to shape his daughter's character so as to determine what she will do with her life lies in the subsequent thirty-four chapters. But clues into how the good doctor will behave in the decades that follow are already apparent. Knowing what is best for his daughter, he has a prescription good for a lifetime, one determined by his reading of her character through "physiognomy" (74). He knows all too well that Catherine is dull and bovine and that she will not change. Typing people, particularly those in and around his family, he readily sizes up Catherine's suitor, and decides that he belongs to the "wrong category" (98). As a physician his task is to take the measure of patients, to codify them, dividing them "into classes, into types" (115). It may turn out that he is "mistaken" about Catherine's suitor "as an individual,'" he will allow, but he has no doubt that "his type is written on his whole person" (115).

All too fitting, then, is the surname of this physician-father that James has given him. If to "slope" is "to take, to move as proceed in, an oblique direction," how appropriate that in sewing, a "sloper" is a "basic pattern" for the making of other patterns. In short, it is a template, a pattern, a prescription, that the fictive Dr. Sloper will employ to curtail Catherine's will and determine her behavior over the length of her adult life.

If James could not read all the way through *Washington Square* when considering it for inclusion in the New York Edition and deciding to exclude it, perhaps it was not because he found it to be early work that no longer measured up to standards but that he found it to be too directly personal, its source in the annals of the James family being much too autobiographical to be put on display anew. Early on the novelist warns the reader that much like the elder Henry James, Dr. Sloper was not one to ask "for explanations which he could entertain himself any day with inventing" (10). A motto that the novelist in the James family would never follow.

22

The Double Bind

There is much to admire in Ross Posnock's *Henry James and the Problem of Robert Browning* (Athens: University of Georgia Press, 1985). It proceeds from the recognition that James's personal and literary involvement with the work (and life) of Browning was problematic for the younger writer and that it was problematic to a degree far in excess of that felt by James when confronted with the work or example of any other competing writer, contemporary or not. The argument runs, as I see it, that James found in Browning's work a handling of themes and situations that he felt compelled to treat in his own fiction, even to the point of rewriting two of Browning's poems and a play. Those rewritings, moreover, served James personally as the means by which he tried to come to terms with the two-sided Browning—the esoteric and the exoteric—who was not only privately a great artist but a fully integrated social being as well. Indeed, to put the matter differently, James was deeply disturbed that the Browning who was the artist not only wrote brilliantly and complexly on the theme of men and women but that he had done so without sacrificing one bit of his opportunity to participate in life's own complications and pleasures of the same sort. In short, Browning—unlike James—had renounced nothing. Yet Browning was still, as James wrote admiringly to friends he shared with Browning, "on the whole the writer of our time of whom, in the face of the rest of the world, the English tongue may be most proud—for he has touched everything, and with a breadth!" With no hesitation, James put him "very high—higher than anyone."

For all its fine qualities, this book is not—*pace* its author—"the first full examination" of the connection between James and Browning. (For "full" it would be more accurate, perhaps, to read "book-length.") If it does not tell the whole story, it nevertheless accomplishes a great deal. Acknowledging the work of others who have worked at bits and pieces of the puzzle—among them, Michael Ross, Mario D'Avanzo, Barbara and Giorgio Melchiori and Sidney E. Lind—

Posnock brings to his task additional evidence, new cases, detailed analyses, and fresh theories.

Of his extensive analyses of Jamesian texts previously associated with Browning, the most incisive is a "realistic" reading of "The Private Life," which he calls a "mimetic narrative." Based on the "new" evidence he adduces, we have carefully argued cases for connecting Browning's *The Inn Album* to "The Lesson of the Master," *In a Balcony* to *The Wings of the Dove*, and *Fifine at the Fair* to *The Golden Bowl*. In an excellent final chapter, moreover, he analyzes how in his 1912 address to the members of the Royal Society of Literature ("The Novel in *The Ring and the Book*") James, the sixty-nine-year-old "Master," negotiated brilliantly his final "appropriation" of the great poem by the author of *Men and Women*.

All this is more or less valid as far as it goes. But Posnock could have enhanced his case by taking into account other available evidence (some of it established in print). For instance, as early as 1869—seven years before James reviewed *The Inn Album*—he had already "taken over" and rewritten a Browning poem. Displaying an epigraph from Browning, "A Light Man" reworks and sometimes parodies "A Light Woman" (from *Men and Women*). Not only does Browning's poem stand unmistakably as the source for this early James story but it stands just as solidly behind James's first major novel, *Roderick Hudson*, published in the year in which Browning published *The Inn Album*, with its paradigmatic situation of an "older" man, a "younger" man, and a beautiful woman of questionable motivation, shadowy background, and ferocious sexual appetites. James named the woman Christina Light, drawing again on "A Light Woman" as well as Browning's poem "Cristina."

Yet there is no question that this canny book will be decidedly useful to students of both the novelist and the poet. There are insights into the work of both "Masters" that are intrinsically valuable. But there is another way in which this study should attract the attention of anyone concerned with contemporary literary criticism and its application to specific texts. To an impressive degree Posnock has successfully married current theory to practical criticism, and he has done so not to create new problems but to solve an existing literal and biographical problem. To do so, he has drawn judiciously upon the theories of Harold Bloom, Theodor Adorno, Leo Bersani, Stanley Fish, Erving Goffman, Stephen Greenblatt, Samuel Weber, Dorrit Cohn, Freud, Lacan, and Rene Girard. It is Girard's theory of the "double-bind," however, that enables Posnock's own interpretation of the way in which simultaneously Browning's life and achievement attracted and repulsed James. In Girard's notion of the "double-bind," he finds an explanation for the psychological and aesthetic dynamics of the master-disciple relationship tacit in James's reaction to Browning and his work. In its most direct form, Browning's very existence and literary example spoke to James in unmistakably contradictory terms: "Imitate me, but don't imitate me."

James, of course, wrote stories about this "bind"—brilliantly and most complexly in "The Lesson of the Master" (incidentally, Posnock errs when he says that James's use of Browning in this story "has gone unnoticed")—but for James personally (if Posnock is right, and I think he is) the "double-bind" seemed to be impervious to solution. That James finally "solved" the matter for himself, in his address in 1912 before the Royal Society—though Browning's death in 1890 had long since made the poet himself more "accessible" to the artist in James—is one of the burdens of Posnock's concluding chapter. The centenary of Browning's birth turned out to be a good time for resolution (and for his most audacious piece of rewriting, if only in the prospect of rewriting of *The Ring and the Book*, an act which would, of course, never take place), and that resolution, coming twenty-two years after the poet's death, argues Posnock, was fostered by the deaths recently of his brother William (a great admirer of Browning) and John LaFarge, the artist and friend who had first unlocked the secrets of *Men and Women* for both Henry and William.

It is indisputable, of course, that these deaths delivered the brother and friend into James's aesthetic possession, even as her death had at once made Minny Temple available to his writer's imagination. But something else had happened to James after 1890, and that something had changed his side of the one-way argument with the once-happily-married paterfamilias and master poet he had been conducting since the late 1860s. James "discovered" the fact (or faced up to it, perhaps) that the nature of his own sexuality differed markedly from that of Browning. If Browning's poetry would always be worthy of the serious writer's imitation and inspired reach, his life might not be. The poet had not told the whole truth about human love and sexuality. He had omitted from his work all consideration of other conflicting sexual passions. The answer to the "double-bind" James had felt had been there from the start in his own work, though encoded to keep such matters from, most likely, himself, as well as his readers. It is neither anachronistic nor critically irresponsible to take another look, given this advantage, at the behavior of the three males in "A Light Man," the dynamics of the tricky relationship Rowland Mallet enjoys with Roderick Hudson, or even that of Paul Overt and Henry St. George in that secularized Pauline allegory of sexuality and celibacy called "The Lesson of the Master."

In the years following Browning's death, it should have dawned upon James that by sticking exclusively, when dealing with sex, to the theme of man's relationship to women, Browning had cut himself off from the less public theme of a man's passionate relationship to other men. James had always acknowledged

22. The Double Bind

Browning's primacy (in both senses of the term) in the literary treatment of heterosexual relationships. "If Browning had spoken for us in no other way," wrote James in 1890, "he ought to have been made sure of, tamed, and chained as a classic, on account of the extraordinary beauty of his treatment of the special relation between man and woman. It is a complete and splendid picture of the matter, which somehow places it at the same time in the region of conduct and responsibility." Yet it could not have escaped James's late notice that when Browning had been confronted with the evidence indicating the possibility that Shakespeare was a pederast, he was reported as having replied with animus: "If so the less Shakespeare he!" Was it simply, in James's case, that his subsequent "discovery" of similar truths about himself (as well as others) promoted a sexual tolerance (which in the late 1890s he extended to Walt Whitman, whom he had savaged in a review of *Drum-Taps* in 1865) that released him personally once and for all from the "double-bind" under which he, artist and man, had so long labored? Surely, whether or not such self-knowledge contributed to his decision not to rewrite *The Ring and the Book* but merely to sketch out imperiously how he would go about rewriting it as a Jamesian novel if he wanted (or needed) to do so, there is every indication that James's final act of "appropriating" Browning was a grand gesture marked less by generosity than out-and-out audacity.

Chapter Notes

Chapter 1

1. Owen Canfield, "A Busy Day at the Archives," *Hartford Courant* (Oct. 28, 1994), p. E1.
2. Henry James, *The Aspern Papers*, in *The Novels and Tales of Henry James* (New York Edition), 24 vols. (New York: Scribner's, 1907–09), XII, 117–18.
3. L. H. Butterfield, "The Papers of the Adams Family: Some Account of Their History," *Proceedings of Massachusetts Historical Society*, 71 (Boston: Published by the Society, 1959), 338.
4. Nathaniel Hawthorne, *The American Notebooks*, ed. Randall Stewart (New Haven: Yale University Press, 1932), p. 280.
5. Margaret Drabble, *The Realms of Gold* (New York: Knopf, 1975), pp. 22–23.
6. William Carlos Williams, "Comedy Entombed: 1930," in *Make Light of It: Collected Stories* (New York: Random House, 1950), p. 327.

Chapter 2

1. *The Complete Notebooks of Henry James*, ed., intr., and notes by Leon Edel and Lyall H. Powers (New York: Oxford University Press, 1987), p. 216.
2. *Henry James Letters*, 4 vols., ed. Leon Edel (Cambridge: Harvard University Press, 1974–80), IV, 77.
3. Henry James, *The American* (Boston: James R. Osgood, 1877), pp. 40, 27.
4. Henry James, "Americans Abroad," *The Nation* (Oct. 3, 1878), p. 27.
5. Edel and Powers, *Notebooks*, 217.
6. Oscar Cargill, *The Novels of Henry James* (New York: Macmillan, 1961), pp. 46, 61. As one example, Cargill points to the caricature of Americans in *L'Etrangère*, a play by Alexandre Dumas, *fils*, put on at the Théâtre Français on Feb. 14, 1876 (43–46).
7. James, *American*, 200.
8. James, *American*, 44, 278–79.
9. James, *American*, 34. His brother William was ever alert to the possibility that he was being used as a source for Henry's portraits of Americans. "The morbid little clergyman [Benjamin Babcock] is worthy of Ivan Sergeitch. I was not a little amused to find some of my own attributes in him," recognized William. "I think you found my 'moral reaction' excessive when I was abroad" (*The Correspondence of William James, Volume I: William and Henry, 1861–1884*, ed. Ignas K. Skrupskelis and Elizabeth M. Berkeley [Charlottesville: University Press of Virginia, 1992], p. 268).
10. "Literary Gossip," *Athenaeum*, 25 May 1878, p. 671.
11. Leon Edel, *Henry James: The Conquest of London: 1870–1881* (Philadelphia and New York: Lippincott, 1962), pp. 249–50. Of course, the *Athenaeum* writer may well have been playing off *The Innocents Abroad*, Mark Twain's well-known 1869 book.
12. Henry James, *The Art of the Novel*, ed. R. P. Blackmur (New York: Scribner's, 1934), pp. 21–23.
13. *Art of the Novel*, 23–24. If Christopher Newman "rose before" him in the Louvre in 1876, Hyacinth Robinson of *The Princess Casamassima* "sprang up" before James "out of the London pavement" the very next year by which time James had left Paris for London (*Art of the Novel*, 60).

14. "Gustave Flaubert," *Notes on Novelists with Some Other Notes* (New York: Scribner's, 1914), pp. 74–75.
15. *Art of the Novel*, 33.
16. "James's French Poets and Novelists," *The Nation* (Apr. 25, 1878), p. 274.
17. "Gustave Flaubert," in *Madame Bovary*, trans. W. Blaydes (New York: Collier, n.d.), p. xv.
18. "Gustave Flaubert," xxii.
19. Lionel Trilling, *The Liberal Imagination* (Garden City: Doubleday, 1953), pp. 67–68. See also Edmund Wilson, "Ambiguity of Henry James," *The Hound & Horn* (April-June 1934), 7: 384–406 (especially pp. 389–401); Philip Grover, *Henry James and the French Novel: A Study in Inspiration* (New York: Barnes & Noble, 1973), pp. 92–107; and Pierre A. Walker, *Reading Henry James in French Cultural Contexts* (DeKalb: Northern Illinois University Press, 1995), pp. 42–56. *The Princess Casamassima* was linked with Flaubert's *L'Éducation sentimentale* in an unsigned review of James's novel in the *Athenaeum* on November 6, 1886; see *Henry James: The Contemporary Reviews*, ed. Kevin J. Hayes (Cambridge: Cambridge University Press, 1996), pp. 175–76.
20. *Art of the Novel*, 119.
21. Gustave Flaubert, *A Sentimental Education: The Story of a Young Man*, trans., intr., and notes by Douglas Parmée (Oxford: Oxford University Press, 1989), p. 39. In the original this passage reads: "*Arnoux s' était raissis et gourmandait un vieillard d'aspect sordide, en lunettes bleues. —Ah! vous êtes joli, père Isaac! Voilà trois oeuvres décrées, perdues! Tout le monde se fiche de moi! On les connait maintenant! Que voulez-vous que j'en fasse? Il faudra que je les envoie en Californie!... au diable! Taisez-vous! La spécialité de ce bonhomme consistait à mettre au bas de ses tableaux des signatures de maîtres anciens. Arnoux refusait de le payer; il le congédia brutalement*" (Flaubert Oeuvres, Pléiade Edition, II, ed. A. Thibaudet and R. Dumesnil (Paris: Gallimard, 1952), pp. 66–67).
22. Dixon Wecter, "Literary Culture on the Frontier," in *Literary History of the United States*, 2nd ed., rev., ed. Robert E. Spiller et al. (New York: Macmillan, 1953), p. 662.
23. *American*, 26.
24. "Current Literature [*The American*]" *The Galaxy* (July 1877), 24:135–38: reprinted in Henry James, *The American* (Norton Critical Edition), ed. James W. Tuttleton (New York: Norton, 1978), pp. 394–97. Quotation from pp. 394–95 of the latter.
25. *Contemporary Reviews*, 27. On the subject of Newman's French, as well as James's use of the language, see Edwin Sill Fussell, *The French Side of Henry James* (New York: Columbia University Press, 1990), pp. 25–57.
26. *John Hay-Howells Letters: The Correspondence of John Milton Hay and William Dean Howells 1861–1905*, ed. George Monteiro and Brenda Murphy (Boston: Twayne, 1980), pp. 22, 24.
27. William Dean Howells, "Henry James, Jr.," *Century Magazine*, 25 (Nov. 1882); reprinted in Michael Anesko, *Letters, Fictions, Lives: Henry James and William Dean Howells* (New York: Oxford University Press, 1997), pp. 229–35. Quotation from p. 233 of the latter.
28. Edel and Powers, *Notebooks*, 53.
29. Edel and Powers, *Notebooks*, 55.
30. *The American*, in *The Complete Plays of Henry James*, ed. Leon Edel (Philadelphia and New York: Lippincott, 1949), p. 209.
31. *Complete Plays*, p. 108.
32. [Editorial Note], *The Nation* (Jan. 11, 1877), p. 29.
33. *Henry James Letters*, II, 306.
34. Brenda Murphy, *American Realism and American Drama, 1880–1940* (Cambridge: Cambridge University Press, 1987), p. 60.
35. Quoted in Gay Wilson Allen, *William James* (New York: Viking, 1967), p. 328.

Chapter 3

1. Wallace Stevens, "Three Academic Pieces" (1947), *Collected Poetry and Prose*, ed. Frank Kermode and Joan Richardson (New York: Library of America, 1997), pp. 690, 692.
2. John Ciardi, "Wallace Stevens' Absolute Music,'" *Nation*, 179 (Oct. 16, 1954): 346–47; reprinted in *Wallace Stevens: The Critical Heritage*, ed. Charles Doyle (London: Routledge & Kegan Paul, 1985). The quotation comes from Doyle, pp. 398–99.
3. Jonathan Strange, "Six Stevens Letters," *Wallace Stevens Journal*, 18 (Spring 1994), 21.
4. *Letters of Wallace Stevens*, ed. Holly Stevens (New York: Knopf, 1966), p. 121.
5. *Letters of Wallace Stevens*, 122.
6. Email, Glen MacLeod to George Monteiro, Oct. 22, 2009.
7. *Letters of Wallace Stevens*, 506.
8. Preface, *The Portrait of a Lady* (2 vols.), in *The Novels and Tales of Henry James*, I, xv-xvi.

9. Preface, *Portrait of a Lady*, xx-xxi.
10. *Henry James: A Life in Letters*, ed. Philip Horne (New York: Viking, 1999), p. 130.
11. Alfred Kreymborg, *Troubadour: An Autobiography* (New York: Liveright, 1925), pp. 218–19.
12. Samuel French Morse, Informal Talk, "English Club," sponsored by the Department of English, Brown University, ca. 1960s.
13. Preface, *Portrait of a Lady*, xix.
14. *Collected Poetry*, 47.
15. *Collected Poetry*, 106,
16. *Collected Poetry*, 50.
17. *Collected Poetry*, 53.
18. *Collected Poetry*, 417.
19. *Collected Poetry*, 747.

Chapter 4

1. "Kane and Abel," *Frank Leslie's Illustrated Newspaper*, Apr. 22, 1871, 281–93, and Apr. 29, 1871, 106–07.
2. *Complete Notebooks*, 140–41.
3. To Howells, on 22 Jan. 1895, James wrote:"I have two good things— and have had them for some time—to thank you for. One is John's charming paper about the Beaux Arts which I was delighted you should have sent me—so lovely it is and young and fresh and vivid and in every way calculated to minister to the 'fondness of a father' and the frenzy of a mother ... The dear boy seems to have been born to invent new ways of being filially gratifying—generally delectable. Happy you— happy, even if you had only him!" (*Henry James Letters*, III, 511). There's a hint here that in *The Ambassadors* Chad Newsome (James's reimagined John Howells) will at the last turn out fine by Woollett's American standards.
4. Leon Edel, *Henry James: The Middle Years, 1882–1895* (Philadelphia and New York: Lippincott, 1962), p. 312.
5. Quoted in Robert L. Gale, *A Henry James Encyclopedia* (New York: Greenwood, 1989), p. 635.
6. *Notebooks*, 141.
7. W. D. Howells, *Selected Letters*, 6 vols., ed. Robert C. Leitz III and others (Boston: Twayne, 1980), III, 175–76.
8. Preface, *The Ambassadors*, 2 vols., (New York Edition), I, xiii-xiv.
9. *Life in Letters*, II, 52–53.
10. See *A Little Bit of Heaven: An Irish-American Anthology*, ed. Sean McMahon (Cork, Ireland: Mercier Press, 1999), p. 99.
11. James employs the phrase in his preface to *The Ambassadors*, I, xiv.

Chapter 5

1. *The Letters of Ernest Dowson*, ed. Desmond Flower and Henry Maas (London: Cassell, 1967), p. 146.
2. Henry James, *Notes of a Son and Brother* (New York: Scribner's, 1914); reprinted in *Henry James: Autobiography*, ed. Frederick W. Dupee (New York: Criterion Books, 1956), pp. 291–92.
3. See James's essays,"Browning in Westminster Abbey," *The Speaker*, 1 (4 Jan. 1890), 10–12, and "The Novel in *The Ring and the Book*," *Transactions of the Royal Society of Literature*, 2nd series, 31, part 4 (1912), 269–98, as well as his autobiographical fragment, *The Middle Years* (1917), in *Autobiography*, 594.
4. *A Browning Handbook*, 2nd ed. (New York: Appleton-Century-Crofts, 1955), p. 33.
5. For general essays on Browning and James, see Giorgio Melchiori, "Browning e Henry James," *Friendship's Garland: Essays Presented to Mario Praz*, ed. Vittorio Gabrieli (Roma: Edizioni di Storia e Letteratura, 1966), pp. 143–80; and Philip Drew, *The Poetry of Browning: A Critical Introduction* (London: Methuen, 1970), pp. 385–96. Two noteworthy studies of indebtedness in specific works are Mario L. D'Avanzo,"James's 'Maud-Evelyn': Source, Allusion, and Meaning," *Iowa English Yearbook*, 13 (Fall, 1968), 24–33; and Michael L. Ross, "Henry James' 'Half-man': The legacy of Browning in 'The Madonna of the Future," *Browning Institute Studies*, 2 (New York: Browning Institute, 1974), 25–42.
6. *The Poetry of Robert Browning*, ed. Jacob Korg (Indianapolis and New York: Bobbs-Merrill, 1971), pp. 192–94.
7. "A Light Man," *Galaxy*, 8 (July, 1869), 49–68; reprinted in *Complete Tales of Henry James*, ed. Leon Edel (Philadelphia and New York: Lippincott, 1962), II, 61–96. Quotations derive from the *Galaxy* printing.
8. Leon Edel, *Conquest of London*, 330; *Henry James Letters*, II, 107, 302; and Maisie Ward, *Robert Browning and His World: Two Robert Brownings? [1861–1889]* (New York: Holt, Rinehart and Winston, 1969), p. 180.
9. *Notebooks*, 87.
10. "The Lesson of the Master," *Universal Review*, 1 (16 July and 15 Aug., 1888), 342–65, 494–523; reprinted in *Complete Tales*, VII, 213–84. Quotations derive from *Complete Tales*.

11. *Poetry of Robert Browning*, 58–59.
12. See William G. DeVane, "The Virgin and the Dragon," *Robert Browning: A Collection of Critical Essays*, ed. Philip Drew (Boston: Houghton Mifflin, 1966), pp. 96–109.
13. "The Private Life," *Atlantic Monthly*, 69 (Apr. 1892), 463–83; reprinted in *Complete Tales*, VIII, 189–227.
14. *William Wetmore Story and His Friends* (Boston: Houghton Mifflin, 1903), II, p. 227.
15. *William Wetmore Story*, II, 89.

Chapter 6

1. *Art of the Novel*, 247, 246.
2. *The Writings of Henry David Thoreau* (Boston and New York, 1906), II, 11.
3. "The Beast in the Jungle," *Henry James: Selected Fiction*, ed. Leon Edel (New York, 1953), pp. 482–536. References are to this text.
4. *Partisan Review*, 7 (Nov.-Dec., 1940), 412–424; reprinted in Philip Rahv, *Image and Idea* (Norfolk, CT: New Directions, 1957), pp. 7–25.
5. Jessie Ryon Lucke, "The Inception of The Beast in the Jungle," *New England Quarterly*, 36 (Dec. 1953), 529–32.
6. *Hawthorne* (London, 1879; New York, 1880), reprinted in *The Shock of Recognition*, ed. Edmund Wilson (New York, 1955), p. 530; quoted in Lucke, "Inception of the Beast," 529.
7. Lucke, "Inception," 532.
8. *Hawthorne*, in *Shock of Recognition*, 530.
9. *American Renaissance* (New York: Oxford University Press, 1941), p. 297.
10. *American Renaissance*, 298.
11. References to Hawthorne's work, unless otherwise noted, are to *The Complete Novels and Selected Tales of Nathaniel Hawthorne*, ed. Norman Holmes Pearson (New York, 1937).
12. Edgar Allan Poe, reviewing Hawthorne's *Twice-Told Tales* in Nov. 1847, recognized in "Wakefield" the working up of "an old idea—a well-known incident" (see "Hawthorne's Tales," *Shock of Recognition*, 166). In "Hawthorne's Literary Borrowings" (*PMLA*, 51 [June, 1936]), H. Arlin Turner points out that this incident is recounted in William King's *Political and Literary Anecdotes of His Own Times*, which was written around 1760 (555). Hawthorne may have been familiar with the second edition of this work published in London in 1819.
13. *The Phoenix and the Spider* (Cambridge: Harvard University Press, 1957), p. 28.
14. "The Antique Ring," *Complete Works of Nathaniel Hawthorne*, ed. G. P. Lathrop (Boston: Houghton Mifflin, 1883), XII,
15. *The Best Short Stories of Dostoevsky*, trans. David Magarshack (New York: Random House, n.d.), p. 107.
16. Preface to *The American*, in *Art of the Novel*, 37.
17. Edel and Powers, *Notebooks*, 312.
18. "Three Commentaries: Poe, James, and Joyce," *Sewanee Review*, LVIII (Winter, 1950), 5.

Chapter 7

1. Review of *The Siege of London*, *The Pension Beaurepas*, and *The Point of View*. *Boston Evening Transcript* (Feb. 23, 1883), p. 6.
2. *Hay-Howells Letters*, 66.
3. *The Letters of Mrs. Henry Adams 1865–1883*, ed. Ward Thoron (Boston: Little, Brown, 1936), p. 403. Incidentally, James sent Mrs. Adams a copy of the American edition of *The Siege of London*, inscribing it: "Marian Adams / from the author / Feb. 16, 1883."
4. "Fiction," *Literary World*, 14 (Mar. 24, 1883), 90.
5. "Recent American Fiction," *Atlantic Monthly*, 51 (May 1883), 707.
6. *Hay-Howells Letters*, 66.
7. "The Point of View," *Complete Tales*, IV, 509, 512. Subsequent quotations from this text are indicated in the text by page number.
8. "Personal," *New York Tribune* (Apr. 20, 1881), p. 4.
9. *Henry James Letters*, II, 412.
10. *Notebooks*, 15.
11. *Notebooks*, 101.
12. *Letters of Mrs. Henry Adams*, 320.
13. *Letters of Mrs. Henry Adams*, 493.
14. "Pandora," *New York Sun* (June 1, 1884), p. I:7, (June 8, 1884), p. I:7.
15. Quoted in Anna Robeson Burr, *Weir Mitchell, His Life and Letters* (New York: Duffield, 1929), p. 322.
16. George Washburn Smalley, "Mr. Henry James, Jr.—The Publishers," *New York Tribune* (Dec. 19, 1881), p. 6.
17. "Personal," *New York Tribune* (Feb. 28, 1882), p. 4.
18. *Letters of Mrs. Henry Adams*, 329.
19. Henry James is "very well meaning but very slow minded. 'Laborious' describes him I think, his manners and his conversation alike," reported one of John Hay's friends. Oscar Wilde, in contrast, "burst upon our view one

Sunday—tights—yellow silk handkerchief and all. He is the most gruesome object I ever saw, but he was very amusing. Full of Irish keenness and humor and really interesting…" (quoted in George Monteiro, "A Contemporary View of Henry James and Oscar Wilde, 1882," *American Literature*, 35 [Jan. 1964], 530).

20. *Life in Letters*, I, 271; "A New York Satire," *New York Tribune* (July 3, 1881), p. 8.

21. *Letters of Mrs. Henry Adams*, 241, 294.

22. "A New York Satire," *New York Tribune* (Sept. 13, 1880), p. 6.

23. "Literary Notes," *New York Tribune* (May 9, 1883), p. 6.

24. *Notebooks*, 56.

25. Review of *Daisy Miller*. *Nation*, 27 (Dec. 19, 1878), 387.

26. *The Nation, Volumes 1–105, New York, 1865–1917: Indexes of Titles and Contributors*, ed. Daniel C. Haskell (New York, 1951–1953), II, 390. (Incidentally, on page 85 of the first volume [*Index of Titles*] this review is mistakenly attributed to Mary E. Parkinson, a contributor to the journal at a much later date.) Mary Eliot (Dwight) Parkman (d. 1879), the wife of Dr. Samuel Parkman and the sister-in-law of the historian Francis Parkman, was a friend and Beverly Farms neighbor of Henry and "Clover" Adams. (See *Letters of Mrs. Henry Adams*, 110, 122, 165, 222; *Henry Adams and His Friends: A Collection of His Unpublished Letters*, ed. Harold Dean Cater [Boston, 1947], pp. 88–89; and Ernest Samuels, *Henry Adams: The Middle Years* [Cambridge: Harvard University Press, 1958], p. 47.) James is credited with the authorship of the review of *Macleod of Dare* in Leon Edel and Dan H. Laurence, *A Bibliography of Henry James* (London: Rupert Hart-Davis, 1957), p. 315.

27. The issue printing Mrs. Parkman on *Daisy Miller* and James on *Macleod of Dare* also carried an unsigned notice of Geraldine MacPherson's *Memoirs of Ann Jameson*, the first two paragraphs of which were written by James and the third (and last) by Mrs. Parkman (*Bibliography*, 315). In an earlier review Mrs. Parkman had predicted that when James's "works are brought out in 'blue-and-gold,' or in any form or hue, we trust that but small space will be allotted to *Watch and Ward*" ("Recent Novels," *Nation*, 27 [Aug. 22, 1878], 118).

28. "Pandora," *Complete Tales*, V, 361. Subsequent references to this edition are incorporated in the text.

29. *Notebooks*, 56.

30. Quoted in Edel, *Middle Years*, 166.

31. For "Clover" Adams's reaction to her "presence" in James's "The Point of View," see *Letters of Mrs. Henry Adams*, 403.

32. *The Letters of Henry Adams*, 6 vols., ed. J. C. Levenson, Ernest Samuels, Charles Vandersee, and Viola Hopkins Winner (Cambridge: Harvard University Press, 1982), II, 420–21.

33. For the New York Edition James revised Alfred Bonnycastle's statement to read: "Hang it, there's only a month left; let us be vulgar and have some fun—let us invite the President"—XVIII, 131). On James's revisions of the story, see Charles Vandersee, "James's 'Pandora': The Mixed Consequences of Revision," *Studies in Bibliography*, 21 (1968), 93–108; and on James's "Presidents," see Robert L. Gale, "'Pandora' and Her President," *Studies in Short Fiction*, 1 (Spring, 1964), 222–24.

34. *Letters of Henry Adams (1858–1891)*, ed. Worthington Chauncey Ford (Boston and New York, 1930), p. 302.

35. For day-to-day examples of Adams's largely unfavorable assessments of these historical figures, see *Letters of Henry Adams*, 284–85, 335, 355 (Hamilton); 278, 284, 323, 335, 338 (Jefferson); 285, 325, 335, 341, 344, 345 (Burr); 338, 341 (Randolph); and Samuels, *Middle Years*, 215, 264 *et passim* (Madison).

36. "Literary Notes," *New York Tribune* (July 9, 1884), p. 6; "Recent Fiction," *The Independent*, 27 (Apr. 9, 1885), 459; and "Fiction," *The Literary World*, 16 (Mar. 21, 1885), 102.

37. Lilian Whiting, "Life at the Hub," Chicago *Daily Inter Ocean* (Nov. 26, 1887), p. 12.

38. The exception that proves the rule is offered by Peter Buitenhuis. Although he calls "Pandora" "a fanciful story," he finds it to be "nonetheless a significant exemplum of American experience. It gave him [James] an opportunity to analyze some aspects of social life and politics in a way which may seem ephemeral on the surface but which in fact cuts deeply into the facts of post–Civil War Washington reality"—*The Grasping Imagination: The American Writings of Henry James* (Toronto: University of Toronto Press, 1970), p. 125.

39. *Henry James Letters*, III, 74, 111; quoted in Arline Boucher Tehan, *Henry Adams in Love: The Pursuit of Elizabeth Sherman Cameron* (Garden City: Hanover House, 1962), p. 89; Edel, *Middle Years*, 167.

40. References to the United States as "the Great Republic" were not always hostile. Robert Louis Stevenson, for example, complimented James: "your little boy [in "The Pupil"] is admirable; why is there no little boy like that unless he hails from the Great Republic?" (quoted in Janet Adam Smith, *Henry James and Robert Louis Stevenson: A Record of Friendship and Criticism* [London: Rupert Hart-Davis, 1948], p. 210).

41. Sir Lepel Henry Griffin, *The Great Republic* (New York: Scribner's and Welford, 1884), pp. 8–9. See also his essay, "A Visit to Philistia," *Fortnightly Review* (Jan. 1884), 35: 50–64.

42. John Kendrick Bangs, "Literary Notes," *Harper's Magazine* (May 1895), 98: 1002; Goldwin Smith, "The Hatred of England," *North American Review* (May 1890), 150: 555.

43. Henry James, "Two Countries," *Harper's Magazine* (June 1888), 77: 83–116; as "The Modern Warning," in *The Aspern Papers [,] Louisa Pallant [,] The Modern Warning* (London and New York: Macmillan, 1888).

44. *Notebooks*, 29–30.

45. "Two Countries," 91.

46. "Two Countries," 49.

47. "Two Countries," 97.

48. "Two Countries," 97.

49. Henry James, "Paris Revisited," *The Galaxy* (Jan. 1878), 25: 5–13; reprinted as "Occasional Paris," in *The Art of Travel: Scenes and Journeys in America, England, France and Italy from the Travel Writings of Henry James*, ed. Morton Dauwen Zabel (Garden City, New York: Doubleday, 1958), pp. 213–29. Quotation from p. 213 of Zabel's collection.

50. Matthew Arnold, "Civilisation in the United States," *Nineteenth Century* (Apr. 1888), 23: 491. See also Arnold's earlier essays in *Nineteenth Century*, "A Word About America" (May 1882, 11: 680–96) and "A Word More About America" (Feb. 1885, 17: 219–36), along with Henry James, "Matthew Arnold," *English Illustrated Magazine* (Jan. 1884), 241–46.

51. See Linda J. Taylor, *Henry James, 1866–1916: A Reference Guide* (Boston: G. K. Hall, 1982), items, in 1888, 10. (*Portland Morning Oregonian*), 54. (*New York Tribune*), 63. (*The Literary World*), 68. (*New York Times*), 71. (*Hartford Courant*), and, in 1889, 1. (*Critic*).

52. James, *American*, 103; [Review.] *Scottish Review* (Apr. 1889), 13: 448 (reprinted in *Contemporary Reviews*, 217).

53. [Review.] *Life* (July 26, 1888), 12: 48.

54. S. Gorley Putt, *Henry James: A Reader's Guide*, intr. Arthur Mizener (Ithaca: Cornell University Press, 1967), p. 129.

55. *Notebooks*, 38.

56. "Minor Notices: *The Aspern Papers*," *The Literary World* (Dec. 8, 1888), 19: 451. See also the *Saturday Review, Academy, New York Tribune, Critic*, and *Scottish Review*–collected in *Contemporary Reviews*, 211–13, 216–17.

57. William Dean Howells, "Editor's Study," *Harper's New Monthly* (Oct. 1888), 77: 799–800; "Current Literature," *San Francisco Bulletin* (Jan. 12, 1889), p. 5.

58. Henry James, "An International Episode," *Complete Tales*, IV, 265–66.

59. Constance Rourke, *American Humor: A Study of the National Character* (Garden City: Doubleday, 1953), pp. 190–91.

60. *Letters of Mrs. Henry Adams*, 384.

Chapter 8

1. *The Letters of Katherine Mansfield*, ed. J. Middleton Murry (New York: Knopf, 1932), p. 355.

2. Robert L. Gale, "A Note on Henry James's 'The Real Thing,'" *Studies in Short Fiction*, 1:65–66 (Fall 1963). Its magazine publication reads: "in those days there were not so many serious workers in black and white" (p. 247); in the New York Edition, which is what Gale quotes, the text reads "in those days there were few serious workers in black-and-white" (p. 330) In both instances, he means that later there were serious workers in black and white but not back then. In 1892 *Black and White* was only in its third volume. Gale does not quote the opening phrase "in those days."

3. "The Real Thing," *Complete Tales*, VIII, 231.

4. In an early 1990s reading Bruce Henricksen writes: "In discussing 'The Real Thing' I argued that the narrator's unconscious desire to be rid of the Monarchs precedes and in fact produces the distorted drawings that become his excuse for firing them. In saying that this illustrates Lacan's argument for the ethical status of the unconscious, I conflated the ethical and the ideological, since my point was that the narrator was acting as a relay for a transindividual power mechanism" ("'The Real Thing': Criticism and the Ethical Turn," *Papers on Language and Literature*, 27 [Fall 1991], 473–95). Quotation from p. 490. Most readers would take James's conscious point in the

story to be at once both more direct and more nuanced than Henricksen's reading will allow. Similarly, they would find limitations in those earlier readings of "The Real Thing" in the 1960s and 1970s that zeroed in on James's having decided to tell his story from the point of view of an unreliable narrator. See, for example, David Toor, "Narrative Irony in Henry James' 'The Real Thing,'" *University Review*, 34:95–99 (Winter 1967); M. D. Uroff, "Perception in James's 'The Real Thing," *Studies in Short Fiction*, 9:41–46 (Winter 1972); and Ronald L. Lycette, "Perceptual Touchstones for the Jamesian Artist-Hero," *Studies in Short Fiction*, 14:55–62 (Winter 1977). James's story is interpreted within the context of a continuing public debate over art and realism in Martha Banta, "Artists, Models, Real Things, and Recognizable Types," *Studies in the Literary Imagination*, 16:7–34 (Fall 1983). For an interpretation of how James's story works as a system of signs and referents, in which the Monarchs are characterized as a "metonymy trying to pass for a metaphor," see Moshe Ron, "A Reading of 'The Real Thing,'" *Yale French Studies*, 58 (1979), 190–212.

5. "The Real Thing," *Complete Tales*, VIII, 249.

Chapter 9

1. *Henry James Letters*, III, 194.
2. *Henry James Letters*, III, 308.
3. *Selected Fiction*, 480.
4. *Complete Tales*, VII, 12.
5. Leon Edel, *Henry James: The Treacherous Years: 1895–1901* (Philadelphia and New York: Lippincott, 1969), p. 100.
6. *Henry James Letters*, III, 301–302, 307–308, and 338–339.
7. Houghton Mifflin Letter-Book (2) [12 Feb. 1890–17 Oct. 1890]; Letter-Book (3) [18 Oct. 1890–8 June 1891]; quoted with the permission of Houghton Mifflin.
8. Ellen B. Ballou's transcription of Horace E. Scudder's manuscript diary..
9. Ellen B. Ballou, "Scudder's *Atlantic*," *Harvard Library Bulletin* (Oct. 1968), 16: 339.

Chapter 10

1. T. S. Eliot, "Sweeney Among the Nightingales," in *Complete Poems and Plays* (New York: Harcourt, Brace, 1952), p. 35.
2. *Bibliography*, 360.
3. "Travels in Portugal," *The Nation* (Oct. 21, 1875), 21: 264–65. "John Latouche" is a pseudonym for Oswald Crawfurd. Curiously, in the story "Four Meetings" (1877) James assigns the name Latouche to his narrator's traveling friend, who takes him to visit his mother in New England.
4. *The Portrait of a Lady* (New York Edition), IV, 39.
5. *The Ambassadors*, ed. Leon Edel (Boston: Houghton Mifflin, 1960), p. 127.
6. *Ambassadors*, 127.
7. See H. L. Mencken, *The American Language*, 4th ed. (New York: Knopf, 1937), p. 461. "Portugee" is one of Mencken's examples, along with "Chinee" and "Japanee." In Thomas Wentworth Higginson's 1867 story, "The Haunted Window," the young boy of Bavarian and Portuguese parentage speaks of "Portegee" and "Portegees," while his immigrant mother identifies herself as "Portuguese" (*Atlantic Monthly* [Apr. 1867], 19: 434).
8. See A. A. Roback, *A Dictionary of International Slurs (Ethnophaulisms)* (Cambridge, MA: Sci-Art Publishers, 1944), p. 59.
9. Donald E. Ericson, "Preface," *The Portuguese Letters: Love Letters of a Nun to a French Officer*, 3rd ed. (New York: Bennett-Edwards, 1986), p. 10.
10. "Travels in Portugal," 264.
11. Mark Twain, *The Innocents Abroad*, intr. Edward Wagenknecht (New York: Heritage Press, 1962), p. 30.
12. *Hawthorne*, 42–43.
13. W. D. Howells, "James's Hawthorne," *Atlantic Monthly* (Feb. 1880), 45: 282–85; reprinted in *Discovery of a Genius: William Dean Howells and Henry James*, ed. Albert Mordell (New York: Twayne, 1961), pp. 92–97. Quotation is from the latter (p. 96).
14. *Henry James Letters*, II, 266–67.
15. Edel and Powers, *Notebooks*, 28.
16. Henry James, "Preface," *The Aspern Papers[,] The Turn of the Screw[,] "The Liar[,]" and "The Two Faces"* (New York Edition), XII, xxiii-xxiv. In *Henry James: A Critical Study* (London: Martin Seeker, 1913) Ford Madox Hueffer quotes the same paragraph from James's preface to illustrate the Master's fictional "methods." Perhaps it is Hueffer's use of James's statement of the "germ" for "The Liar" that prompts Leon Edel to see in the character of the romancing Colonel Capadose the invention of Hueffer "long before" James "met him" in 1895 (*The Life of Henry James* [Hammondsworth: Penguin Books, 1977], II, 387). See also Joseph Wiesenfarth, "Henry James

and Ford Madox Ford: A Troubled Relationship," *Henry James Review* (Spring 1992), 13: 175.

17. Quoted in Bertram Brewster, "The Capadose Family," in Isaac da Costa, *Noble Families Among the Sephardic Jews* (London: Oxford University Press, 1936), p. 187, note 1. The original of this letter seems not to have survived. The text as given in *Noble Families* is the basis for the text in *Henry James Letters,* IV, 89.

18. "Capadose Family," 187.
19. "Capadose Family," 186.
20. "Capadose Family," 187.
21. "The Liar," 343.
22. Cecil Roth, "An Excursus on the History of the Capadose Family," in *Noble Families,* 181.
23. "Travels in Portugal," 265.
24. "Capadose Family," 163.
25. On James's anti–Semitism and his views on race, see Leo B. Levy, "Henry James and the Jews," *Commentary* (Sept. 1958), 26: 243–49, and Elsa Nettels, "Henry James and the Idea of Race," *English Studies* (Feb. 1978), 59: 35–47. Neither of these studies makes reference to "The Liar" or Colonel Capadose.
26. "Excursus," 189.
27. Introduction to *The Mirror of the New Christians (Espelho de Cristãos Novos) of Francisco Machado,* ed., trans., and intr. by Mildred Evelyn Vieira and Frank Ephraim Talmage (Toronto: Pontifical Institute of Mediaeval Studies, 1977), pp. 15–16.
28. Recent scholars have differed sharply over the nature and extent of the religious beliefs and commitment of the New Christians. One school, whose strong advocate is A. J. Saraiva (*A Inquisição Portuguesa,* 1956), maintains that the judaizing of the New Christians was a fabrication of the Inquisition: since these "converts" are to be identified in the main with the well-to-do middle class, the Inquisition, supported by the State, wished to eliminate them and confiscate their wealth. The other view, advanced by I. S. Réah ["Les Marranes," *Revue des Juives* (1959), 118: 27–77] and reaffirmed by Y. H. Yerushalmi ["Prolegomenon" to *History of the Origin and Establishment of the Inquisition in Portugal* by A. Herculano (1972, New York photoprint of 1936 Stanford edition)], insists on "the essential reality of the Judaism—or at least the judaizing—of most of the New Christians of Portugal" (*Mirror,* 16).
29. "Capadose Family," 187, note 1.

30. "Capadose Family," 165. The original reads:
Gallardo Abraham
Capadoce Galan de la Ley bendita,
a la ciencia galantea
com gala, y galanteria

31. See Judith E. Funston, "James's Portrait of the Artist as Liar," *Studies in Short Fiction* (Fall 1989), 26: 431–38, as well as Ora Segal, *The Lucid Reflector: The Observer in Henry James' Fiction* (New Haven: Yale University Press, 1969), pp. 93–106.

32. *Letters of Henry Adams,* III, 113. The editors gloss this statement: "In Henry James's 'The Liar,' the narrator detests a habitual but harmless teller of lies and wonders if the liar's wife condones the lies or masks an aversion" (113, n. 5).

33. "The Liar," 323.
34. "Excursus," 189.
35. "The Liar," 350.
36. "The Liar," 374.
37. In "A Note on The Liar," in *Selected Short Stories of Henry James,* ed. Clifton Fadiman (New York: Random House, 1945), p. 186. Fadiman writes: "A final note—the point on which the action hinges—the narrator's ability to expose in oils the true character of Capadose is, I am assured by a competent portrait painter of my acquaintance, quite implausible. It is interesting, however, to reflect on how little this admitted improbability, or impossibility, detracts from the value of the story." It is also possible that James's use of the motif of the "revealing" portrait derives from Nathaniel Hawthorne's use of it in "The Prophetic Pictures" and in *The House of the Seven Gables;* see F. O. Matthiessen, "James and the Plastic Arts," *Kenyon Review* (Winter 1943), 5: 35; Robert J. Kane, "Hawthorne's 'The Prophetic Pictures' and James's 'The Liar,'" *Modern Language Notes* (Apr. 1950), 65: 257–58; and Edward Rosenberry, "James' Use of Hawthorne in 'The Liar,'" *Modern Language Notes* (Mar. 1961), 76: 234–38.
38. "Capadose Family," 182.
39. Ezra Pound, "Henry James," in *Instigations of Ezra Pound* (Freeport, NY: Books for Libraries Press, 1967, p. 142). Pound's essay was first published in the *Little Review* in 1918.

Chapter 11

1. Edgar Allan Poe, "The Purloined Letter," in *Short Fiction,* p. 231.
2. *French Side,* 167.

3. Henry James, "Preface," *The Spoils of Poynton* (New York Edition), X, vii.
4. May Sinclair, "The Reputation of Ezra Pound," *North American Review* (May 1920), 211: 659.
5. *Spoils*, X, 24. Further quotations refer to this edition and are indicated parenthetically by page number in the body of this chapter.
6. "Books and Authors," *Outlook* (Feb. 27, 1897), 55: 610.
7. "Mr. James's Latest Tendency," *The Chap-Book* (Feb. 15, 1897), 6: 296.
8. *The Literary World* (Apr. 17, 1897), 26: 126–27.

Chapter 12

1. There are names that recall earlier names. For instance, "Strether" in *The Ambassadors* plays off "Marcher" in "The Beast in the Jungle," which, in turn, recalls "Archer" of *The Portrait of a Lady*. James was wont to compile lists of names that caught his fancy and might be used in some future piece of fiction. See, for example, *Complete Notebooks*, 32, 57, 60 et passim.
2. *Webster's New World Dictionary of the American Language*, Second College Edition (New York: Simon and Schuster, 1980).
3. Henry James, "Preface," *Novels and Tales*, XII, v-xxiv.
4. Jeremy Tambling, "Henry James's American Byron," *Henry James Review*, 20 (Winter 1999), 43–50.
5. *Aspern Papers*, *Novels and Tales*, XII, 48. Subsequent references are indicated in the text by page numbers.
6. Adeline R. Tintner, *The Book World of Henry James: Appropriating the Classics* (Ann Arbor: UMI Research Press, 1987), p. 95.
7. William Veeder, "The Aspern Portrait," *Henry James Review*, 20 (Winter 1999), 39.
8. Hays, *Contemporary Reviews*, 217.
9. *Henry James Letters*, IV, 541.

Chapter 13

1. This letter is in the collections of the Harry Ransom Humanities Research Center, University of Texas at Austin, and is published with consent.
2. [Edward Garnett], "As Subtle as Life," *The Outlook*, 3 (10 June 1899), 620.
3. Further references to Ford Madox Hueffer's 1914 study of James appear in the text. Hueffer also refers to James's "figure in the carpet" in *Thus to Revisit: Some Reminiscences* (New York: Dutton, 1921). There he writes: "I dare say, if we could only perceive it, Life has a pattern. I don't mean that of birth, apogee, and death, but a woven symbolism of its own. The Pattern in the Carpet, Henry James called it—and that he saw something of the worth was no doubt the secret of his magic" (p. 46). And in a discussion of Stephen Crane's friendship with James, he writes: "[Crane] gave you the pattern in—and the reverse of—the carpet in physical life" (p. 119).
4. *The Letters of Henry James*, ed. Percy Lubbock, 2 vols. (New York: Scribner's, 1920), I, 333.
5. Henry James, Preface," *The Awkward Age*, (New York Edition), IX, xviii. Further references to this work appear numerically in the text.
6. In *The Autobiography of Alice B. Toklas* (New York: Harcourt, Brace and Co., 1933), Gertrude Stein confesses: "When I was about nineteen years of age I was a great admirer of Henry James. I felt that *The Awkward Age* would make a very remarkable play and I wrote to Henry James suggesting that I dramatise it. I had from him a delightful letter on the subject and then, when I felt my inadequacy, rather blushed for myself and did not keep the letter" (3–4). For a discussion of what Thornton Wilder did with James's hint that *The Awkward Age* had the structure of a play, see Lyall H. Powers, "Thornton Wilder as Literary Cubist: An Acknowledged Debt to Henry James," *Henry James Review*, 7 (1985), 34–44.
7. *Awkward Age*, 358.
8. Preface, *Awkward Age*, vii.
9. See *Henry James and Edith Wharton: Letters: 1900–1915*, ed. Lyall H. Powers (New York: Scribner's 1990), p. 103, n. 3.
10. Leon Edel, *Henry James: The Master, 1901–1916* (Philadelphia and New York: Lippincott, 1972), p. 372.

Chapter 14

1. *The Master*, 501.
2. *Notebooks*, 88.
3. *Notebooks*, 169.
4. *Notebooks*, 179.
5. "A Round of Visits," *Complete Tales*, XII, 430.
6. "Introduction: 1903–1910," *Complete Tales*, XII, 8.
7. *Complete Tales*, XII, 432, 433, 434.

8. "Henry James' Double," *San Jose Sunday Mercury and Herald* (June 25, 1905), p. 20.
9. Quoted in Edel, "Introduction: 1903–1910," *Complete Tales*, XII, 9.

Chapter 15

1. *The Labyrinth*, ed. S. H. Hooke (London: Society for Promoting Christian Knowledge, 1935), p. 42.
2. *Tanglewood Tales* (Boston: James R. Osgood, 1876), p. 44.
3. "Venice," *Century Magazine*, 25 (Nov. 1882), 3–23.
4. *Henry James Letters*, II, 392.
5. *Henry James Letters*, III, 547.
6. *Henry James Letters*, III, 548 and 550.
7. "Henry James, Jr.," *Century Magazine*, 25 (Nov. 1882), 25–29.
8. *Henry James Letters*, II, 391.
9. Howells, "Henry James, Jr.," 28.
10. *Henry James Letters*, II, 392.
11. Frank R. Stockton, "The Lady, or the Tiger?" *Century Magazine*, 25 (Nov. 1882), 83–86.
12. "Inception," 532.
13. *Selected Fiction*, 497, hereafter cited parenthetically as "B."
14. "The Lady or the Tiger?" in *Stories I, The Novels and Stories of Frank R. Stockton* (New York: Scribner's, 1900), p. 3, hereafter cited parenthetically as "L."
15. Stockton insisted that he himself did not know the answer. See Walter L. Pforzheimer, "The Lady, The Tiger and the Author," *Colophon*, n.s, 1 (Autumn 1935), 261–70.
16. *Notebooks*, 182–83.
17. *Notebooks*, 311.
18. Sylvia L. Horwitz, *The Find of a Lifetime: Sir Arthur Evans and the Discovery of Knossos* (New York: Viking, 1981), p. 6.
19. *Find of a Lifetime*, 1.
20. *Henry James Letters*, I, 4.
21. Walter Pater, *The Renaissance: Studies in Art and Poetry* (London: Macmillan, 1910), pp. 238–39.
22. *Notebooks*, 183–239.
23. *Renaissance*, 236.
24. *Art of the Novel*, 247. On Pater's influence on James, see Adeline R. Tintner's "Henry James's Mona Lisa," *Essays in Literature*, 8 (Spring 1981), 105–08, and "Pater in *The Portrait of a Lady* and *The Golden Bowl*, Including Some Unpublished Henry James Letters," *Henry James Review*, 3 (Winter 1982), 80–95.
25. "Introduction: 1900–1903," *Complete Tales*, XI, 10.
26. See *Middle Years*, 356–77. So central to James's biography did Edel find the Woolson/James relationship that while he entitled this volume *The Middle Years*, he did so "with the distinct feeling that they [its pages] had, all the while, still another, a hidden title—*The Beast in the Jungle*" (p. 18).
27. These essays were collected in *Mentone, Cairo, and Corfu*, published posthumously in 1896.
28. Constance Fenimore Woolson's letters to James, 1882–1883, are published in an appendix to *Henry James Letters*, III, 525–61.
29. "'Always, Your Attached Friend': The Unpublished Letters of Constance Fenimore Woolson to John and Clara Hay," ed. Alice Hall Petry, *Books at Brown*, 29–30 (1982–1983), 102–03.
30. Quoted in George Monteiro, *Henry James and John Hay: The Record of a Friendship* (Providence: Brown University Press, 1965), p. 182.
31. *Art of the Novel*, p. 246.
32. *Henry James Letters*, III, 550.
33. *Notebooks*, 226.
34. Quoted in *Notebooks*, 228.
35. *Henry James Letters*, III, 511.
36. Quoted in *Notebooks*, 228.
37. *Henry James Letters*, III, 283.

Chapter 16

1. *The Correspondence of Henry James and Henry Adams 1877–1914*, ed. George Monteiro (Baton Rouge: Louisiana State University Press, 1992), p. 33.
2. Of Machiavelli, Adams wrote: "Education founded on mere self-interest was merely Guelph and Ghibelline over again—Machiavelli translated into American"— *The Education of Henry Adams*, ed. Ernest Samuels and Jayne N. Samuels (Boston: Houghton Mifflin, 1973), p. 85.
3. *Henry James Letters*, II, 110–11.
4. *Henry James Letters*, II, 125–26.
5. *Letters of Henry Adams*, II, 448.
6. *Ccorrespondence of James and Adams*, 42
7. *The Education*, 228–29.
8. "Abbeys and Castles," *Lippincott's Magazine* (Oct. 1877), 20:434–42.
9. *Letters of Henry Adams*, II, 344.
10. *Letters of Henry Adams*, II, 515.
11. *Letters of Henry Adams*, II, 512–13.
12. *Letters of Henry Adams*, III, 113.

13. "The Liar," *Complete Tales*, VI, 408–09.
14. *The Education*, 180.
15. *The Education*, 164.
16. *The Education*, 151.
17. *The Education*, 167, 170.
18. *Letters of Henry Adams (1892–1918)*, ed. Worthington Chauncey Ford (Boston: Houghton Mifflin, 1938), p. 333.
19. "The Liar," 383, 396; *The Sacred Fount*, intr. Leon Edel (New York: Grove Press, 1953), p. 98.
20. *Sacred Fount*, 23.
21. *Letters of Henry Adams (1892–1918)*, 490.
22. *Correspondence of James and Adams*, 73.
23. *Correspondence of James and Adams*, 74.
24. *The Education*, 163.
25. Quoted in Ernest Samuels, *Henry Adams: The Major Phase* (Cambridge: Harvard University Press, 1964), p. 338.
26. *Correspondence of James and Adams*, 69–70.
27. *Letters of Henry Adams (1892–1918)*, 622.
28. *The Education*, 209.

Chapter 17

1. The Decker and Wasser papers were read at "Henry Adams and the Need to Know," a conference sponsored by the Massachusetts Historical Society, Boston, Massachusetts, in May 2001. "A Martyr to the Disease of Omniscience," an expanded version of William Merrill Decker's paper, appears in *Henry Adams & the Need to Know*, ed. William Merrill Decker and Earl N. Harbert (Boston: Massachusetts Historical Society, 2005), pp. 315–44.
2. *Letters of Henry Adams*, VI, 638.
3. *Correspondence of James and Adams*, pp. 88–89.
4. *Correspondence of James and Adams*, p. 69.
5. T. S. Eliot, "Henry James," *The Little Review* (Aug., 1918), in *Shock of Recognition*, 856.
6. R. P. Blackmur, *Henry Adams*, ed. Veronica Makowsky (New York and London: Harcourt, Brace Jovanovich, 1980), p. 316.
7. Quoted in *James and Hay*, 4–5.

Chapter 18

1. L. W., "Concerning Kettledrums," *Lippincott's Magazine*, 23 (Mar. 1879), 384, 383. Emphasis added.
2. "Preface," *Novels and Tales*, XVIII, vi.
3. F. W. Dupee, *Henry James* (Garden City: William Morrow, 1956), pp. 94–95.
4. *Hawthorne*, ed. Tony Tanner (London: Macmillan / New York: St. Martin's, 1967), p. 55.
5. "The Trotting at Cleveland To-Day," New York *Times*, July 25, 1876, p. 1; see also "Races at Pittsburg," New York *Times*, July 18, 1877, p. 5; and "Events on the Trotting Courses," New York *Times*, July 19, 1877, p. 5. The name "Daisy Miller" shows up as well in the lineage of a different horse ("Trotters Go at Auction," New York *Times*, Mar. 4, 1897, p. 11).

Chapter 19

1. Marius Bewley, *The Complex Fate: Hawthorne, Henry James and Some Other American Writers*, 2d ed. (New York: Gordian, 1967), p. 39.
2. "My heart is sore pained within me; and the terrors of death are fallen upon me / Fearfulness and trembling are come upon me, and horror hath overwhelmed me. / And I said, Oh that I had wings like a dove! for then would I fly away, and be at rest" (Psalms 55:6).
3. James, *Hawthorne*, in Wilson, *Shock of Recognition*, 554.
4. James, *Hawthorne*, 476.

Chapter 20

1. Quoted in Peter Coveney, *The Image of Childhood: The Individual and Society: A Study of the Theme in English Literature*, rev. ed., intr. F. R. Leavis (Baltimore, Maryland: Penguin Books, 1967), p. 399. Originally published as *Poor Monkey* (1957).
2. *The Poetical Works of Wordsworth*, ed. Thomas Hutchinson, rev. ed. Ernest de Selincourt (London: Oxford University Press, 1960), p. 461.
3. E. E. Cummings, *Poems: 1923–1954* (New York: Harcourt, Brace, 1954), p. 370.
4. Mark Twain, *Adventures of Huckleberry Finn*, ed. Henry Nash Smith (Boston: Houghton Mifflin, 1958), p. 85.
5. *The Poetical Works of Longfellow*, intr. George Monteiro (Boston: Houghton Mifflin, 1975), p. 201.

Chapter 21

1. "Henry James the Elder," New York *Times*, Jan. 25, 1885, p. 4.

2. See, respectively, Edel, *Conquest of London*, 397–98, and Alfred Habegger, *The Father: A Life of Henry James, Sr.* (New York: Farrar, Straus and Giroux, 1994), p. 44. James recorded Mrs. Kemble's gossip in his *Notebooks* (pp. 12–13).
 3. *The Father*, 46.
 4. *The Father*, 46.
 5. *The Father*, 351.
 6. Henry James, *Washington Square*, intr. Clifton Fadiman (New York: Modern Library, 1950), p. 33. All subsequent page references to this edition appear in the text within parentheses.
 7. *Henry James Letters*, II, 316. Perhaps William's suspicions were stoked by Dr. Sloper's observation that "people are not always so fond of their brothers" (105).
 8. "New Publications," Philadelphia *Public Ledger and Daily Transcript*, Dec. 4, 1880), Supplement, p. 2; quoted in Taylor, *Reference Guide*, p. 53.

Bibliography

Adams, Henry. *The Education of Henry Adams.* Ed. Ernest Samuels and Jayne N. Samuels. Boston: Houghton Mifflin, 1973.

———. *Henry Adams and His Friends: A Collection of His Unpublished Letters.* Ed. Harold Dean Cater. Boston: Houghton Mifflin, 1947.

———. *Letters of Henry Adams (1858–1891).* Ed. Worthington Chauncey Ford. Boston: Houghton Mifflin, 1930.

———. *Letters of Henry Adams (1892–1918).* Ed. Worthington Chauncey Ford. Boston: Houghton Mifflin, 1938.

———. *The Letters of Henry Adams*, 6 vols. Ed. J. C. Levenson, Ernest Samuels, Charles Vandersee, and Viola Hopkins Winner. Cambridge: Harvard University Press, 1982.

Allen, Gay Wilson. *William James.* New York: Viking, 1967.

Anesko, Michael. *Letters, Fictions, Lives: Henry James and William Dean Howells.* New York: Oxford University Press, 1997.

Arnold, Matthew. "Civilisation in the United States." *Nineteenth Century* (Apr. 1888), 23: 491.

———. "A Word More About America." *Nineteenth Century*, 11 (May 1882), 680–96, and 17 (Feb. 1885), 219–36.

Ballou, Ellen B. "Scudder's *Atlantic.*" *Harvard Library Bulletin* (Oct. 1968), 16:326–53.

———. Unpublished transcription of Horace E. Scudder's diary.

Bangs, John Kendrick. "Literary Notes," *Harper's Magazine* (May 1895), 98: 1002.

Banta, Martha. "Artists, Models, Real Things, and Recognizable Types." *Studies in the Literary Imagination*, 16: 7–34 (Fall 1983).

Bewley, Marius. *The Complex Fate: Hawthorne, Henry James and Some Other American Writers*, 2d ed. New York: Gordian, 1967.

Blackmur, R. P. *Henry Adams.* Ed. Veronica Makowsky. New York and London: Harcourt, Brace Jovanovich, 1980.

"Books and Authors." *Outlook* (Feb. 27, 1897), 55: 610.

Brewster, Bertram. "The Capadose Family." In Isaac da Costa, *Noble Families Among the Sephardic Jews.* London: Oxford University Press, 1936.

Buitenhuis, Peter. *The Grasping Imagination: The American Writings of Henry James.* Toronto: University of Toronto Press, 1970.

Burr, Anna Robeson. *Weir Mitchell, His Life and Letters.* New York: Duffield, 1929.

Butterfield, L. H. "The Papers of the Adams Family: Some Account of Their History," *Proceedings of Massachusetts Historical Society*, 71 (Boston: Published by the Society, 1959), 328–56.

Canfield, Owen. "A Busy Day at the Archives." *Hartford Courant* Oct. 28, 1994), p. E1.

Cargill, Oscar. *The Novels of Henry James.* New York: Macmillan, 1961.

Ciardi, John. "Wallace Stevens' 'Absolute Music,'" *The Nation*, 179 (Oct. 16, 1954): 346–47.

Coveney, Peter. *The Image of Childhood: The Individual and Society: A Study of the Theme in English Literature.* Rev. ed., intr. F. R. Leavis. Baltimore: Penguin, 1967.

Cummings, E. E. *Poems: 1923–1954.* New York: Harcourt, Brace, 1954.

"Current Literature [*The American*]." *The Galaxy* (July 1877), 24:135–38.

"Current Literature." *San Francisco Bulletin* (Jan. 12, 1889), p. 5.

D'Avanzo, Mario L. "James's 'Maud-Evelyn': Source, Allusion, and Meaning." *Iowa English Yearbook*, 13 (Fall, 1968), 24–33.

Decker, William Merrill, and Earl N. Harbert, eds. *Henry Adams & the Need to Know*. Boston: Massachusetts Historical Society, 2005.

DeVane, William C. *A Browning Handbook*. 2nd ed. New York: Appleton-Century-Crofts, 1955.

_____. "The Virgin and the Dragon." In Drew, *Robert Browning: A Collection of Critical Essays*, pp. 96–109.

Dostoyevsky, Fyodor. *The Best Short Stories of Dostoyevsky*. Trans. David Magarshack. New York: Random House, n.d.

Dowson, Ernest. *The Letters of Ernest Dowson*. Ed. Desmond Flower and Henry Maas. London: Cassell, 1967.

Doyle, Charles, ed. *Wallace Stevens: The Critical Heritage*. London: Routledge & Kegan Paul, 1985.

Drabble, Margaret. *The Realms of Gold*. New York: Knopf, 1975.

Drew, Philip. *The Poetry of Browning: A Critical Introduction*. London: Methuen, 1970.

_____. ed., *Robert Browning: A Collection of Critical Essays*. Boston: Houghton Mifflin, 1966, pp. 96–109.

Dupee, F. W. *Henry James*. Garden City: William Morrow, 1956.

_____. Ed. *Henry James: Autobiography*. New York: Criterion Books, 1956.

Edel, Leon. *Henry James: The Conquest of London: 1870–1881*. Philadelphia and New York: Lippincott, 1962.

_____. *Henry James: The Middle Years, 1882–1895*. Philadelphia and New York: Lippincott, 1962.

_____. *Henry James: The Treacherous Years: 1895–1901*. Philadelphia and New York: Lippincott, 1969.

_____. *Henry James: The Master, 1901–1916*. Philadelphia and New York: Lippincott, 1972.

_____. *The Life of Henry James*. 2 vols. Hammondsworth: Penguin Books, 1977.

Edel, Leon, and Dan H. Laurence. *A Bibliography of Henry James*. London, Rupert Hart-Davis, 1957.

[Editorial Note]. *The Nation* (Jan. 11,1877), p. 29.

Eliot, T. S. "Henry James." *The Little Review* (Aug., 1918). In Wilson, *Shock of Recognition*, pp. 854–65.

_____. "Sweeney Among the Nightingales." In *Complete Poems and Plays*. New York: Harcourt, Brace, 1952. P. 35.

Ericson, Donald E."Preface." *The Portuguese Letters: Love Letters of a Nun to a French Officer*, 3rd ed. New York: Bennett-Edwards, 1986.

"Events on the Trotting Courses." *New York Times*, July 19, 1877, p. 5.

Fadiman, Clifton. "A Note on The Liar," in *Selected Short Stories of Henry James*. Ed. Clifton Fadiman. New York: Random House, 1945.

"Fiction." *The Literary World*, 14 (Mar. 24, 1883), 90.

"Fiction." *The Literary World*, 16 (Mar. 21, 1885), 102.

Flaubert, Gustave. *Flaubert Oeuvres*. Pléiade Edition. Ed. A. Thibaudet and R. Dumesnil. Paris: Gallimard, 1952.

_____. *A Sentimental Education: The Story of a Young Man*. Trans., intr., and notes by Douglas Parmée. Oxford: Oxford University Press, 1989.

Funston, Judith E. "James's Portrait of the Artist as Liar." *Studies in Short Fiction* (Fall 1989), 26: 431–38.

Fussell, Edwin Sill. *The French Side of Henry James*. New York: Columbia University Press, 1990.

Gale, Robert L. *A Henry James Encyclopedia*. New York: Greenwood, 1989.

_____. "A Note on Henry James's 'The Real Thing.'" *Studies in Short Fiction* (Fall 1963), 1: 65–66.

_____. "'Pandora' and Her President." *Studies in Short Fiction*, 1 (Spring, 1964), 222–24.

[Garnett, Edward]. "As Subtle as Life." *The Outlook*, 3 (June 10, 1899), 620.

Griffin, Sir Lepel Henry. *The Great Republic*. New York: Scribner's and Welford, 1884.

_____."A Visit to Philistia." *Fortnightly Review* (Jan. 1884), 35: 50–64.

Grover, Philip. *Henry James and the French Novel: A Study in Inspiration*. New York: Barnes & Noble, 1973.

Habegger, Alfred. *The Father: A Life of Henry James, Sr*. New York: Farrar, Straus and Giroux, 1994.

Haskel, Daniel C., ed. *The Nation, Volumes 1–105, New York, 1865–1917: Indexes of Titles and Contributors*, 2 vols. New York, 1951–1953.

Hawthorne, Nathaniel. *The American Notebooks*. Ed. Randall Stewart. New Haven: Yale University Press, 1932.

_____. "The Antique Ring," *Complete Works of Nathaniel Hawthorne*. 12 vols. Ed. G. P.

Lathrop. Boston and New York: Houghton Mifflin, 1883.

———. *The Complete Novels and Selected Tales of Nathaniel Hawthorne.* Ed. Norman Holmes Pearson. New York, 1937.

———. *Tanglewood Tales.* Boston: James R. Osgood, 1876.

Hay, John. "Kane and Abel," *Frank Leslie's Illustrated Newspaper*, Apr. 22, 1871, 281–93; Apr. 29, 1871, 106–07.

Hayes, Kevin J., ed. *Henry James: The Contemporary Reviews.* Cambridge: Cambridge University Press, 1996.

Henricksen, Bruce. "'The Real Thing': Criticism and the Ethical Turn," *Papers on Language and Literature*, 27 (Fall 1991), 473–95.

"Henry James' Double." San Jose *Sunday Mercury and Herald*, June 25, 1905, p. 20.

"Henry James the Elder." *New York Times*, Jan. 25, 1885, p. 4.

Higginson, Thomas Wentworth. "The Haunted Window." *Atlantic Monthly* (Apr. 1867), 19: 429–37.

Hoffman, D. G. *Form and Fable in American Fiction.* New York: Oxford University Press, 1961.

Hooke, S. H., ed. *The Labyrinth.* London: Society for Promoting Christian Knowledge, 1935.

Horne, Philip, ed. *Henry James: A Life in Letters.* New York: Viking, 1999.

Horwitz, Sylvia L. *The Find of a Lifetime: Sir Arthur Evans and the Discovery of Knossos.* New York: Viking, 1981.

Houghton Mifflin Letter-Book (2) [12 Feb. 1890–17 Oct. 1890].

Houghton Mifflin Letter-Book (3) [18 Oct. 1890–8 June 1891].

Howells, William Dean. "Editor's Study," *Harper's New Monthly* (Oct. 1888), 77: 799–800.

———. "Henry James, Jr.," *Century Magazine*, 25 (Nov. 1882), pp. 25–29.

———. "James's Hawthorne." *Atlantic Monthly* (Feb. 1880), 45: 282–85.

———. *Selected Letters*, 6 vols. Ed. Robert C. Leitz III and others. Boston: Twayne, 1980–83.

Hueffer, Ford Madox [Ford, Ford Madox]. *Henry James: A Critical Study.* London: Martin Seeker, 1913.

———. *Thus to Revisit: Some Reminiscences.* New York: Dutton, 1921.

James, Henry. "Abbeys and Castles." *Lippincott's Magazine* (Oct. 1877), 20: 434–42.

———. *The Ambassadors.* Ed. Leon Edel. Boston: Houghton Mifflin, 1960.

———. *The American.* Boston: James R. Osgood, 1877.

———. *The American* (Norton Critical Edition), Ed. James W. Tuttleton. New York: Norton, 1978.

———. *The American*, in *Complete Plays*.

———. "Americans Abroad." *The Nation* (Oct. 3, 1878), 208–09.

———. *The Art of the Novel.* Ed. R. P. Blackmur. New York: Scribner's, 1934.

———. "The Beast in the Jungle." *Henry James: Selected Fiction.* Ed. Leon Edel. New York, 1953, pp. 482–536.

———. "Browning in Westminster Abbey." *The Speaker*, 1 (Jan. 4, 1890), 10–12.

———. *The Complete Notebooks of Henry James.* Ed., intr., and notes by Leon Edel and Lyall H. Powers. New York: Oxford University Press, 1987.

———. *The Complete Plays of Henry James.* Ed. Leon Edel. Philadelphia and New York: Lippincott, 1949.

———. *Complete Tales of Henry James*, 12 vols. Ed. Leon Edel (Philadelphia and New York: Lippincott, 1962).

———. "Gustave Flaubert." In *Madame Bovary*. Trans. W. Blaydes. New York: Collier, n.d, pp. v–xlii.

———. "Gustave Flaubert." *Notes on Novelists*, pp. 65–108.

———. *Hawthorne.* London, 1879; New York, 1880; In *The Shock of Recognition*. Ed. Edmund Wilson. New York: 1955, pp. 427–565.

———. *Hawthorne.* Ed. Tony Tanner. Lon-don: Macmillan / New York: St. Martin's, 1967.

———. *Henry James Letters*, 4 vols. Ed. Leon Edel. Cambridge: Harvard University Press, 1974–80.

———. "The Lesson of the Master." *Universal Review*, 1 (July 16 and Aug. 15, 1888), 342–65, 494–523.

———. "A Light Man," *Galaxy*, 8 (July, 1869), 49–68.

———. "Matthew Arnold." *English Illustrated Magazine* (Jan. 1884), 241–46.

———. "The Modern Warning." In *The Aspern Papers [,] Louisa Pallant [,] The Modern Warning.* London and New York: Macmillan, 1888.

———. *Notes of a Son and Brother.* New York: Scribner's, 1914.

———. *Notes on Novelists with Some Other Notes.* New York: Scribner's, 1914.

———. "The Novel in *The Ring and the Book.*" *Transactions of the Royal Society of Literature*, 2nd series, 31, part 4 (1912).

———. *The Novels and Tales of Henry James* (New York Edition). 24 vols. New York: Scribner's, 1907–09.

———. "Occasional Paris." In *The Art of Travel: Scenes and Journeys in America, England, France and Italy from the Travel Writings of Henry James.* Ed. Morton Dauwen Zabel. Garden City, New York: Doubleday, 1958, pp. 213–29.

———. "Pandora." *New York Sun* (June 1, 1884), p. I:7, and (June 8, 1884), p. I:7.

———. "Paris Revisited." *The Galaxy* (Jan. 1878), 25: 5–13.

———. "Preface," *The Aspern Papers[,] The Turn of the Screw[,] "The Liar[,] " and "The Two Faces."* (New York Edition), XII, pp. xxiii-xxiv.

———. *The Sacred Fount.* Intr. Leon Edel. New York: Grove Press, 1953.

———. "Travels in Portugal." *The Nation* (Oct. 21, 1875), 21: 264–65.

———. "Two Countries." *Harper's Magazine* (June 1888), 77: 83–116.

———. "Venice." *Century Magazine*, 25 (Nov. 1882), 3–23.

———. *Washington Square.* Intr. Clifton Fadiman. New York: Modern Library, 1950.

———. *William Wetmore Story and His Friends.* Boston: Houghton Mifflin, 1903.

James, William. *The Correspondence of William James, Volume I: William and Henry, 1861–1884.* Ed. Ignas K. Skrupskelis and Elizabeth M. Berkeley. Charlottesville: University Press of Virginia, 1992.

"James's French Poets and Novelists." *The Nation* (Apr. 25,1878), p. 274.

Kane, Robert J. "Hawthorne's 'The Prophetic Pictures' and James's 'The Liar.'" *Modern Language Notes* (Apr. 1950), 65: 257–58.

King, William. *Political and Literary Anecdotes of His Own Times. ca. 1760.*

Kreymborg, Alfred. *Troubadour: An Autobiography.* New York: Liveright, 1925.

Levy, Leo. "Henry James and the Jews." *Commentary* (Sept. 1958), 26: 243–49.

"Literary Gossip." *Athenaeum*, 25, May 1878, p. 671.

"Literary Notes." *New York Tribune*, May 9, 1883, p. 6

"Literary Notes." *New York Tribune*, July 9, 1884, p. 6.

The Literary World (Apr. 17, 1897), 26: 126–27.

Longfellow, Henry Wadsworth. *The Poetical Works of Longfellow.* Intr. George Monteiro. Boston: Houghton Mifflin, 1975.

Lucke, Jessie Ryon. "The Inception of *The Beast in the Jungle.*" *New England Quarterly*, 36 (Dec. 1953), 529–32.

Lycette, Ronald L. "Perceptual Touchstones for the Jamesian Artist-Hero." *Studies in Short Fiction* (Winter 1977), 14: 55–62.

MacLeod, Glen. Email to George Monteiro. Oct. 22, 2009.

McMahon, Sean, ed. *A Little Bit of Heaven: An Irish-American Anthology.* Cork, Ireland: Mercier Press, 1999.

Machado, Francisco. *The Mirror of the New Christians (Espelho de Cristãos Novos) of Francisco Machado.* Ed., trans., and intr. Mildred Evelyn Vieira and Frank Ephraim Talmage. Toronto: Pontifical Institute of Mediaeval Studies, 1977.

Mansfield, Katherine. *The Letters of Katherine Mansfield.* Ed. J. Middleton Murry. New York: Knopf, 1932.

Matthissen, F. O. *American Renaissance.* New York: Oxford University Press, 1941.

———. "James and the Plastic Arts." *Kenyon Review* (Winter 1943), 5: 533–50.

Melchiori, Giorgio. "Browning e Henry James." *Friendship's Garland: Essays Presented to Mario Praz.* Ed. Vittorio Gabrieli. Roma: Edizioni di Storia e Letteratura, 1966, pp. 143–80.

Mencken, H. L. *The American Language*, 4th ed. New York: Knopf, 1937.

"Minor Notices: *The Aspern Papers.*" *The Literary World* (Dec. 8, 1888), 19: 451.

"Mr. James's Latest Tendency." *The Chap-Book* (Feb. 15, 1897), 6: 296.

Monteiro, George. "A Contemporary View of Henry James and Oscar Wilde, 1882." *American Literature*, 35 (Jan. 1964), pp. 528–30.

———. *The Correspondence of Henry James and Henry Adams 1877–1914.* Baton Rouge: Louisiana State University Press, 1992.

———. *Henry James and John Hay: The Record of a Friendship.* Providence, RI: Brown University Press, 1965.

———. "The Limits of Professionalism; A Sociological Approach to Faulkner, Fitzgerald and Hemingway." *Criticism*, 15 (Spring, 1973), 145–55.

Monteiro, George, and Brenda Murphy, eds. *John Hay-Howells Letters: The Correspondence of John Milton Hay and William Dean Howells 1861–1905.* Boston: Twayne, 1980.

Mordell, Albert, ed. *Discovery of a Genius: William Dean Howells and Henry James*. New York: Twayne, 1961, pp. 92–97.

Morse, Samuel French. Informal Talk, "English Club," sponsored by the Department of English, Brown University, ca. 1960

Murphy, Brenda. *American Realism and American Drama, 1880–1940*. Cambridge: Cambridge University Press, 1987.

Nettels, Elsa. "Henry James and the Idea of Race." *English Studies* (Feb. 1978), 59: 35-47.

"New Publications." *Philadelphia Public Ledger and Daily Transcript*, Dec. 4, 1880, Supplement, p. 2. In Taylor, *Reference Guide*.

"A New York Satire." *New York Tribune*, July 3, 1881, p. 8.

Pater, Walter. *The Renaissance: Studies in Art and Poetry* (London: Macmillan, 1910).

"Personal." *New York Tribune*, Apr. 20, 1881, p. 4.

"Personal." *New York Tribune*, Feb. 28, 1882, p. 4.

Pforzheimer, Walter L. "The Lady, The Tiger and the Author." *Colophon*, n.s, 1 (Autumn 1935), 261–70.

Poe, Edgar Allan. "Hawthorne's Tales." In Edmund Wilson, *Shock of Recognition*, pp. 154–69.

———. "The Purloined Letter." In *The Short Fiction of Edgar Allan Poe*. Ed. Stuart and Susan Levine. Indianapolis: Bobbs-Merrill, 1976.

Poggioli, Renato. *The Phoenix and the Spider*. Cambridge: Harvard University Press, 1957.

Posnock, Ross. *Henry James and the Problem of Browning*. Athens: University of Georgia Press, 1985.

Pound, Ezra. "Henry James." In *Instigations of Ezra Pound*. Freeport, NY: Books for Libraries Press, 1967, pp. 106–07.

Powers, Lyall H., ed. *Henry James and Edith Wharton: Letters: 1900–1915*. New York: Scribner's 1990.

———."Thornton Wilder as Literary Cubist: An Acknowledged Debt to Henry James." *Henry James Review*, 7 (1985), 34–44.

Putt, S. Gorley. *Henry James: A Reader's Guide*. Intr. Arthur Mizener. Ithaca: Cornell University Press, 1967.

"Races at Pittsburg." *New York Times*, July 18, 1877, p. 5.

Rahv, Philip. "The Cult of Experience." *Partisan Review*, VII (Nov.-Dec., 1940), 412–24.

———. *Image and Idea*. Norfolk, Connecticut: New Directions, 1957.

Réah, I. S. "Les Marranes," *Revue des Juives* (1959), 118: 27–77.

"Recent American Fiction." *Atlantic Monthly*, 51 (May 1883), 706–07.

"Recent Fiction." *The Independent*, 27 (Apr. 9, 1885), 459.

"Recent Novels." *The Nation*, 27 (Aug. 22, 1878), 117–18.

Review of *Daisy Miller*. *The Nation*, 27 (Dec. 19, 1878), 386–89.

Review of *The Siege of London, The Pension Beaurepas*, and *The Point of View*. *Boston Evening Transcript*, Feb. 23, 1883, p. 6.

Review. *Life* (July 26, 1888), 12: 48.

Review. *Scottish Review* (Apr. 1889), 13: 448.

Roback, A. A. *A Dictionary of International Slurs (Ethnophaulisms)*. Cambridge, MA: Sci-Art Publishers, 1944.

Ron, Moshe. "A Reading of 'The Real Thing.'" *Yale French Studies*, 58 (1979), 190–212.

Rosenberry, Edward. "James' Use of Hawthorne in 'The Liar.'" *Modern Language Notes* (Mar. 1961), 76: 234–38.

Ross, Michael L. "Henry James' 'Half-man': The Legacy of Browning in 'The Madonna of the Future.'" *Browning Institute Studies*, 2. New York: Browning Institute, 1974, pp. 25–42.

Roth, Cecil. "An Excursus on the History of the Capadose Family." In *Noble Families*.

Rourke, Constance. *American Humor: A Study of the National Character*. Garden City: Doubleday, 1953.

Samuels, Ernest. *Henry Adams: The Major Phase* (Cambridge: Harvard University Press, 1964.

———. *Henry Adams: The Middle Years*. Cambridge: Harvard University Press, 1958.

Segal, Ora. *The Lucid Reflector: The Observer in Henry James' Fiction*. New Haven: Yale University Press, 1969.

Sinclair, May. "The Reputation of Ezra Pound." *North American Review* (May 1920), 211: 658–68.

Smalley, George Washburn. "Mr. Henry James, Jr.—The Publishers." *New York Tribune* (Dec. 19, 1881), p. 6.

Smith, Goldwin. "The Hatred of England." *North American Review* (May 1890), 150: 547–62.

Smith, Janet Adam. *Henry James and Robert Louis Stevenson: A Record of Friendship and Criticism*. London: Rupert Hart-Davis, 1948.

Stein, Gertrude. *The Autobiography of Alice B. Toklas*. New York: Harcourt, Brace, 1933.

Stevens, Wallace. *Letters of Wallace Stevens.* Ed. Holly Stevens. New York: Knopf, 1966.

———. "Three Academic Pieces" (1947), *Collected Poetry and Prose,* ed. Frank Kermode and Joan Richardson. New York: Library of America, 1997.

Stockton, Frank R. "The Lady, or the Tiger?" *Century Magazine,* 25 (Nov. 1882), 83–86.

———. "The Lady or the Tiger?" In *Stories I, The Novels and Stories of Frank R. Stockton.* New York: Scribner's, 1900.

Strange, Jonathan. "Six Stevens Letters," *Wallace Stevens Journal,* 18 (Spring 1994), pp. 18–26.

Tambling, Jeremy. "Henry James's American Byron." *Henry James Review,* 20 (Winter 1999), 43–50.

Tate, Allen. "Three Commentaries: Poe, James, and Joyce." *Sewanee Review,* 58 (Winter, 1950), pp. 1–15.

Taylor, Linda J. *Henry James, 1866–1916: A Reference Guide.* Boston: G. K. Hall, 1982.

Tehan, Arline Boucher. *Henry Adams in Love: The Pursuit of Elizabeth Sherman Cameron.* Garden City: Hanover House, 1962.

Thoreau, Henry David. *The Writings of Henry David Thoreau.* 20 vols. Boston and New York: Houghton Mifflin, 1906.

Thoron, Ward, ed. *The Letters of Mrs. Henry Adams 1865–1883.* Boston: Little, Brown, 1936.

Tintner, Adeline R. *The Book World of Henry James: Appropriating the Classics.* Ann Arbor: UMI Research Press, 1987.

———. "Henry James's Mona Lisa." *Essays in Literature,* 8 (Spring 1981), 105–08.

———. "Pater in *The Portrait of a Lady* and *The Golden Bowl,* Including Some Unpublished Henry James Letters." *Henry James Review,* 3 (Winter 1982), 80–95.

Toor, David. "Narrative Irony in Henry James' 'The Real Thing.'" *University Review* (Winter 1967), 34: 95–99.

Trilling, Lionel. *The Liberal Imagination.* Garden City: Doubleday, 1953.

"Trotters Go at Auction." *New York Times,* Mar. 4, 1897, p. 11.

"The Trotting at Cleveland To-Day." *New York Times,* July 25, 1876, p. 1.

Turner, H. Arlin. "Hawthorne's Literary Borrowings," *PMLA,* 51 (June, 1936), pp. 543–62.

Twain, Mark. *Adventures of Huckleberry Finn.* Ed. Henry Nash Smith. Boston: Houghton Mifflin, 1958.

———. *The Innocents Abroad.* Intr. Edward Wagenknecht. New York: Heritage Press, 1962.

Uroff, M. D. Uroff. "Perception in James's 'The Real Thing.'" *Studies in Short Fiction* (Winter 1972), 9: 41–46.

Veeder, William. "The Aspern Portrait." *Henry James Review,* 20 (Winter 1999), pp. 22–42.

W., L. "Concerning Kettledrums." *Lippincott's Magazine,* 23 (Mar. 1879), pp. 381–84.

Walker, Pierre A. *Reading Henry James in French Cultural Contexts.* DeKalb: Northern Illinois University Press, 1995.

Ward, Maisie. *Robert Browning and His World: Two Robert Brownings? [1861–1889].* New York: Holt, Rinehart and Winston, 1969.

Webster's New World Dictionary of the American Language, Second College Edition. New York: Simon & Schuster, 1980.

Wecter, Dixon. "Literary Culture on the Frontier," in *Literary History of the United States.* Ed. Robert E. Spiller et al. 2nd ed., rev. New York: Macmillan, 1953, Vol. II, pp. 653–61.

Whiting, Lilian. "Life at the Hub." *Chicago Daily Inter Ocean* (Nov. 26, 1887), p. 12.

Wiesenfarth, Joseph. "Henry James and Ford Madox Ford: A Troubled Relationship." *Henry James Review* (Spring 1992), 13

Williams, William Carlos. "Comedy Entombed: 1930," in *Make Light of It: Collected Stories.* New York: Random House, 1950, pp. 322–32.

Wilson, Edmund. "Ambiguity of Henry James." *The Hound & Horn* (Apr.-June 1934), 7: 384–406.

———. Ed. *The Shock of Recognition.* New York: Doubleday Doran, 1943.

Woolson, Constance Fenimore. "'Always, Your Attached Friend': The Unpublished Letters of Constance Fenimore Woolson to John and Clara Hay." Ed. Alice Hall Petry. *Books at Brown,* 29–30 (1982–1983), pp. 11–107.

Wordsworth, William. *The Poetical Works of Wordsworth.* Ed. Thomas Hutchinson, rev. ed. Ernest de Selincourt. London: Oxford University Press, 1960.

Yerushalmi, Y. H. "Prolegomenon" to *History of the Origin and Establishment of the Inquisition in Portugal* by A. Herculano. Stanford edition 1936. Reprint; New York, 1972.

Index

Adams, Charles Francis, Sr. (U.S. minister to England) 120, 126
Adams, Henry Brooks 6, 8–10, 29, 31, 53–68, 62–63 (quoted), 81, 91 (quoted), 117, 120–29, 122 (quoted), 123 (quoted), 124 (quoted), 126 (quoted), 127–28 (quoted), 129 (quoted), 130–34 (quoted), 159ch7n26, 164ch16n2 (quoted); "Buddha and Brahma" 133; *Democracy* 132; *The Education of Henry Adams* 121–23 (quoted), 124–27 (quoted), 129 (quoted), 132; *History of the United States of America During the Administrations of Jefferson and Madison* 9, 63, 130; *John Randolph* 63; "A Letter to American Teachers" 133; *Mont-Saint-Michel and Chartres* 127–28, 131–32; "Prayer to the Virgin of Chartres" 133
Adams, Marian "Clover" Hooper 29, 53–68, 54 (quoted), 58–60 (quoted), 67–68, 123, 159ch7n26, 159ch7n31
Adorno, Theodor 151
Alcott, Louisa May: *Little Men* 142; *Little Women* 142
Aldrich, Thomas Bailey: *The Story of a Bad Boy* 142
Ariadne 113, 114
Armenia 81, 82, 85
Arnold, Matthew 64, 66 (quoted)
Arvin, Newton 2
Ascot 84–85, 135
Athenaeum (journal) 14 (quoted)
Athens (Greece) 118
Atlantic Monthly (journal) 18–19, 53–54, 72–78, 85, 94
Auchincloss, Louis 130
Austen, Jane: Catherine Olney (character) 122–23; *Northanger Abbey* 122

Bacon, Sir Francis 130
Ballou, Ellen B. 78 (quoted)
Barrett (Browning), Elizabeth 39
Barzun, Jacques 2

Beaux Arts (Paris) 30, 119, 157ch4n3
Beowulf 12
Bernhardt, Sarah 56
Bersani, Leo 151
Bewley, Marius: *The Complex Fate* 136
Bishop of Capadocia 89
Black, William: *Macleod of Dare* 61, 159ch7n27
Black and White (journal) 69, 70, 77, 160ch8n2
Blackmur, R.P. 2, 132 (quoted)
Blaine, James G. 60
Blake, William 140–41; *Songs of Innocence and Experience* 140
Bloom, Harold 151
bordereau (French) 95–97
Bosanquet, Theodora 1
Boscobel (England) 123
Boston 61, 79, 120
Boston Evening Transcript 53
Boston Gazette 59 (quoted)
Bourget, Paul 33
Brewster, Bertram: "The Capadose Family" 87–88 (quoted), 92 quoted)
British Museum (General Catalogue) 88
Brooks, Van Wyck 143; *The Ordeal of Mark Twain* 1; *The Pilgrimage of Henry James* 1, 18
Brown University 6–7, 27
Browning, Robert 33–40, 69, 106, 150–53; "Andrea del Sarto" 37, 69; "Christina" 151; *Fifine at the Fair* 151; "Fra Lippo Lippi" 69; "In a Balcony" 151; *The Inn Album* 39, 151; "A Light Woman" 33–37 (quoted), 151; *Men and Women* 33, 36, 151–52; "My Last Duchess" 33, 39; *The Ring and the Book* 33, 39, 152–53; *Sordello* 33, 36
Buitenhuis, Peter 159ch7n38 (quoted)
Butterfield, Lyman 9–10 (quoted)
Byron, Allegra 95
Byron (Lord) 8, 95

Cairo 117
California 13–15, 17–20

173

Cambridge (Massachusetts) 7, 80, 120, 127, 131
Cameron, Elizabeth 124–26, 131
Campbell, Roy 12
Camus, Albert 51
Capadose (family) 83, 87–92
Capadose, Aaron Abraham 89 (quoted), 91
Capadose, Antonius Everdinus 87–90
Capadose, Col. Henry 87–88, 99; *Kindred, a Comedy* (translation of A.F.F. von Kotzebue play) 88; *Organs of the Brain, a Comedy* (translation of A.F.F. von Kotzebue play) 88; *Sixteen Years in the West Indies* 88; *Travels in India* 88
Capadose, Jacob 87–88
Capadose, Isaac (coadjutor to the Apostles in the 'Catholic Apostolic Church) 88, 92
Capote, Truman 142
Cargill, Oscar 14 (quoted), 155*ch*2*n*6 (quoted)
Cathcart, Aeneas 5
Century Magazine 53, 86–87, 91, 108–9, 124
The Chap-Book (journal) 94 (quoted)
Cheever, Benjamin 10
Cheever, John 10
Cheever, Susan 10
Chiardi, John 21–22 (quoted)
Chicago 54, 60
Child, Theodore 37
Clairmont, Jane 95
Clark, Sir John 8
Clemens, Samuel Langhorne *see* Twain, Mark
Cohn, Dorrit 151
Coleridge, Samuel Taylor 22, 141
Columbia University 6–7
Compton, Edward 19–20
Concord (Massachusetts) 85
Conrad, Joseph 51
Cooper, James Fenimore 55
Corfu 118
Cornhill Magazine 134
Cosmopolis (journal) 99
Crane, Stephen 6, 163*ch*13*n*3
Crawford, Francis Marion: *Mr. Isaacs: A Tale of Modern India* 110
Crete 108, 114
Cummings, E.E. 141 (quoted)
Cunliffe, Sir Robert (and wife) 121

Daedalus 108, 114
Daiches, David 2
"Daisy Miller" (racehorse) 135
Dana, Charles A. 58
Danes 85
Daudet, Alphonse 37, 91; *Numa Roumestan* 86, 91
D'Avanzo, Mario 150
"De Fuerte salió Dulce" (Capadose family motto) 92
de Balzac, Honoré: *Lost Illusions* 17; *Père Goriot* 17

Decker, William Merrill 130 (quoted), 132 (quoted), 165*ch*17*n*1; "A Martyr to the Disease of Omniscience" 130, 165*ch*17*n*1
Deedes, C.N.: *The Labyrinth* 108 (quoted)
Delane, John Thaddeus 125
Dennery (Adolphe d'Ennery) 19
de Tocqueville, Alexis 57–58, 64
DeVane, William C. 33 (quoted)
Dickens, Charles 17, 64, 109, 123; *Great Expectations* 17
Dickinson, Emily 9
Disraeli, Benjamin (First Earl of Beaconsfield) 91
Dorat, Jean 16
Dostoevsky, Fyodor 47–48; *Notes from the Underground* 48 (quoted)
Dowson, Ernest 33 (quoted)
Drabble, Margaret: Frances Wingate (character) 11–12; *The Realms of Gold* 11 (quoted)
Drayfus, Alfred 95
Dumas, *fils*, Alexandre: *L'Etrangère* 155*ch*2*n*6
Dupee, F.W. 2, 7, 134 (quoted); *The Question of Henry James* 2
Dusty Miller (flower) 60

Ecclesiastes 21 (quoted)
Edel, Leon 6–8, 10, 15 (quoted), 64 (quoted), 72–73 (quoted), 77, 104–6, 117 (quoted), 146, 161*ch*10*n*6, 164*ch*15*n*26; *Henry James Letters* 73
Edict of Expulsion 90
The Egoist (journal) 1
Egypt 117–18
Eliot, T.S. 1, 26, 79–80, 132 (quoted); "Sweeny Among the Nightingales" 79 (quoted)
"Eliot Among the Sweeneys" 80
Emerson, Ralph Waldo 25 (quoted), 32
Emmanuel (King Manuel) 89, 90
England 65–66, 77, 80, 85
Epson 84, 85, 135
Eton 84
Europe (Continent) 13–15, 18–20, 29, 32, 35, 38, 51, 55–56, 64, 80, 83–84, 143
Evans, Arthur (Little Evans, son of John Evans the Great") 114–15, 118

Fadiman, Clifton 92, 162*ch*10*n*37 (quoted)
Faulkner, William 7, 51
Ferdinand (Archduke) 103
Fergusson, Francis 2
Fielding, Henry 109
Fish, Stanley 151
Flaubert, Gustave 15–17; *L'Education sentimentale: Histoire d'une Jeune Homme* 16–17; *Flaubert Oeuvres* (Pléiade Editions) 156*ch*2*n*21 (quoted); *Madame Bovary* 15–16; *Salammbô* 16; *La Tentation de Saint-Antoine* 16
Florence (city) 95, 120

Ford, Ford Madox *see* Hueffer, Ford Madox
France, French 80, 85
Freud, Sigmund 151
Friendship Park 135
Frost, Robert 21–22 (quoted), 130
Fussell, Edwin Sill 93 (quoted)

The Galaxy 18 (quoted)
Gale, Robert L. 70 (quoted), 160*ch*8*n*2 (quoted)
Garnett, Edward 98–99 (quoted), 100–2 (quoted), 103
Gaskell, Lady Catherine 121–22
Gaskell, Sir Charles Milnes 120–23
Germany 80, 91
Gide, Andre 51
Gilmore, Patrick Sarsfield ("Louis Lambert"): "When Johnnie Comes Marching Home" 32
Girard, Rene 151–52
Gladstone, William Ewart 125, 128, 146
Godwin, Mary 95
Goffman, Erving 151
Gomez, Enrique 1
Gosse, Edmund 31
Greece 117
Greenblatt, Stephen 151
Gregory's Gulch (Colorado) 18
Griffin, Sir Lepel Henry: *The Great Republic* 64–66 (quoted)
Gyp (Sibylle Aimée Marie-Antoinette Gabrielle de Riquetti Mirabeau) 101

Habegger, Alfred 146–47 (quoted)
Hamilton, Alexander 63
Hankin, St. John: *The Charity That Began a Home (A Comedy for Philanthropists)* 104; *The Last of the De Mullins* 104
Harper & Brothers 106
Harper's Magazine 65
Harper's Monthly 117
Harper's Weekly 78, 102
Harrow (England) 84
Hartford, Connecticut 27
Hartford Courant: The Resurrection of Caleb Quine (by Owen Canfield) 5; "A Busy Day at the Archives" (by Owen Canfield) 5 (quoted)
Harvard University 3, 6, 56, 79
Hatcher, Geoffrey 5
Hawthorne, Nathaniel 10 (quoted), 43–53, 84, 108–10, 113–14, 136–39 (quoted), 142, 162*ch*10*n*37; *The Blithedale Romance* 44–45 (quoted), 109; "Ethan Brand" 51; "The Gentle Boy" 142; *The House of the Seven Gables* 162*ch*10*n*37; *The Marble Faun; Or the Romance of Monte Beni* 136–39; "The Minotaur" 108 (quoted); "My Kinsman, Major Molineux" 142; "Prophetic Pictures" 162*ch*10*n*37; *The Scarlet Letter* 142; "Wakefield" 47–52 (quoted), 158*ch*6*n*12

Hawthorne, Sophia 10
Hay, Adelbert (Del) 29
Hay, Clara Stone 29, 117
Hay, John 6–8, 11, 19 (quoted), 29, 31, 54–55 (quoted), 81, 117–18, 124, 126, 158*ch*6*n*19; *The Bread-Winners* 124; "Kane and Abel" 29–30
Haymarket Theatre 104
Hemingway, Ernest 10
Hemingway, Mary 10
Henricksen, Bruce 160–61*ch*8*n*4 (quoted)
Henry (Prince) 90
"Henry Adams and the Need to Know" (conference) 165*ch*17*n*1
"Henry James Among the Portingales" 79–80
"Henry James' Double" 106 (quoted)
The Henry James Society 2
Hesse, Herman 51
Higginson, Thomas Wentworth: "The Haunted Window" 161*ch*10*n*7
Hoffman, Daniel 6
Holmes, Oliver Wendell 29, 31
Horwitz, Sylvia L. 114 (quoted)
Houghton (Lord) *see* Milnes, Richard Monckton
Houghton Library 6–7, 9
Houghton Mifflin 73
The Hound and Horn (journal) 1, 2
Howells, John Mead 30–32, 119, 157*ch*4*n*3
Howells, William Dean 5, 19 (quoted), 29–32 (quoted), 67 (quoted), 85 (quoted), 109 (quoted), 118–19, 123–24, 157*ch*4*n*3; *A Hazard of New Fortunes* 119; "Henry James, Jr." 109; *Indian Summer* 29; *Their Silver Wedding Journey* 119; *Their Wedding Journey* 119
Hoytem, van der 92
Hudson River (New York) 18
Hueffer, Ford Madox (Ford Madox Ford) 1, 98–100, 102–4 (quoted); *Henry James: A Critical Study* 161*ch*10*n*6; *Thus to Revisit: Some Reminiscences* 163*ch*13*n*3 (quoted)
Hugo, Victor 115
Hyde Park (London) 31

Ibsen, Henrik: "A Doll's House" 101; "The Wild Duck" 101
idée fixe 126
Imperial Garde Meuble 94
Incorporated Stage Society 104
India 27, 88
Inquisition 90
Iron City Jockey Club Day 135
Irving, Washington 81
Isabel (Queen) 90
Italy 80

Jackson, Catherine Charlotte (Lady): *Fair Lusitania* 83
James, Alice (sister) 146–47 (quoted)

Index

James, Alice (Mrs. William James) 26, 29, 118
James, Bay 3
James, Henry 13–17 (quoted), 19–20 (quoted), 22–23 (quoted), 25–32 (quoted), 33–47, 49–69 (quoted), 81 (quoted), 83–86 (quoted), 90–91, 98 (quoted), 100–2 (quoted), 105–6 (quoted), 108–10 (quoted), 112–13 (quoted), 118–23, 131 (quoted), 126, 128 (quoted), 132 (quoted), 139 (quoted), 143, 144, 147–48 (quoted), 150 (quoted), 153 (quoted), 157ch4n3 (quoted), 158ch6n19, 160ch8n2, 163ch13n3; "The Altar of the Dead" (movie) 2; "The Altar of the Dead" ("The Altars of the Dead") 99, 116; *The Ambassadors* 2, 22, 25, 30 (quoted), 31, 32 (quoted), 43, 44, 46, 82, 89, 93, 112, 118, 119, 128, 132, 163ch12n1; *The American* 13–20, 66 (quoted), 81, 85, 123, 137; *The American* (play) 19–20; *The American Scene* 79, 81, 104; *The Aspern Papers* 8–9 (quoted), 89, 95–97; "The Author of Beltraffio" 144; *The Awkward Age* 89, 98–100, 102–3, 163ch13n6; "The Beast in the Jungle" 41–44 (quoted), 50–51, 109–12, 114–15 (quoted), 117–19, 128, 163ch12n1; *The Better Sort* 109; *The Bostonians* 55, 123; *The Bostonians* (movie) 2; "Brooksmith" ("The Servant") 76, 78; "The Californian" (rejected title) 20; "The Chaperon" 78; "Covering End" 89; "Daisy Miller" 53, 59, 60- 61, 63–64, 67, 109, 123, 134–35, 143, 146, 159ch7n27; *Daisy Miller* (movie) 2; *English Hours* 81; *The Europeans* 85, 123, 137; *The Europeans* (movie) 2, 53; "The Figure in the Carpet" 93, 98–104; "Four Meetings"161ch10n6; "Gabrielle de Bergerac" 19; "Glasses" 89; *The Golden Bowl* 21, 84, 89, 94, 151; *Guy Domville* 3; *Hawthorne* 55, 60, 84–85 (quoted), 109 (quoted), 134–36 (quoted); *The Heiress [Washington Square]* (movie) 2; *The Heiress [Washington Square]* (play) 2; *The High Bid* 104; "An International Episode" 59, 67; *Italian Hours* 81; *The Ivory Tower* 22, 105; "The Jolly Corner" 22, 107; "The Lesson of the Master" 33, 37–40 (quoted), 151–52; letters to Antonius Everdinus Capadose 87; letters to Ford Madox Hueffer 98; letters to Horace E. Scudder 74–77; "The Liar" 71, 79–92, 124–26, 161ch10n6; "A Light Man" 33, 35–36 (quoted), 151–52; *A Little Tour in France* 81; *A London Life* 67, 86; "The Marriages" 78; "The Modern Warning" ("A Modern Warning") ("Two Countries") 53, 64–65, 67–68 (quoted); *Notes of a Son and Brother* 129, 131; "The Novel in *The Ring and the Book*" 151; *The Old Things* 94; "Pandora" 53, 58–60-61 (quoted), 63–64, 68, 121, 123, 157ch7n38; *A Passionate Pilgrim* 84; "The Pension Beaurepas" 53; "The Point of View" 53–59 (quoted), 62, 68, 123, 140 (quoted); "Poor Richard" 109; *The Portrait of a Lady* 1, 23–24 (quoted), 27, 59, 81–82, 85, 103, 123, 132, 163ch12n1; *The Portrait of a Lady* (movie) 2; "Prefaces" (New York edition) 15–17 (quoted), 30 (quoted), 32, 41 (quoted), 95, 99 (quoted), 100–3, 116, 124, 134; *The Princess Casamassima* 17, 67, 123, 155ch13n13, 156ch2n19; "The Private Life" 36, 39–40, 106, 151; "The Pupil" 160ch7n40, 72–78, 89, 144; "The Real Thing" 69–71, 161ch8n2; *The Real Thing and Other Tales* 69; *Roderick Hudson* 69, 81, 123, 151; "A Round of Visits" 105–7 (quoted); *The Sacred Fount* 25, 93, 126–27 (quoted); *The Saloon* 104; *The Siege of London* 53; *A Small Boy and Others* 129; *The Spoils of Poynton* 89, 93–94; *The Tragic Muse* 73–74, 78, 89; *The Turn of the Screw* 2, 80, 86, 93, 144; "Two Faces" 86; "Venice" 108–9; *Washington Square* 2, 22–23, 82, 146–49 (quoted); *Watch and Ward* 159ch7n27; *What Maisie Knew* 2, 89, 143–44; *The Wings of the Dove* 22, 136–39, 151
James, Henry (English jurist) 146
James, Henry (Henry James's nephew) 29
James, Henry, Sr. 56, 131, 146, 147; *The Literary Remains of the Late Henry James* 146
James, William (grandfather) 147
James, William (brother) 155ch2n9 (quoted), 25, 26, 29, 31, 56, 127, 128, 146, 147, 152, 166ch21n7
James, William (Henry James's nephew) 7, 8, 29
James Family Collection (Houghton Library) 7, 12
Jefferson, Thomas 63
Jews 79, 82, 83, 89, 90, 92
John Hay Library (Special Collections) 6–7
John III (King) 90
Judaism 92

Kafka, Franz 51
Kemble, Fanny 146–47
Kentucky Derby 135
Kenyon Review 2
King, Clarence 11
King, William: *Political and Literary Anecdotes of His Own Times* 158ch6n12
Kirstein, Lincoln 1, 2 (quoted)
Knossos (Crete) 114
Kossuth, Lajos 47
Kotzebue, A.F.F. von: *Kindred, A Comedy* (translation by Henry Capadose) 88; *Organs of the Brain, a Comedy* (translation by Henry Capadose) 88
Kreymborg, Alfred ("Krimmie") 26–27 (quoted)
Krutch, Joseph Wood 47

Index

labyrinth 108, 113, 114
Lacan, Jacques 151
LaFarge, John 152
Lamb House 7, 10, 29
Laplanders 85
Latouche, John (Oswald Crawford) 81–85, 161ch10n6; *Travels in Portugal* 81, 83, 84, 85, 89
Leite, Jacinto 80
Levenson, J.C. 130
Life (journal) 66 (quoted)
Lincoln, Abraham 6, 29
Lind, Sidney E. 151
Lion d'Or (Paris) 11
Lippincott's Magazine 134 (quoted)
Lisbon 12, 80, 90
The Literary World (journal) 54 (quoted), 67 (quoted), 94 (quoted)
The Little Review 1
Locke, John 140 (quoted)
London 29, 37, 43, 58–59, 69, 71, 77, 83, 86, 88, 100, 105, 109, 120–22, 134, 155ch2n13
London Stock Exchange 88
London *Times* 39, 87
Longfellow, Henry Wadsworth 81, 143; "The Children's Hour" 140, 144 (quoted)
"Louis Lambert" *see* Gilmore, Patrick Sarsfield
Louis Seize (furniture) 93
Louvre (Salon Carré) 15, 20, 155ch2n13
Lowell, James Russell 81
Lubbock, Percy 1, 131
Lucke, Jessie Ryon: "The Inception of *The Beast in the Jungle*" 44 (quoted)
Ludlow (England) 122
Ludlow Castle 123

MacLeish, Archibald 5
MacPherson, Geraldine: *Memoirs of Ann James* 159ch7n27
McCullers, Carson 142
Machado, Francisco: *Espelho de Cristão Novos* (*The Mirror of the New Christians*) 89–90 (quoted)
Machiavelli, Niccolò 120, 164ch16n2; *The Prince* 121
Madison, James 63
Madrid (Spain) 81
Maeterlinck, Maurice 23
Malamud, Bernard 10
Mansfield, Katherine 69 (quoted)
Marches (borderland between England Wales) 123
Marie Antoinette 93
Marranos 89, 90
Matthiessen, F.O. 2, 51 (quoted); *American Renaissance* 45–46 (quoted); *Henry James: The Major Phase* 23 (quoted)
Mayne, Ethel Coburn 1
Melchiori, Barbara 150

Melchiori, Giorgio 150
Mencken, Henry L.: *The American Language* 161ch10n6
Methuen 109
meubles (definition) 93–94
Milnes, Richard Monckton (Lord Houghton) 121
Milton, John: "On the Morning of Christ's Nativity" 117
Minotaur 114
Mitchell, John 59 (quoted)
Mitchell, S. Weir 59 (quoted)
Modern Fiction Studies 2
Modern Language Studies 2
Moll, Elsie (Mrs. Wallace Stevens) 22, 23
Moore, Arthur 33
Moore, Marianne 2
Morse, Samuel French 27 (quoted)
Mount Vernon (George Washington's home) 59
Murdock, Kenneth B. 51 (quoted)
Murphy, Brenda 20 (quoted)

Naples 113
The Nation (journal) 16 (quoted), 20 (quoted), 61 (quoted), 83
New Christians 79–92, 162ch10n28
New England Magazine 47
New Review (journal) 105
New York (city) 60, 61, 86, 109, 148
New York *Sun* 58
New York Times 18–19 (quoted), 146 (quoted)
New York Tribune 13, 56 (quoted), 59 (quoted), 60 (quoted), 64 (quoted), 117
Newby, T.C. 88
Newmarch 126
Newport 131
Nile (river) 117, 118
Norton, Charles 131
Nortons (family) 26, 27 (quoted), 80

O Mentiroso 80
O'Connor, Flannery 142
Oedipus 113
Oporto (city) 89
Orage, A.R. 1
Oshkosh 56
The Outlook (journal) 94, 98, 99
Oxford (England) 84, 128
Oxford English Dictionary 83, 93

Palais Royal (Paris) 58
Palgrave, Sir Francis: *Golden Treasury of Songs and Lyrics* 121
Palmerston (Henry John Temple, 3rd Viscount Palmerston) 125, 128
Paris 11, 13, 14, 15, 17, 29, 30, 31, 32, 43, 81, 118, 119, 155ch2n13
Parkinson, Mary E. 159ch7n26

Parkman, Francis 159*ch7n*26
Parkman, Mary Eliot (Dwight) 61, 159*ch7n*27 (quoted)
Parkman, Samuel 159*ch7n*26
Pater, Walter 23–24, 115–16, 118; *The Renaissance* 115 (quoted)
Perry, Thomas Sergeant 13
Perseus 39
Pessoa, Fernando 12
Pittsburgh 135
Plath, Sylvia 10
Poe, Edgar Allan 93, 158*ch6n*12
Poggioli, Renato 47 (quoted)
Poles (Polish) 82
Pompeii 114
Porter, Katherine Anne 2
Portugal 81, 82, 83, 84, 85, 89, 90
Portugalia 80
Portugees 82, 161*ch10n*7
Portuguese (Lusitanians) 79, 80, 81, 82, 83, 85, 89
Portuguese Letters (novel) 83
Posnock, Ross: *Henry James and the Problem of Robert Browning* 150–53
Potomac (river) 59
Pound, Ezra 1, 92, 94 (quoted)
Princeton University 31
Psalms 55:6 165*ch19n*2
Public Ledger and Daily Transcript (Philadelphia newspaper) 148 (quoted)
Punch (journal) 126
Putt, S. Gorley 66 (quoted)

Rahv, Philip 43, 143; "The Cult of Experience in American Writing" 43
Réah, I.S. 162*ch10n*28
Robeson, George Maxwell 60
Rodker, John 1
Rogue (magazine) 26
Rome 29, 118
Roosevelt, Theodore 6, 132–33 (quoted)
Ross, Michael 150
Roth, Cecil 89 (quoted), 91–92 (quoted)
Rothschild, Ferdinand 11
Rourke, Constance: *American Humor: A Study of the National Character* 67 (quoted)
Rousseau, Jean-Jacques: *Confessions* 115
Royal Society of Literature (London) 151, 152
Russell, John (Earl) 125, 126, 127, 128
Russian 85
Rye (Sussex) 29

St. George 39
Salem (Massachusetts) 85
Salinger, J.D. 10, 142
San Francisco Evening Bulletin 67 (quoted)
Saraiva, J.A. 162*ch10n*28
Sarajevo 103
Saratoga (New York) 32

Sardou, Victorien 19
Saturday Morning Club (Boston) 60
Schenectady (New York) 18, 63, 143
Schliemann, Heinrich 114
Scottish Review 66 (quoted), 97 (quoted)
Scribe, Eugène 19
Scribner's 109
Scripture 136
Scudder, Horace E. 54 (quoted), 57, 72, 73, 76, 77 (quoted), 78; letters (to Henry James) 73–76
Semitic 92
Sephardim 83, 89, 90, 92
Sexton, Anne 10
Shakespeare, William 47, 123–24, 153
Shrewsbury (England) 123
Shropshire 121–22
Sicily 118
Simões, João Gaspar: *Calafrio* 80
Smalley, George Washburn 59 (quoted)
Smith, Goldwin 64–65 (quoted)
Spain 81, 90
Spender, Stephen 2
Sphinx 113
Stayes (fictional place) 125, 126
Stein, Gertrude: *The Autobiography of Alice B. Toklas* 163*ch13n*6 (quoted)
Stendhal (Mari-Henri Beyle): *The Red and the Black* 17
Stevens, Wallace 12, 21–28 (quoted), 133 (quoted); "Connoisseur of Chaos" 12 (quoted); "The Emperor of Ice-Cream" 27 (quoted); "A High-Toned Old Christian Woman" 27 (quoted); "The Idea of Order at Key West" 27 (quoted); "On Modern Poetry" 24 (quoted), 133 (quoted); "An Ordinary Evening in New Haven" 28 (quoted); "Peter Quince at the Clavier" 27; "Sunday Morning" 27 (quoted), 28; "Tea" 27; "Thirteen Ways of Looking at a Blackbird" 25
Stevenson, Robert Louis 160*ch7n*40
Stockton, Frank R. 114, 164*ch15n*15; 'The Lady, or the Tiger?' 109–12 (quoted), 118
Stokesay (England) 122, 123
Stone Library (Quincy, Massachusetts) 9
Sturges, Jonathan 30, 31, 118–19
Sweeney, John L. 2
Switzerland 80, 135

Taine, Hippolyte 57 (quoted)
Taj Mahal 27
Tate, Allen 51 (quoted)
Tauchnitz (publishers) 61, 63
Temple, Minny 152
Thackeray, William Makepeace 23, 123, 124; *Henry Esmond* 109; *Vanity Fair* 109
Theseus 113
Thoreau, Henry David: *Walden* 42 (quoted)
Tiber (river) 91

Time (magazine) 7
Titians 55
Trasteverina (Rome) 91
Trilling, Lionel: "Young Man from the Provinces" (phrase) 17
Trinidad 88
Trinity College (Hartford, Connecticut) 27
Trollope, Frances Milton (Mrs.) 58, 64
Troy 114
Turgenev, Ivan 15, 33, 53, 57, 155*ch*2*n*9
Turks 82
Turner, H. Arlin 158*ch*6*n*12
Turner, J.M.W. 120
Twain, Mark 10, 20, 54, 83–84 (quoted), 142, 143, 155*ch*2*n*11; *Adventures of Huckleberry Finn* 142–43 (quoted); *The Adventures of Tom Sawyer* 142; *The Innocents Abroad: The New Pilgrims' Progress* 83–84 (quoted), 155*ch*2*n*11; *The Mysterious Stranger* 142; *Roughing It* 142

Union College 56
United States 55, 57, 80, 81, 160*ch*7*n*40
United States Capitol (Washington, D.C.) 58
United States Department of State 81
United States House of Representative 83
Uriconium (England) 123
Utica (New York) 18, 61, 63
University of Nebraska Press 2
University of Rhode Island 6
University of Texas 12

Vasari, Giorgio 120–21
Venice 30, 108, 117–18
Vivas, Eliseo 2

Wales 123
Waley, Arthur 1
Ward, Theodora 9
Warren, Austin 2
Warren, Robert Penn 2
Washington, George 59
Washington (D.C.) 54, 58–60, 62–63, 159*ch*7*n*38
Wasser, Henry 130, 131, 132, 165*ch*17*n*1; "Henry Adams, Intellectual" 130
Weber, Samuel 151
Webster's New World Dictionary 95 (quoted)
Wecter, Dixon 18 (quoted)
Wenlock Abbey 120–23, 127
Whistler, James 30, 32
Whiting, Lilian 64 (quoted)
Whitman, Walt: *Drum-Taps* 153
Wilde, Oscar 60, 72, 158–59*ch*6*n*19
Wilder, Thornton 163*ch*13*n*6
Williams, William Carlos: "Comedy Entombed: 1930" 12 (quoted)
Wilson, Edmund 2
Woollett (fictional place) 32, 82, 83, 157*ch*4*n*3
Woolner, Thomas 121
Woolson, Constance Fenimore 7, 108, 117–18
Wordsworth 141–42; "Ode: Intimations of Immortality from Recollections of Early Childhood" 141 (quoted)
World War I 80
Wrekin (England) 123

Yerushalmi, Y.H. 162*ch*10*n*28
"Young Man from the Provinces" *see* Trilling, Lionel

www.ingramcontent.com/pod-product-compliance
Ingram Content Group UK Ltd.
Pitfield, Milton Keynes, MK11 3LW, UK
UKHW042015140426
5217IPUK00015B/1180